A **WESTERN H**

MW01098583

Legends
VOLUME 4

Outstanding Quarter Horse Stallions and Mares

Contributors

Mike Boardman   Frank Holmes
Diane Ciarloni   Betsy Lynch
Alan Gold   A.J. Mangum
Jim Goodhue   Susan Scarberry
Sally Harrison   Larry Thornton

Edited by Pat Close and Roy Jo Sartin

Legends

VOLUME 4

Published by
WESTERN HORSEMAN® magazine

3850 North Nevada Ave.
Box 7980
Colorado Springs, CO 80933-7980

www.westernhorseman.com

Design, Typography, and Production
Western Horseman
Colorado Springs, Colorado

Cover painting by
Orren Mixer

Printing
Branch Smith
Fort Worth, Texas

©*1999 by Western Horseman*
a registered trademark of
Morris Communications Corporation
725 Broad Street
Augusta, GA 30901

Seventh Printing: June 2005

ISBN 0-911647-63-5

INTRODUCTION

THIS IS the fourth volume in our ongoing, ever-popular series of books on outstanding Quarter Horse stallions and mares who have had a significant impact on the breed. The era in which the horses were bred and used ranges from 1917, when Zantanon was foaled, to the 1990s, when the progeny of more contemporary horses such as Zan Parr Bar and Diamonds Sparkle competed. In fact, Diamonds Sparkle is still alive as this is written in early October 1999. The phenomenal palomino mare is 25 years old.

We have several guidelines for determining which horses to include in a *Legends* volume. One of them is that the horse must be deceased, for at least five years. In the case of Diamonds Sparkle, we waived the rule since Blondy's Dude, her grandsire, and Zan Parr Bar, the stallion who sired several of her most outstanding foals, are both in this book. It was only fitting that we also include this great mare.

This volume features three more terrific mares: Fillinic, Miss Bank, and Miss Princess. Quarter racing fans will recognize the names of the latter two mares, as they were two of the very best race horses in the 1940s.

Fillinic's name will be readily recognizable to reined cow horse enthusiasts because she was the cornerstone of Californian Greg Ward's breeding program. That program has produced many horses who have dominated not only reined cow horse events, but also cutting and reining.

Racing Classifications

Legends, Vol. 1, includes an informative history of the American Quarter Horse Association, including registration rules and the standards for grading Quarter race horses. It was written by Jim Good-

hue, who was the AQHA registrar for many years. Since *Legends, Vol. 4,* includes many references to the early day speed classifications, I am excerpting a portion of Jim's explanations regarding the history behind the system for those classifications.

> *The system, which was loosely based on classification of Greyhounds at dog racing tracks, designated certain times within each of the seven distances recognized at that time—mid-1940s—(220 yards through 440 yards) as either D, C, B, A, or AA.*
>
> *If a horse finished a 350-yard race in 17.8 seconds, for instance, he was given a grade of A, no matter how he placed in the race. Then, he was qualified to run in races written specifically for A horses. Such grading was designed to provide close competition—appealing to both horsemen and the general public.*
>
> *Because A and AA were the faster grades on this scale, the horses who officially received such grades were placed in the Register of Merit (ROM). This was for recognition of superior race horses and was thought to be a means for helping select breeding stock to produce future runners.*
>
> *In later years, as horses and tracks became faster, an even faster category was*

INTRODUCTION

added. This was AAA, and then to qualify for the Register of Merit horses had to be AA or AAA. Some years later, an even faster category was specified and given the name Top AAA. This came to be designated in the computer era as TAAA or AAAT.

At an even later date (1969), when tracks were no longer using these grades to any large extent as gauges for writing races for Quarter Horses, and the ROM was used primarily for advertising or to advance a horse within the registry, the letter grade system was dropped. A speed index (SI) rating by number, based on speed within each distance as compared to the track record for that distance, was then adopted. At that point, horses with speed ratings of 80 or higher were included in the Register of Merit.

Keep in mind that today there are three Registers of Merit: one for racing, one for halter, and one for performance events—but not a separate Register of Merit for each performance event. An ROM in halter or performance is earned when a horse wins a certain number of points in competition.

For more details on AQHA titles and awards, contact AQHA at Box 200, Amarillo, TX 79168; 806-376-4811; www.AQHA.com.

Special Acknowledgments

Publishing these *Legends* books would be difficult, if not impossible, without the help of free-lance writers, whose profiles begin on page 206, the many photographers who have granted us permission to use their photographs, and popular artist Orren Mixer of Arcadia, Oklahoma. Orren, a legend himself, has painted the cover for each volume in the *Legends* series.

Special thanks also to the folks at *The Quarter Horse Journal* and the American Quarter Horse Heritage Center & Museum for loaning us so many photographs from their files. To be more specific, Paula Sarrett at the *Journal* and David Hoover, collections manager at the Heritage Center. Richard Chamberlain, assistant editor of *The Quarter Racing Journal*, also answered many of our questions about racing stats for several horses.

Here at *WH*, Associate Editor Roy Jo Sartin helped to coordinate production of this book, Assistant Art Director Jeanne Mazerall did the design and layout, and Glenn Mattingly and Richard Smith handled the photographic work in our production department.

As with previous books in this series, if you see a mistake in this one, or a person incorrectly identified, or not identified at all, in a photo caption, let us know and we can make corrections in the next printing.

Finally—yes, there will be a *Legends, Vol. 5*, but the release date has not been set at this time. Probably it will be in the year 2001.

Patricia A. Close
Western Horseman

CONTENTS

Page

6	1/ ZANTANON
20	2/ ED ECHOLS
32	3/ ZAN PARR BAR
42	4/ BLONDY'S DUDE
56	5/ DIAMONDS SPARKLE
66	6/ MISS PRINCESS/ WOVEN WEB (TB)
72	7/ MISS BANK
78	8/ REBEL CAUSE
90	9/ TONTO BARS HANK
102	10/ HARLAN

Page

114	11/ LADY BUG'S MOON
126	12/ DASH FOR CASH
138	13/ VANDY
150	14/ IMPRESSIVE
162	15/ FILLINIC
174	16/ ZIPPO PINE BAR
190	17/ DOC O'LENA
206	AUTHOR PROFILES
211	PHOTO INDEX
214	NOTES

1 ZANTANON

By Jim Goodhue

He became known as the Mexican Man O' War.

IN 1917 TWO COLTS were foaled who were to make lasting impressions on their respective breeds.

One of those colts came into this world on a luxurious Thoroughbred breeding farm, raced brilliantly on the finest tracks in the eastern United States, and made headlines around the world. Winning 20 of his 21 starts, he became the leading American Thoroughbred money-earner of the time, with $249,465. His name was Man O' War. He was so good that he played a part in persuading the English Thoroughbred authorities to

Zantanon was often referred to as "The Man O' War of Mexico." This is the most frequently seen picture of the renowned early day sire.

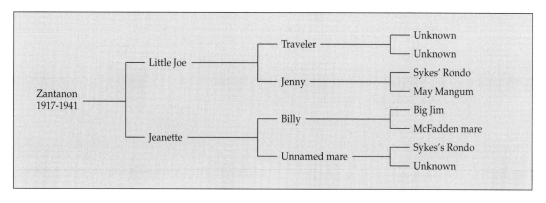

Tree diagram:
- Zantanon 1917-1941
  - Little Joe
    - Traveler
      - Unknown
      - Unknown
    - Jenny
      - Sykes' Rondo
      - May Mangum
  - Jeanette
    - Billy
      - Big Jim
      - McFadden mare
    - Unnamed mare
      - Sykes's Rondo
      - Unknown

change their rules in order to accept American bloodlines.

The second colt was dropped on a small ranch in south Texas, raced on makeshift match-race tracks in Mexico, and was known only to the small group of people who were excited by short-distance sprinting. His name was Zantanon, but because he also won so consistently, he came to be known as "The Man O' War of Mexico."

In the breeding ranks, however, Zantanon may have come out ahead. Man O' War sired some outstanding foals, such as War Admiral and Crusader. But for some reason he was not given the finest quality mares and his breeding record was not as consistent as his racing record.

Zantanon, on the other hand, proved outstanding as a sire, even with a limited band of broodmares and fewer crops of offspring. His sons and daughters helped provide the foundation on which the modern American Quarter Horse breed has been built.

The colt called Zantanon was foaled March 17, 1917, on the ranch of premier breeder Ott Adams near the small town of Alfred. Adams' expertise guaranteed that the dark sorrel colt's breeding was as good as could be found for a Quarter Horse in that era.

Zantanon's sire was Little Joe, a legendary sprinter who was sired by the great Traveler (see his story in *Legends, Vol. 2*). Little Joe's dam was Jenny, by Sykes' Rondo. Jenny's dam was May Mangum, a granddaughter of Old Billy. Since Little Joe was related to some of the finest families of sprinters, it came as no surprise when Little Joe sired such famous speedsters and progenitors as Joe Moore, Grano De Oro, and Cotton Eyed Joe. Little Joe was a full brother to the good horse successfully raced in Texas

as King (not King P-234) and later known as Possum in Arizona, where he became an outstanding sire.

The dam of Zantanon was Jeanette, who was both a granddaughter and great-granddaughter of Sykes' Rondo. From other matings to Little Joe, Jeanette also produced the good sire Pancho Villa, as well as the mares Black Annie and Little Sister.

A common practice for Adams was to sell his young race prospects. So, at 11 months, Zantanon was sold with two other potential runners to Erasmus Flores of Nuevo Laredo, Mexico. Flores' uncle, Don Eutiquio Flores, selected Zantanon from this group and successfully offered his nephew a profit three months later when the colt showed indications of speed. The

In this photograph
Zantanon was
24 years old.

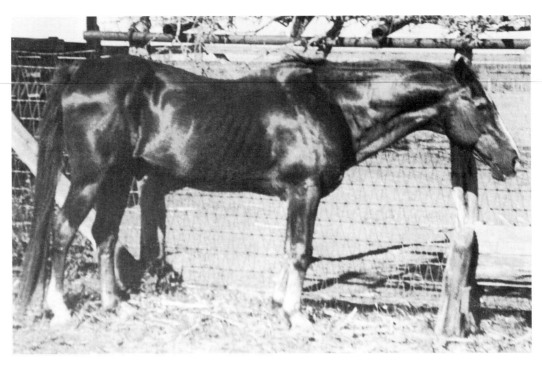

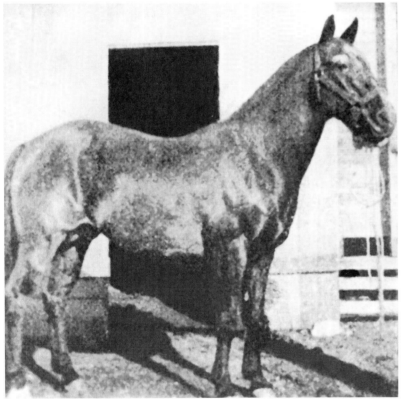

Little Joe, the sire of Zantanon, was foaled in 1905 and bred by Dow and Will Shely, Alfred, Texas. This picture was reproduced from AQHA Studbook No. 2, with permission of the AQHA.

colt was put into training immediately.

The senior Flores raced Zantanon until he was 14 years old. Usually he was ridden by Flores' 140-pound son. During those years, Flores became a man of property—accumulating both a ranch and several buildings in town. Zantanon was a consistent winner against all comers, while recording such times as :15⅖ for 300 yards. His challengers came from hundreds of miles around, only to meet defeat.

Zantanon's last race was against a fast young daughter of Ace Of Hearts named Coneza. Since Coneza had twice defeated the reputable runner named Pancho Villa, a full brother to Little Joe, she was considered a favorite by many. The wily old horse, however, scored perfectly and broke on top. As usual, he stayed in front to the finish line.

One of the men who tried to beat Zantanon was the father of Manuel Benavides Volpe of Laredo, Texas. He wanted so badly to beat the son of Little Joe that he bought eight well-bred, top-quality race horses to match against him. These horses were purchased one at a time and then each was replaced as he/she lost to the mighty Zantanon.

The senior Volpe, thwarted so many times, developed a strong aversion to the horse. His son, however, after seeing the

San Siemon was perhaps Zantanon's greatest breeding son. Foaled in 1934, he was out of Panita, by Possum. The handler is either Thomas or Warren Wilson.

This ad for H.H. Darks, in AQHA Studbook No. 5, includes a picture of San Sue Darks, who was by San Siemon. Reproduced with permission of the AQHA.

horse and hearing how he won despite mishandling, made purchasing Zantanon his ambition. Once he had accomplished this and got the game speedster back across the Rio Grande, the younger Volpe gave him the kind of care he had not known since his first year.

Volpe then made known the full story about the mishandling of this famed runner. He related that on a typical train-ing day, Zantanon was walked on hard gravel streets the four miles out to a track, and then was walked, trotted, and galloped before jogging him until his sweat dried. He then was walked back

*The great Leo San traced back to Zantanon through his dam, San Sue Darks,
who was by San Siemon. Leo San's sire was the renowned Leo.*

Photo Courtesy *The Quarter Horse Journal*

those same four miles and tied to a tree
through the heat of the day until about
4 o'clock when he was ridden on the
gravel streets until dark.

At night, Zantanon received just a small
amount of oats and corn, along with corn
fodder for roughage. By race day, he was
so poor that his ribs were starkly visible.

Volpe stated that the first time he saw
Zantanon, the horse was so thin and
weak that he wavered as he walked. His
head hung listlessly until he was led onto

the track. Noted horseman John Arm-
strong was quoted as saying that Zantanon had won his races on breeding
alone, since the horse's racing condition
was such that other horses in that shape
couldn't catch a cow.

When Volpe purchased him, Zantanon
was so weak, poor, and infested with
ticks that he could barely walk. Volpe
believed that a horse who could win
consistently under such conditions was
a phenomenon who deserved a better
life and a chance to show his potential
at stud. Once back in Texas, Zantanon
never knew an empty manger.

Although Volpe did not breed Zantanon
to any outside mares, and although many
of Volpe's mares were related to Zantanon,
the horse was getting his first chance to
prove himself at stud. Used as a sire for
only 10 years with that small group of
mares, Zantanon showed he was as
incredible a sire as he was a runner.

Because Zantanon died the year after
the AQHA was formed, his opportunities
of getting foals into the registry and into
the mainstream of the Quarter Horse
industry were further limited.

The fact that Zantanon was linebred
to the extent of having three crosses to
Sykes' Rondo may help explain the con-
sistency of quality in his foals. Sykes'
Rondo was a son of McCoy Billy and
therefore was a member of the famed
Billy family of early Quarter Horse history. Helen Michaelis, one of the first
AQHA secretaries and a very careful historian of the breed, has written that the
Billy family was at one time the most popular strain of Quarter Horses in Texas.

In Volpe's care, Zantanon sired King
P-234 (*Legends, Vol. 1*), another immortal
in the history of Quarter Horses. This
bay colt, foaled in 1932, was successfully
matched for a couple of races before being
converted to a calf-roping horse. His foals
and subsequent descendants excelled in
all kinds of performance, but their domi-
nation of cutting horse contests was so
strong that the family name has become
almost synonymous with that event.

San Siemon

In 1934 Zantanon's great breeding son,
San Siemon, was foaled. His dam was a
daughter of Possum named Panita.

Peppy San, who traced back to Zantanon, was a 1959 son of Leo San and out of Peppy Belle, by Pep Up. Trained and shown by Matlock Rose, Peppy San became an AQHA Champion, the 1967 NCHA World Champion Cutting Horse, and a successful sire. That's Matlock in the saddle.

San Siemon's daughters are the reason he receives the most acclaim in today's Quarter Horse circles.

Possum, a full brother to Little Joe (Zantanon's sire), was one of the foundations of top-quality Quarter Horses in Arizona.

Typical of the good sons sired by San Siemon were Bras d'Or, Joe Barrett, and Black Hawk. San Siemon's daughters, however, are the reason that he receives the most acclaim in today's Quarter Horse circles.

Bras d'Or, out of the famous producer Lady Coolidge, sired the AQHA Champion Ann d'Or and several ROM performers in working events. His daughters produced the AQHA Champions Skipper Bar 2, Casey Tivio, Fairfax Suzie, Rosada Bars, and Robin Tivio, as well as several race and working ROM qualifiers.

Joe Barrett, by San Siemon and out of Little Sue, was the grand champion stallion at Fort Worth in 1944. At stud, he sired both racing and working ROM qualifiers. Among the offspring of his daughters were the AQHA Champions Poco Mo, Jody Cord, and Julio Bar, in addition to the Superior-earning cutting horse Hollywood Bill. Joe Barrett daughters also produced ROM performers in both racing and arena work.

Black Hawk, another son of San Siemon and Little Sue (a daughter of Sam Watkins, by Hickory Bill), sired many capable rodeo performers in addition to his offspring with AQHA records. In AQHA-recognized events, he sired two racing and six arena ROM qualifiers.

San Siemon's daughters produced many racing and arena ROM qualifiers—including the AQHA Champion Dixie Siemon, who also was a Superior-earning

Peppy San Badger, better known as Little Peppy, traces back to Zantanon through his sire, Mr San Peppy, who was a son of Leo San and a full brother to Peppy San. Shown here with Buster Welch in the saddle, Peppy San Badger won the 1977 NCHA Futurity and 1978 NCHA Derby, then went on to become a successful sire.

Joe Barrett was another good son of San Siemon—and grandson of Zantanon. During his show career he was named the grand champion stallion at Fort Worth in 1944. His offspring were ROM qualifiers in both racing and working events.

Photo by Williamson, Courtesy *The Quarter Horse Journal*

SONNY KIMBLE 1169

This R.C. Tatum ad, featuring a picture of Sonny Kimble, appeared in AQHA Studbook No. 2. Sonny Kimble was another outstanding son of Zantanon and particularly successful as a sire of rope horses. Reproduced with permission of the AQHA.

halter horse. Other Superior-earning halter horses from these dams were San's Jo and Cutter Smokey.

Little Sue, the dam of Joe Barrett and Black Hawk, also produced San Siemon's two most prominent daughters: Sue Hunt and San Sue Darks.

Sue Hunt produced the performance ROM qualifiers Continental King and Sansue Bert. Continental King, a Superior reining horse, became an important progenitor in the cutting and reining horse industries.

San Sue Darks produced the great sire Leo San. Among Leo San's many working and racing ROM offspring are Wimpy Leo San (1961 High-Point Halter Stallion), Leo San Van (1961 High-Point Cutting Gelding and High-Point Halter Gelding, as well as 1962 High-Point Cutting Gelding), and Tabor's Leo (1962 High-Point Barrel Racing Stallion).

Peppy San and Mr San Peppy

Leo San capped his breeding career, however, when he sired the full brothers Peppy San and Mr San Peppy—both out of Peppy Belle, a daughter of Pep Up.

The AQHA awarded Peppy San the titles of AQHA Champion, Superior

Zantanon Jr., foaled in 1937, was out of the Thoroughbred mare Dorothy E. Not as popular as his full brother Ed Echols, Zantanon Jr. did achieve some success as a sire. **Photo Courtesy** *The Quarter Horse Journal*

Here's an own daughter of Zantanon named Chapparita Menada. Foaled in 1932, she was out of Panita, by Little King. This picture was reproduced with permission from AQHA Studbook No. 3.

Zandy, foaled in 1934, was the only son of Zantanon to earn a ROM in performance. He was out of a mare by the Strait Horse.

Photo Courtesy *The Quarter Horse Journal*

Cutting Horse, and High-Point Cutting Stallion of 1967. The NCHA named him World Champion Cutting Horse of 1967 and inducted him into the NCHA Hall of Fame. He had placed second in the 1962 NCHA Futurity.

At stud, Peppy San continued to be a leader. His spectacular cutting son Peponita was placed in the NCHA Hall of Fame and was the 1977 and 1979 NCHA World Champion Cutting Horse. He was also the AQHA World Champion Senior Cutting Horse in both 1977 and 1978.

Peppy San also sired Peppy's Desire (1975 NCHA World Champion Cutting Horse), Peppy Lena San (1986 NCHA Derby Champion), Tip It San (1977 NCHA Derby Champion), and Chunky's Monkey (1974 NCHA Derby Co-Champion).

AQHA title-winners sired by Peppy San include Sanacee (1985 and 1986 AQHA World Champion Amateur Cutting Horse), Miss Peppy Gay Bar (1983 AQHA High-Point Amateur Cutting Horse), and Royal Santana (1986 High-Point Amateur Cutting Horse).

Mr San Peppy was the NCHA World Champion Cutting Horse of both 1974 and 1976. He was the 1972 NCHA Derby Champion. An AQHA Superior-earning cutting horse, Mr San Peppy was the 1976 AQHA World Champion Senior Cutting Horse and the AQHA High-Point Cutting Stallion.

As a progenitor, Mr San Peppy also was top class. His most acclaimed son is Peppy San Badger (known in cutting circles as Little Peppy). Peppy San Badger won the 1977 NCHA Futurity and then came back to win the 1978 NCHA Derby. He was the NCHA Reserve World Champion in 1980 and has been placed in the NCHA Hall of Fame.

As a sire, Peppy San Badger continued to add honors to the family's credit. Among his foals is Peppymint Twist, co-champion of the 1983 NCHA Derby. Many of his foals have placed in the top 10 at the AQHA World Championship Show in reining, calf roping, heeling, and cutting. They have also made their marks in both the NCHA Futurity and the NCHA Derby. Little Peppy also sired the AQHA Superior-earning cutting horse Little Marvel and many AQHA ROM qualifiers.

Mr San Peppy also sired Tenino San, the 1982 NCHA World Champion. Other outstanding foals sired by Mr San Peppy include Peppy Rancho, Peppy San Chato, Peppys Pluma, Organ Grinder, and Peppys Regona.

Zandy

Another notable son of Zantanon was Zandy, out of a mare by the Strait Horse. Foaled in 1924 and the only foal of Zantanon to earn a performance ROM title, Zandy sired both racing and working ROM foals. His most noted breeding offspring, Sport and Lorane, however, did not win any such awards.

Sport sired Sporty Pedro, an AQHA Champion and Superior-earning halter horse, and several other arena ROM performers. In turn, Sporty Pedro sired the Superior-earning western pleasure horse Sporty O'Kings and other ROM performance horses. Sport's daughters added several more arena ROM horses to the family.

Lorane's top son was Grey Question. This gray stallion was a AAA stakes

Sport, a son of Zandy and grandson of Zantanon, was pictured in this Haythorn ad in AQHA Studbook No. 4. Reproduced with permission of the AQHA.

winner and held the 330-yard track record at the Sonoma (Calif.) County Fair. Grey Question sired numerous race ROM horses and his daughters produced many more.

Lorane's AAA daughter Miss Okmulgee produced such classy runners as Lotta Charge (Top AAA), Three Gee's (AAA stakes winner), and Bita Charge (AAA and dam of the AAA Pokey Charge). Lorane also produced three other ROM runners, including

Bob Cuatro, foaled in 1957, was by Cuatro de Julio, by Zantanon, and out of Leota W, by Leo. He's shown here, with trainer John Hoyt in the saddle, when he was named the 1963 All-Around Performance Horse Champion in the state of Arizona. He was owned by Dr. and Mrs. T.O. Plummer of Montrose, Colo., and that's Mrs. Plummer receiving the trophy from Pat O'Leary. Hoyt, who now lives in Texas, was living in Arizona at the time. **WH File Photo**

the AAA Lorane's Vandy.

Another of Lorane's outstanding broodmares was Lorane's Question. She produced Junior Reed (AAA stakes winner and holder of 300-yard track record at the Cochise County Fair), and Vandy's Question (AA stakes winner).

Also a notable sire, Junior Reed climaxed his breeding career by siring the AQHA Supreme Champion Mach I. To earn this title, Mach I not only ran Top AAA and won grand and reserve halter championships while in race training, but he also garnered points in reining, heading, heeling, and western pleasure.

Chico

In 1936, Zantanon and Panita produced a full brother to San Siemon. His name was Chico. The grand champion stallion at one of the Oklahoma Quarter Horse Association's earliest shows, Chico became a prominent sire in that state.

Probably the most successful son of Chico was Chico Dawson. Top among foals from this stallion was Dawson's Slats (known also in cutting arenas as Slats

Dawson). Dawson's Slats was the AQHA High-Point Cutting Gelding of 1958.

Sonny Kimble

Another outstanding son of Zantanon was Sonny Kimble, foaled in 1936. He was out of Queen, a daughter of Valentino, and his second dam was Jabalina, the dam of King P-234.

Sonny Kimble was particularly successful as a sire of rope horses. They proved capable both in rodeo arenas and AQHA show rings. A versatile sire, Sonny Kimble also sired the AQHA Superior-earning cutting horse Baldy Gus and the ROM racers Baby Doll Jones and Sonny Rondo, as well as ROM performers in other events.

Zantanon Jr. and Ed Echols

When bred to Zantanon, the Thoroughbred mare Dorothy E, by Flying Squirrel, foaled Zantanon Jr. in 1937 and Ed Echols in 1940. (See Ed Echols' story in this book.)

Zantanon Jr. did not achieve the popularity of his brother, but through him the blood of Zantanon was passed down to many winning horses. Volpe thought enough of the bright sorrel stallion that he not only gave him his sire's name, but also used him in his own breeding program. For Volpe, Zantanon Jr. sired the ROM campaigners Peggy Dean, Miss Glory, and Red Gravey. In those early days of recognized racing, when official races were few and far between, Zantanon Jr. also was represented by ROM runners County Billy, Mr Jimmy Hicks, and Patty Ann Yeager.

Red Gravey was the top breeding son of Zantanon Jr., siring several race and performance ROM horses. His daughters also proved to be all-around producers of both working and race ROM horses.

Zantanon Jr. was successful, too, as a broodmare sire. His daughter Shov Zan produced the noted cutting horse

Sporty Pedro, by Sport, was an AQHA Champion and Superior halter horse
Photo by Moore, Courtesy *The Quarter Horse Journal*

Jose Uno, an AQHA Superior-earning cutting horse.

Zantanon's Daughters

Zantanon deservedly fits into that acclaimed category of horses known as a sire of sires. As broodmares, however, his daughters did their share to maintain the family traditions.

Maria Elena, by Zantanon, produced Hi Maria, Zantanon H, and Leozan. Hi Maria won the Eagle Pass Derby and

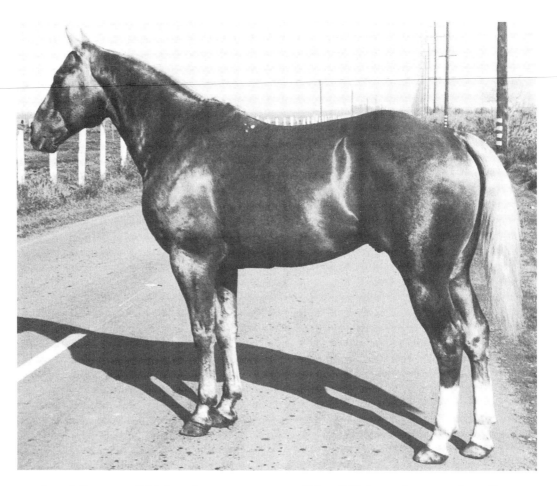

Bras d'Or, foaled in 1940, was an outstanding son of San Siemon, by Zantanon, and out of Lady Coolidge, by Beach's Yellow Jacket. He was bred by Bert Benear of Tulsa, Oklahoma.

Photo Courtesy Phil Livingston

produced the arena ROM-performer Little Dynamite.

Zantanon H gained most of his reputation as a sire. His progeny include the AQHA Champions Poco Zantanon (sire of Poco Benne Mo, an AQHA Champion and Superior-earning western pleasure horse), Traveler Sam, Zan Hankins (also a Superior-earning halter horse), and Zan Sun (a Superior-earning cutting horse).

Leozan also was best known as an all-around sire. His sons and daughters include the AAA stakes winner Leo Bill, the AQHA Superior-earning halter horse Leozanne Cody, and many other working and racing ROM stars.

Other ROM speedsters produced by daughters of Zantanon include Miss Hasty and El Barril. Winner of $9,641, respectable earnings for those years, the AAA Miss Hasty was the top money-earner produced by Zantanon's daughters.

Zantanon's good daughter Spider M produced Tanon Luck, who was a ROM performer in both open and youth events.

Stormy Lee, out of Zantanon's daughter Babe Cheshewalla, sired the AQHA Champion Quincy Scooter, whose foals earned the titles of AQHA Champion, race ROM, and performance ROM.

Another Zantanon daughter, Uncle's Pet, produced the well-known sire Small Town Dude, who proved himself by siring the great Blondy's Dude. An AQHA Champion, Blondy's Dude became one of the breed's leading sires of AQHA Champions and a leading sire of ROM arena horses. (See the chapter on Blondy's Dude in this book.)

Zantanon, of course, lived out most of his life before there were recognized races or the official Quarter Horse shows in which his descendants carved their illus-

Zorena, foaled in 1952, was a maternal great-granddaughter of Zantanon who earned her AQHA Championship. She was by J.B. King and out of Zantorena, by Zantanon Jr. This 1956 photo was taken at Sonoita, Ariz., where Zorena was named grand champion mare. She was shown by Frank Owenby and owned by Mrs. Rose Fulton of Dragoon, Arizona.

Photo by Richard Schaus

trious careers. At one point, Volpe apparently decided to cut back his horse operation and devote more time to his successful oil business.

As a result, he sold Zantanon and many of his best mares to Byrne James. A rancher, calf roper, and professional baseball player, James is listed in the first AQHA Stud Book as the breeder of King P-234, although Volpe generally is given that credit. After a short time, Volpe regretted the transaction and persuaded James to sell Zantanon and many of the mares back.

Zantanon remained with Volpe until 1941. At that time, the 24-year-old stallion became ill and Volpe sent him to the Hebronville ranch of his friend Alonzo Taylor. The plan was for Dr. J. K. Northway, the very capable King Ranch veterinarian, to treat him. However, before Northway could do anything for the horse, he died. Meanwhile, the legacy of Zantanon and the quality of his descendants continues into the present day.

The AQHA/PRCA Horses of the Year are acknowledged to be professional rodeo's best horses in their respective categories. In 1996 these titleholders included Super San Wood (steer wrestling), Van's Lad (steer roping), Flit's Smokin Dream (heeling), and

French Flash Hawk, better known as Bozo (barrel racing). One thing that all these horses have in common is the fact that Zantanon appears in every one of their pedigrees.

In 1996 racing, AQHA's world champion Quarter running horse, Dashing Folly, and the 2-year-old world champion, Toast To Dash, also trace back to Zantanon. Toast To Dash is of particular note because he was bred and owned by the Angelina Cattle Co. of Laredo. This cattle and horse operation was founded by M. Benavides Volpes' sister Angelina, along with her son and daughter.

These champions and other top horses who demonstrated their winning abilities in 1996 show that Zantanon's outstanding qualities live on. Zantanon's name is quite far back in their pedigrees, but it is there, sparkling like a distant star.

2   ED ECHOLS

By Larry Thornton

**He sired top
horses in many
events, and his
descendants
have made
him a legend.**

IN THE late 1930s and early '40s, the sheriff of Pima County, Ariz., was a former rodeo cowboy named Ed Echols. Echols claimed the title of world champion cowboy by virtue of winning the steer roping at the 1912 Calgary Stampede.

Sheriff Echols was good friends with a horseman named W.D. "Dink" Parker, who named a stallion he owned in honor of his friend. Ed Echols, the horse, went on to make a name for himself as a sire of race horses, halter horses, and performance horses.

The equine Ed Echols was a chestnut bred by Manuel Benevides Volpe and foaled on Volpe's ranch in Laredo, Tex., on April 16, 1940. But the influence of Ed Echols began when he was purchased

*An undated photograph
of Ed Echols, who sired
a number of speedsters,
including several mares
who became outstand-
ing producers.*

**Photo Courtesy
American Quarter
Horse Heritage Center
& Museum**

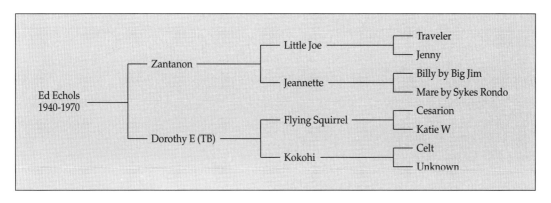

Ed Echols
1940–1970
├─ Zantanon
│ ├─ Little Joe
│ │ ├─ Traveler
│ │ └─ Jenny
│ └─ Jeannette
│   ├─ Billy by Big Jim
│   └─ Mare by Sykes Rondo
└─ Dorothy E (TB)
   ├─ Flying Squirrel
   │ ├─ Cesarion
   │ └─ Katie W
   └─ Kokohi
      ├─ Celt
      └─ Unknown

by Dink Parker. Parker's long-time friend and protégé, Art Pollard, said, "Dink gave more money for Ed Echols than he gave for any other horse he had bought up to that time, and it was something like $1,500. Back then that was a lot of money."

Fay Parker, Dink's wife, wrote in a December 1948 *Quarter Horse Journal* article that they had bought Ed Echols, or "Edward" as she called him, from George Clegg, the breeder of such noted horses as Old Sorrel and Sam Watkins. AQHA records show that Clegg bred a 1944 son of Ed Echols, called Joe Echols, a Register of Merit race horse.

Dink and Fay Parker's friendship with Pollard was instrumental in helping Pollard get a good start in the horse business. Dink became Pollard's mentor and guide in developing the Lightning A Ranch, where Pollard bred horses such as Lightning Bar and Bardella.

"Actually, I was going to the Quarter Horse races while attending the University in Tucson," explained Pollard. "I enjoyed racing and had seen match races in Texas, where I came from originally. I went out and met Dink, because he was winning everything.

"He took a fatherly interest in me, and when I got interested in the horse business, he said he'd help me select some mares. Dink was a great mare man, which rubbed off on me." Pollard went on to own such famous mares as Hula Girl P, Della P, Black Gal P, Miss Panama, Queenie, and Miss Bank.

Pollard remembers Parker as a great cattleman from a family of great cattlemen. Parker had traveled from Texas to New Mexico in his younger days with his family. They reportedly drove several hundred head of horses from their home in Texas to New Mexico.

Halter and Performance Record: Race Register of Merit.

Progeny Record:

Foal Crops: 23	Performance Registers of Merit: 21
Foals Registered: 244	Superior Performance Awards: 4
AQHA Champions: 8	Race Starters: 52
Halter Point-Earners: 24	Race Money Earned: $118,533
Halter Points Earned: 303	Race Registers of Merit: 27
Performance Point-Earners: 38	Superior Race Awards: 3
Performance Points Earned: 657	
Leading Race Money-Earner: Little Smoke Echols ($29,383)	

After World War I Parker moved to Arizona, where at one time he owned as many as 80 sections of land. He established his horse breeding operation on the Apache Springs Ranch, where he had such horses as Ben Hur and Parker's Chicaro.

As for Ed Echols the sheriff, Pollard said, "I guess Ed and Dink knew each other in Texas. Ed was a great lover of horse racing. I remember him coming out to the Lightning A as an old man. He came out to see horses like Miss Bank. He'd grown senile and couldn't recognize the horses anymore. But he loved to come out. He was a grand man and a helluva stockman."

As for Ed Echols the horse, Pollard said, "He could be pretty feisty. He wasn't the best-looking horse. He was a liver chestnut and didn't have the best head in the

Hula Girl P, a sorrel daughter of Ed Echols and Leilani, was foaled in 1947. Shown here with owner Art Pollard, she was rated AA on the track and became an AQHA Champion.

WH File Photo

Here's Hula Girl P with her 1955 foal, a Lightning Bar filly named Hula Baby, who earned a AAA rating on the track.

Photo by Matt Culley

Parker's Trouble, foaled in 1949, was one of Ed Echols' best sons. Out of Little Nellie Bars, who was by Bull Lightning, Parker's Trouble was rated AAA on the track, sired several AAA horses, and became a leading maternal grandsire of ROM race colts. He also sired several AQHA Champions such as Againu, Bar Trouble, Miss Kachina, and Mr Trouble. The fellow in the picture is Blain Lewis of Patagonia, Arizona. Blain and his brother, Greet, bought Parker's Trouble from Dink Parker in 1960.

Photo Courtesy The Quarter Horse Journal

Hula Girl P became a tremendous broodmare and is shown in this 1953 photo with her colt, Arizonan, by Spotted Bull (TB). Arizonan, rated AAAT, was the 1955 Champion Quarter Running Gelding.

Photo by Richard Schaus

War Chant, by Three Bars (TB) and out of Hula Girl P—and thus a grandson of Ed Echols—was bred by Art Pollard and foaled in 1952. Rated AAA+, he was a stakes winner who sired a number of ROM race offspring, such as Sword Play, who also became an AQHA Champion. War Chant reportedly stood 14.2 and weighed 1,200 pounds.

Photo Courtesy Yvonne LeMaitre

world. Might have been a little heavy in the shoulder and a bit short in the hip, but he could sire horses."

Fay Parker gives an indication of the feisty side of Ed Echols with an incident in the 1948 *Quarter Horse Journal* article: "One Sunday a few weeks after Edward had gone into training, he happened to be one in a field of five horses. He got out of the gate well and was leading the pack when a horse named Little Texas … began pulling alongside of Edward. The outcome was near when Ed glanced back and saw Little Texas coming nearer. He put on extra speed, but so did Texas as he started to pass. When he did, Ed, with

nostrils flared, opened his mouth wide and took a firm and vicious bite of Texas and held on like a bulldog." The jockey had to take hold of Ed and the horse lost the race.

Fay Parker's account also states that Ed Echols was green when they put him in the hands of Lyo Lee, a Tucson trainer. The Parkers raced Ed Echols because his "folks were runnin' stock" and they wanted to see what kind of race horse he was before they retired him to stud.

Ed Echols' race record with the American Quarter Racing Association shows that he had six official starts in 1947 with three wins and one second. He was A-rated on the track with a Register of Merit. The *1947 AQRA Year Book* indicates that Ed Echols was also raced under the name "The Sheriff."

Of Running Stock

The "runnin' stock" Fay Parker referred to were Zantanon and Dorothy E, who is thought to have been a Thoroughbred. Zantanon has been labeled the

Ed Heller, foaled in 1947, was a speedy son of Ed Echols out of the mare Glass Eyes. She was by Wild Law (TB) and out of Lady, by Rainy Day. Rated AAAT, Ed Heller sired several ROM race offspring.

Photo by Til Thompson, Courtesy *The Quarter Horse Journal*

"Man O' War of Mexico" for his greatness as a race horse while in Mexico. He was later owned and came to fame in the hands of Manuel Benevides Volpe. (See Zantanon's chapter in this book.)

Volume 10 of the *American Stud Book* shows Dorothy E to be a registered Thoroughbred mare bred by J.A. Hall of Stanberry, Missouri. Her sire was Flying Squirrel, by Cesarion, who was by Faustus, by Enquirer.

The dam of Cesarion was *Cleopatra, by Rosicrucian. AQHA records list the dam of Flying Squirrel as unknown, but historians believe she was Katie W, by Himyar, who sired the great Thoroughbred stallions Plaudit and Domino. The dam of Katie W was Favoress, by *Macaroon.

The dam of Dorothy E was Kokohi, by Celt. Celt was sired by Commando, by Domino, by Himyar. This would make Dorothy E double-bred to Himyar.

Not all researchers agree that Dorothy E was truly a full-blood Thoroughbred. The controversy over her pedigree is noted by Helen Michaelis in a mare binder from the Bob Denhardt

Collection at the American Quarter Horse Heritage Center. This material tells us that Dorothy E was falsely registered as a Thoroughbred out of Kokohi, but that her dam was actually a Quarter mare.

This material also states that Dorothy E's one-time owner, R.C. Row, indicated that she was not bred by J.A. Hall, but by Bud Hall of Iowa. He also indicated that she could do the quarter in 22 seconds. Row told that he was given an affidavit that attested to that fact when he bought the mare from Bud Hall. Dorothy E was later owned by M. Benevides Volpe and Alonzo Taylor of Halletsville, Texas.

Bob Denhardt reaffirms some of this

Gin Echols was an Ed Echols daughter who helped prove that his get could excel in the show ring as well as on the track. After B.F. Phillips bought the mare, he rode her to the 1965 and 1966 NCHA non-pro championships. Gin Echols, foaled in 1954, was out of Gin Squirt (TB).   **Photo by Dalco, Courtesy** *The Quarter Horse Journal*

Ginger Echols, an Ed Echols daughter, earned her ROM in the arena. Foaled in 1952, she was out of Ginger D, who was by Red Tone, by Silvertone, and out of Pal, by Alamo. The rider is not identified. **Photo by Charlie Ray, Courtesy** *The Quarter Horse Journal*

Annie Echols, bred by Frank Vessels and foaled in 1952, was an Ed Echols daughter out of Orphan Annie. She was by Baby King, by Possum, and out of a Ben Hur mare. Annie Echols was rated AAA on the track and earned 40 halter points. One of her sons was Par Three, a Superior halter horse who sired the great Zan Parr Bar.

Photo by Matt Culley

information in his book, *Foundation Dams of the American Quarter Horse*, by stating that Dorothy E was out of a Quarter mare named Kokohi, who was sired by Celt. He also says that she was bred by J.A. Hall and was first run by Bud Hall of Iowa.

New Owners

In 1949 Dink Parker sold Ed Echols to Ray Sence from Burbank, California. "The fact that Father Time was catching up and good help was hard to find prompted Dink to sell Ed Echols and many of his other horses," said Pollard, who explained that Parker's 70 broodmares constituted a big project for a man of his age.

Sence stood Ed Echols until 1956, when

he sold the horse to Jack Clifford from Kelseyville, California. In the beginning, Clifford didn't think he had gotten such a good deal. "Ray Sence, a horse breeder out in California, had a sale," Clifford said. "Ed Echols brought $4,600. I thought it was a pretty bad buy till I sold him to B.F. Phillips Jr. for $10,000.

"We didn't do any good with him," Clifford explained. "We stood him at stud one year or so, and some people liked him and some didn't. I liked him; he was a nice horse, a son of Zantanon. Phillips always said, 'He was a better son of Zantanon than King P-234.' I don't know if that is true or not. But I do know that if Ed Echols had the chance King did, he'd be a famous horse today. He had fine colts."

B.F. Phillips was building a top showing and breeding operation in the 1950s and was assembling some great names in Quarter Horse history. The Phillips Ranch was home to such horses as Steel Bars, Cactus Breeze, L H Quarter Moon, Poco Lynn, Poco Jan, Martha King, and Gold-

Travel Echols was a 1955 sorrel stallion with no AQHA show record. Sired by Ed Echols, he was out of H's Pepsi, who was by Joe Traveler and out of Fran, by King P-234. Travel Echols sired 96 foals, including the AQHA Champion Pepsi Raysen.

Photo by John H. Williamson, Courtesy *The Quarter Horse Journal*

wood. Phillips and his trainer, Matlock Rose, were always on the lookout for top horses, and they went to California to look at Ed Echols.

"Matlock and B.F. Phillips came out to the ranch to look at the horse," Clifford remembered. "Phillips offered me $7,500, and I swallowed hard and said, 'No— $10,000 or nothing.' They bought him, but Phillips said, 'For $10,000, you deliver him.' So we delivered him."

Actually, Phillips formed a partnership with T.F. Larkin until 1959. Then Phillips assumed full ownership of Ed Echols and owned the horse until his death in August of 1970.

Offspring

Ed Echols sired some very fast foals who were major players in the southwestern racing scene. These speedsters included Parker's Trouble, Dandy Z, Ed Heller, Hula Girl P, and Little Smoke Echols.

Little Smoke Echols, a multiple stakes-

winner, won the 1950 Southwestern Futurity at Rillito. Ed Heller, another multiple stakes-winner, captured the 1949 Southwestern Futurity, and Dandy Z won the 1952 Joe Blair Handicap. All three runners either set or equaled at least one track record during their careers.

Parker's Trouble wasn't a track record-setter, but he was a AAA-rated runner. The official race record of Parker's Trouble doesn't show him a winner in the Southwestern Futurity, but reference is made by several people, including Art Pollard, that Parker's Trouble won this race in 1951. This gives Ed Echols and Dink Parker the first three winners of that race.

Parker's Trouble went on to be a great sire for his owner, Blain Lewis, whose

Cherry Echols, a 1949 sorrel mare bred by W.D. Parker, was by Ed Echols and out of Ratona, who was by Ben Hur, by Rainy Day, and out of Lady Ratona. Cherry Echols earned 21 halter points, 26 cutting points, and two racing points. She earned her AQHA Championship in 1957.

Photo by Dick Merfeld, Courtesy *The Quarter Horse Journal*

brother, Greet, trained the stallion. Among Parker's Trouble's foals are Trouble Gal, the fourth dam of 1984 World Champion Quarter Running Horse Dashs Dream; Trouble Fair, dam of Boston Mac; Pima Country, an AQHA Champion; and Big Step, sire of horses such as Trouble Step, the 1965 AQHA High-Point Halter Horse.

B.F. Phillips talked about his purchase of Ed Echols in a December 1980 *Quarter Horse Journal* article. Phillips said, "I think he (Ed Echols) is probably as good a sire of females as I've ever seen." Two of those noted daughters are Hula Girl P and Annie Echols.

Hula Girl P

Bred by Dink Parker, Hula Girl P was out of the mare Leilani, by Parker's Chicaro. The first horse Art Pollard bought from Parker, Hula Girl P started her career as a show horse, winning blue ribbons and grand championships. Pollard believes they won somewhere in the neighborhood of 20 grand championships out of 24 or 25 shows. She officially earned 20 halter points.

Blain Lewis, who had Little Bit L, once told Pollard, "When are you going to stop showing her so the rest of us will have a shot at grand champion mare?"

When Pollard did stop showing his classy mare, he surprised everyone by starting her on the racetrack. She set a track record in her second start. In the 1950 Arizona Derby, Hula Girl P went off at odds of 80 to 1. She won, and Pollard won enough at those odds to build a training track.

Then Hula Girl P proved her value as a broodmare. She produced such noted horses as War Chant, winner of the Pacific Coast QHRA Futurity; Arizonan, the 1955 World Champion Gelding; and Sonoitan, a AAA-rated AQHA Champion.

Jack Clifford's admiration of the Ed Echols horses didn't end when he sold the stallion to Phillips. He would later buy and stand War Chant, Hula Girl P's good son. As he put it, "War Chant took us from hamburger and put us on steaks." War Chant sired horses such as the AAA-rated AQHA Champion Sword Play while Clifford owned him.

Annie Echols

Annie Echols was bred by Frank Vessels Jr. and foaled during Ed Echols' time with Ray Sence. She became an integral part of the famous Finley Ranch breeding program in Arizona. This great mare repeated the pattern set by Hula Girl P as both a race horse and show horse. She earned her ROM and AAA-rating on the track, then went to the show pen to earn 40 halter points.

Annie Echols produced nine performers, including a stakes-winner, two Superior-earning halter horses, and one AQHA Champion. The stakes-winner was Fancy Three, a mare who won the 1965 AQRA Lassie Stakes. The AQHA Champion was Echols' Dandy with 37 halter points and 65.5 performance points, and the two Superior halter horses were Dandy Duz and Par Three.

A great amount of the Ed Echols influence today comes through his grandson Par Three. Par Three sired Zan Parr Bar,

foaled in 1974. Zan Parr Bar became the 1977 AQHA World Champion 3-Year-Old Halter Stallion and the 1979 and 1980 World Champion Aged Halter Stallion. He was also the 1977 AQHA High-Point Halter Stallion and the 1979 AQHA High-Point Steer Roping Horse. For more on Zan Parr Bar, see his chapter in this book.

Phillips Ranch

The last phase of Ed Echols' record as a sire came when he stood at the Phillips Ranch in Frisco, Texas. There he became a noted sire of good performance horses. His foals during this time included Echo Reed, the 1964 AQHA High-Point Calf Roping Horse; Mike Echols, the 1964 AQHA High-Point Reining Stallion; and Echo Ed, the 1981 Reserve World Champion Amateur Reining Horse. Amazingly, Echo Ed won his reserve world championship in 1981 at the age of 20.

When B.F. Phillips bought Ed Echols, he also got a daughter of the stallion, named Gin Echols, who became his personal cutting horse. He rode her to the 1965 and 1966 NCHA non-pro world championships.

Matlock Rose, who trained Gin Echols, describes her as "a really nice mare. She was kind of a Thoroughbred-lookin' mare who had a lot of speed and cow. A real cow horse." In fact, Gin Echols was out of a Thoroughbred mare named Gin Squirt, by Grogg.

Gin Echols became another outstanding Ed Echols broodmare, producing Gins Lena, an NCHA Futurity finalist; Tanquery Gin, an NCHA Futurity finalist and successful sire; and Spot O'Gin, an NCHA Futurity semifinalist. These three horses were sired by Doc O'Lena.

The "feisty stallion" from south Texas named after the sheriff of Pima County left a fitting record as a sire and progenitor of the breed. He sired top horses in many events, and his descendants have made him a legend. He died in 1970.

3 ZAN PARR BAR

By A.J. Mangum

One of the top performance horses of all time, he sired horses with arena records that rivaled his own.

HIS ADMIRERS labeled him a "cowboy's horse" because he combined impeccable conformation with proven talent in the arena. Zan Parr Bar, a chestnut California-bred stallion, rose to prominence in the late 1970s under the ownership of Texas breeder Carol Rose, garnering world halter titles while simultaneously establishing himself as a top roping horse. His get inherited both his looks and his athletic ability, and built their sire's reputation as a leading sire of performance horses.

Bred by Bobbie Silva of Tulare, Calif., Zan Parr Bar was foaled April 30, 1974. He was by Par Three—who was by Three Bars (TB) and out of Annie Echols—and out of Terry's Pal, a mare tracing to Poco Bueno. Californian Bill Gibford, a Cal Poly professor, purchased the foal at 4 months of age and gave him his name, referencing the Quarter Horse sire Zantanon, who appears on both the top and bottom sides of Zan Parr Bar's pedigree.

By his 2-year-old year, Zan Parr Bar,

Before his death at age 13, Zan Parr Bar sired 23 world champions who had earned 30 titles, 24 in roping events.

Photo Courtesy *The Quarter Horse Journal*

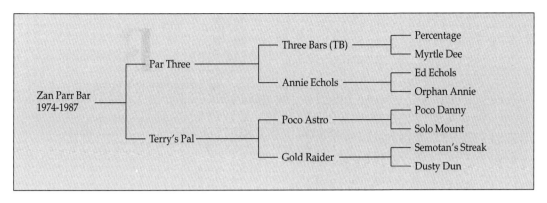

				Percentage
		Three Bars (TB)		Myrtle Dee
	Par Three		Ed Echols
		Annie Echols		Orphan Annie
Zan Parr Bar 1974-1987				Poco Danny
		Poco Astro		Solo Mount
	Terry's Pal		Semotan's Streak
		Gold Raider		Dusty Dun

with Gibford at his lead, had made his debut in California halter competition, earning several grand and reserve titles.

Enter Carol Rose.

The Acquisition

One of the Quarter Horse industry's most influential breeders, Carol Rose has said that Zan Parr Bar put her in the business of breeding Quarter Horses. Based in Gainesville, Tex., Rose had developed a program aimed at producing performance horses with winning halter conformation.

A chance encounter at a California show brought Zan Parr Bar into her program and into her life.

Rose traveled to California in 1976 to shop for broodmares, and happened to stop at a Labor Day show in Norco, where she caught her first glimpse of Zan Parr Bar.

"As I was leaving, I saw the profile of one of the most beautiful horses I've ever seen," Rose said. "I couldn't believe his head and his hip, his whole profile."

Rose looked to see who was holding the horse and recognized Gibford, her former advisor during her days as a student at Cal Poly.

"He'd called me and told me about this horse, but I wasn't really looking for a stallion," she recalled.

Rose watched Zan Parr Bar win the show's grand champion stallion title, and began envisioning the horse as part of her operation in Gainesville.

"I had a plane to catch, but I decided to stay the rest of the day and try to buy the horse," she said. Gibford declined all offers, refusing to even price the colt. "I finally asked him to give me first refusal if he ever decided to sell him."

A month later, Rose received a call

Halter and Performance Record: Performance ROM; 1977 AQHA World Champion 3-Year-Old Stallion; Superior Halter; AQHA Champion; Superior Steer Roping; 1979 AQHA World Champion Aged Stallion; 1980 AQHA World Champion Aged Stallion.

Progeny Record: (As of September 1999)

Foal Crops: 12	Halter Registers of Merit: 5
Foals Registered: 652	Performance Registers of Merit: 204
AQHA Champions: 22	Performance Point-Earners: 293
World Champions: 31	Performance Points Earned: 23,457
Halter Point-Earners: 119	Superior Performance Awards: 143
Halter Points Earned: 1,299	Race Starters: 1
Superior Halter Awards: 6	Race Money Earned: $139

from Gibford, who told her that since the Norco show, interest in Zan Parr Bar had grown rapidly and he was fielding offers on the horse.

"That was at about 9 o'clock at night," Rose said. "I was on a plane at eight the next morning, there by three, and by 5:30, the deal was done. At six, someone else who'd made an offer showed up."

Campaigning

Rose relocated Zan Parr Bar to Texas and the horse's show career moved into high gear. Almost immediately after the colt's arrival, renowned Texas trainer

Foaled in 1974, Zan Parr Bar had the conformation of a halter champion and the athleticism of one of the Quarter Horse breed's top roping horses. Kansas trainer Billy Allen campaigned the horse for owner Carol Rose.

Photo by Alfred Janssen III, Courtesy Carol Rose

Pleasure classes had allowed Zan Parr Bar to showcase his way of traveling, but the stallion's true athletic talent was in the roping arena.

Matlock Rose—Carol Rose's husband at the time—showed him to a grand championship halter title in Houston.

The following year, 1977, Zan Parr Bar stood to a full book of mares in Gainesville, and would continue to be used as a breeding stallion as his show career progressed. Carol Rose hauled

the horse, hitting major shows and circuits. He stood grand at the All American Quarter Horse Congress, then claimed his first world halter title, the 3-year-old stallion championship.

Under trainer Billy Allen, Zan Parr Bar made his western pleasure debut in the fall, earning 19 points before year's end. By the end of 1977, he'd earned his AQHA Superior halter title, AQHA's year-end high-point halter stallion and high-point junior halter horse titles, and a performance ROM.

As a saddle horse, Allen said, Zan Parr Bar was nothing short of remarkable.

"He rode kind of like he looked," the trainer said. "He had a real desire to work. There were times on the ground when he was hard to handle, but when you got a saddle on him, he was happy as a lark. He loved to work."

For Allen, Zan Parr Bar's talent came as no surprise. Before being hired by the Roses to ride the stallion, the Kansas horseman had a good look at Zan Parr Bar as a 2-year-old.

"I'd judged him at a horse show in 1976," Allen said, "before I knew I'd have anything to do with him. He was a nice horse, the kind that fits the industry at any time. He had lots of hip, a nice head, a good eye. He was the kind I like. He fit in then and he'd fit in today."

Although pleasure classes had allowed Zan Parr Bar to showcase his way of traveling and conformation under saddle, the stallion's true athletic talent was in the roping arena. Again teamed with Allen, the stallion earned a fourth in junior heeling at the 1978 AQHA World Show, capping the year by placing sixth in the year-end standings for steer roping, earning a steer roping Superior, and claiming an AQHA Championship. (Note: Until 1982 AQHA's term for dally team roping was steer roping.) That same year, Zan Parr Bar's first full foal crop hit the ground.

The horse's show ring success reached new heights in 1979. In addition to his top-10 finishes in senior heading and senior heeling at the World Show, and his capturing the high-point year-end steer roping title, the stallion earned his second world halter championship, taking the aged stallion

Billy Allen with Zan Parr Bar following the horse's win in the aged stallion class at the 1980 Quarter Horse World Show. In all, Zan Parr Bar earned three halter world titles.

Photo by Harold Campton, Courtesy Carol Rose

title in Oklahoma City.

In 1980, Zan Parr Bar's last year in the show ring, he again captured the aged stallion world title—his third world halter championship—and took third in senior heeling at the World Show.

The stallion exited show competition at the top of his game as a roping horse. Zan Parr Bar's natural talent had given Allen a long series of good, solid runs in the arena.

"In three years of roping on him, I never got outrun by a steer," he said. "I never felt that horse strain to catch up."

When he was retired to stud after the 1980 World Show, Zan Parr Bar's show record included three world titles, 114 grand championships, 13 reserve grand championships, 245 halter points, 160 heeling points, and 118 heading points, in addition to points in western pleasure, calf roping, and reining, all earned before the horse turned 7.

For the rest of his life, Zan Parr Bar's

Carol Rose first encountered Zan Parr Bar by accident at a horse show in Norco, California. After buying the stallion, Rose built her own fame as a breeder around Zan Parr Bar's success.

Photo by Don Trout, Courtesy Carol Rose

Zan Parr Jack, a 1979 stallion by Zan Parr Bar and out of Miss Goldie Jack, also became a renowned roping horse and performance sire. In 1983 the stallion earned the junior working cow horse world championship with trainer Billy Allen before claiming senior heeling world titles in both 1984 and 1985. **Photo Courtesy** *The Quarter Horse Journal*

time under saddle would be spent at Carol Rose Quarter Horses in Gainesville. His showing days were over, but his tenure as one of the Quarter Horse breed's leading sires was just beginning.

Progeny

After Zan Parr Bar's retirement to stud in Gainesville, the 15.3, 1,250-pound stal-

lion remained a fixture in the show barn at Carol Rose's ranch. A typical year's book brought 70 to 90 mares of varying type and breeding. Over the years, Zan Parr Bar proved he could cross well with any mare and produce a winner.

His 1978 daughter Zans Playgirl, out of Hands Off (by Parker's Trouble), had made an early mark for her sire by winning the 1979 reserve world championship for yearling mares, but it wasn't until the 1980s that Zan Parr Bar get began turning heads.

In 1982 Zans Par, out of Miss Spry (by Smokey Elgelo), earned the yearling stallion reserve world halter title, setting the stage for his later wins, the 1984 junior heading world championship and the 1986 senior heeling reserve world title. Also in 1982 Zanza Skip, out of Miss Ann Skipper (by Erna's Skip), earned the youth yearling gelding world champion title and yearling gelding reserve world championship.

Perhaps the most significant 1982 performance for Zan Parr Bar get, though, was that of Reprise Bar. A 1978 gelding out of Dudey Zee (by Blondy's Dude), he took the reserve in junior heeling at the World Show.

Reprise Bar and Zan Parr Jack, another of Zan Parr Bar's most famous sons, were among the stallion's most successful progeny. At the 1983 World Show, Reprise Bar earned the senior heading title, while Zan Parr Jack, a 1979 stallion out of Miss Goldie Jack (by Two Eyed Jack), took the junior working cow horse championship.

On his return to the World Show in 1984, Reprise Bar earned the Superhorse title, along the way claiming the senior heading championship, reserve senior calf roping championship, and top-10 finishes in heeling, working cow horse, and aged geldings. The horse would go on to earn a 1993 heading title at the Quarter Horse Youth World.

Zan Parr Jack's winning streak included back-to-back senior heeling world championships in 1984 and '85, and a 1987 heeling world title in the amateur division.

Throughout the '80s, Zan Parr Bar get continued to excel in competition, with Zans Bueno Bar, Zan Gold Jack, Zans

Like his sire, Zan Parr Jack is blessed with both looks and athleticism. He's owned by the Lazy E Ranch, Guthrie, Oklahoma.

Photo Courtesy Lazy E Ranch

Zan Gold Jack, a 1981 son of Zan Parr Bar and the Two Eyed Jack daughter Miss Goldie Jack, earned the 1985 junior heeling world championship, as well as Superiors for both heading and heeling. The horse was co-owned by Billy Allen and Jerry Riemann.

Photo by Alfred Janssen III

Sunflower, Amazan, Zippin Zanita, Zanador, Zans Parson, Biarritz Bar, Parr Skip Bar, Zan Parr Barb, and Zans Showdown all earning roping world titles that decade.

Sparkles Rosezana, a 1982 mare out of World Show Superhorse Diamonds Sparkle (see her chapter) and one of Zan Parr Bar's best-known daughters, won the 1985 NRHA Futurity and the 1986 junior reining world title. Two years later, she'd take home both the senior heading world championship and reserve senior working cow horse title. In 1989 she finished her show career with the reserve win at the World Show in senior reining.

Zan Parr Bar's 1983 son Zans Diamond Sun, a full brother to Sparkles Rosezana, won the junior reining world title in 1987.

The cross with Diamonds Sparkle proved to be one of the most successful any horseman could imagine. In 1985 the match produced Sparkles Suzana, who won the 1989 NRHA Derby and 1992 senior calf roping world championship.

Zans Misty Skip, a 1985 gelding out of Skips Misty Barb (by Skip A Barb), earned two world titles in 1989, one in junior heading and the other in junior calf roping. The gelding would go on to win two titles at the 1994 World Show—the senior calf roping championship and the amateur calf roping title. He also claimed the 1995 amateur heeling world championship and 1997 reserve world title in senior calf roping.

Other sons and daughters of Zan Parr Bar who claimed world roping titles in the

Reprise Bar proved to be one of Zan Parr Bar's most successful sons. The 1978 gelding out of Dudey Zee, a Blondy's Dude daughter, earned the senior heading title at the 1983 Quarter Horse World Show, then returned the following year to capture the Superhorse title, winning a second senior heading championship in the process. The gelding is shown here with trainer Bobby Lewis, owner Carol Rose, and Clay O'Brien Cooper, who also roped on the horse, following the 1984 Superhorse win.

Photo Courtesy *The Quarter Horse Journal*

1990s include Mr Bar Parr, Ritzy Dollie, Zan Parr Porsche, Seven S Zanaday, Zans Even Parr, and Zans Last Light.

In all, Zan Parr Bar sired 23 world champions who earned 30 open titles, all but six in roping events. (The remaining world championships were in working cow horse, halter, reining, and trail.)

Impact

Although his get have made an indelible mark on roping events, earning 24 open roping world championships, Zan

Parr Bar sired horses who excelled across the board in performance categories, earning honors in events ranging from cutting and working cow horse to reining and western pleasure.

"Their athletic ability, their minds, their conformation all allowed them to go in so many directions," Rose said. "The foals

*Renee Morgan, Spring-
town, Tex., runs barrels
on her Zan Parr Bar
grandson, Zan Gold
Chevas (Zan Gold
Jack x Ima Dry Chex).*

Photo by C. Brown

seemed like they took just a little longer
to train, but once they were trained, their
hearts were as big as Texas. The more
you asked, the more you got."

Specialization has changed the face of
the Quarter Horse industry since Zan
Parr Bar's days in the arena and at stud.
Today, stallions are often targeted at specific niches, capitalizing on their own successes in one event. Because of this, it's
easy for some horsemen to question
whether an all-around sire of Zan Parr
Bar's caliber will be seen again.

But Rose doesn't believe Zan Parr Bar
was part of a long-gone era.

"Since he was shown, people aren't

showing or training as many all-around
horses," she said. "I think there are sires
today who could sire some great all-around
horses. They're just not being tried."

Zan Parr Bar's exceptional athleticism
can't be questioned, though. In Billy
Allen's view, the stallion had the ideal balance of willingness and physical talent.

"His heart and desire to excel made the
difference for him," he said. "You always
need a horse who's physically capable,
but the good ones have to love the challenge. That's what separates the good
ones from the mediocre. You had to let
him learn. I knew Zan Parr Bar was special when we got to the point where he
had to bear down and show he had both
the desire and ability to do it."

Legacy

In 1987, 13-year-old Zan Parr Bar
foundered and was sent to a vet clinic

The cross between Zan Parr Bar and Diamonds Sparkle proved to be nothing short of phenomenal. Their 1983 son, Zans Diamond Sun, won the 1987 junior reining world championship with rider Craig Johnson, shown here with Carol Rose and Dick Steward.

Photo Courtesy *The Quarter Horse Journal*

at Southwest Stallion Station in Elgin, Tex., for two months. Rose had planned to pick up the stallion the Monday before Thanksgiving, but delayed her plans after the clinic called and told her the horse needed more time to rest.

The day after Thanksgiving, November 27, Rose received another call. Zan Parr Bar had died suddenly from colitis X, a noncontagious toxic disease causing severe shock. The horse was buried on-site at South-

west Stallion Station.

At the time of his death, Zan Parr Bar was AQHA's leading sire of performance horses. He left behind 652 foals from 12 crops.

4 BLONDY'S DUDE

By Frank Holmes

He founded an outstanding family of halter and performance horses.

ALTHOUGH he came from two proven Quarter Horse lines—King P-234 and Plaudit—Blondy's Dude founded a family of halter and performance horses that was his and his alone.

Sired by Small Town Dude and out of Blondy Queen, Blondy's Dude was foaled April 30, 1957, on the Minneapolis, Kan., ranch of Homer Foutz. From his 3-year-old year on, he was owned by Morgan Freeman of Skiatook, Oklahoma.

"I first saw Dude here in Skiatook in June of 1960," Freeman said. "Harold Hudspeth was showing him in a reining

contest, and they won it. By this time, I had been raising horses for 20 years, and had assembled what I thought was a pretty nice little band of broodmares. But I needed a stallion.

"At first glance, Dude was sure the type of stud I had been looking for. I've always liked a keen head and neck on a horse, and Dude was outstanding in both those areas. And, for that day and time, he carried a lot of muscle. He was especially deep in the stifle.

"Dude got his outstanding head and neck from his maternal grandsire,

With his longer, leaner profile, Blondy's Dude was the harbinger of a new era in the evolution of the halter horse. He's shown here with owner Morgan Freeman.

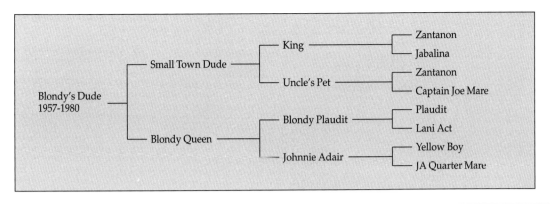

Blondy Plaudit," Freeman continued. "Blondy Plaudit was bred by the Philmont Ranch of Cimarron, N.M., but spent most of his life in northeast Oklahoma. I had the privilege of seeing both Blondy Plaudit and his half-brother Question Mark and, conformation-wise, I rated Blondy the better of the two."

Morgan Freeman

By the time his path crossed that of Blondy's Dude, Morgan Freeman was a highly qualified judge of good horse-flesh. Born in Arkansas, he had first come to northeastern Oklahoma as a 15-year-old to work as a cowboy. A short stint back in Arkansas in the wholesale grocery business was followed by a permanent return to Oklahoma in 1950 as the owner of a livestock feed store.

As a young cowboy in Oklahoma, Freeman had come in contact with such legendary horse breeders as Coke Blake, "Uncle" John Dawson, and Ronald Mason. From them, he learned to appreciate that it was not only how a horse looked, but also what he could do that was important.

"I appreciate a horse with good conformation," Freeman said. "But if a horse can't do anything, I don't care how pretty he is. He's not for me."

On that lucky day in 1960, Blondy's Dude made enough of an impression on Freeman that the man immediately got in touch with his son, Jerald, who had a training facility on the west edge of town.

"I told Jerald that I had just seen the horse that everyone in town had been talking about," Freeman said. "I added that he had great conformation and performance ability and might be something

Halter and Performance Record: AQHA Champion; Performance Register of Merit; 1962 Grand Champion Stallion at Fort Worth; 45 Halter Points; 12 Performance Points.

Progeny Record:

Foal Crops: 21	Superior Halter Awards: 11
Foals Registered: 1,402	Performance Point-Earners: 320
AQHA Champions: 30	Performance Points Earned: 7,074
Supreme Champions: 1	Performance Registers of Merit: 130
World Champions: 2	Superior Performance Awards: 31
Halter Point-Earners: 228	Race Starters: 11
Halter Points Earned: 3,032	Race Money Earned: $70
Leading Race Money-Earner: Chuck Dude ($70)	

we should own. And then I just stewed on it for a while."

Freeman's next contact with Dude was several weeks later at a cutting held at Jerald's.

"J.T. Walters and Nick McNair owned Dude at the time," Freeman said. "J.T. was riding him in the cutting at Jerald's. He had initially just brought him there to ride around, but then decided to cut a few cattle. J.T. cut out one of those ol'

Blondy's Dude and Freeman at Fort Worth in 1962, right after the big sorrel was named grand champion stallion.

Photo by *Fort Worth Star Telegram,* Courtesy *The Quarter Horse Journal*

Brahma cows and worked her for a while. Then she broke out and started down the fence. Dude headed her, dropped his hindquarters into the ground, and came around facing her.

"I told Jerald, then and there, 'I'm going to buy him before they wake up and realize what they have.' "

Walters and McNair were asking

$5,000 for Blondy's Dude—a hefty price for a 3-year-old stallion in 1960. But Freeman and Walters met at the local cafe anyway, and started working on a deal. By the time they were done, some cash, feed, and horses had changed hands, and Dude belonged to Morgan Freeman.

The elder Freeman was justifiably proud of his new acquisition and stood back to wait for the outside mares and money to roll in. At first, the going was slow.

"Right after I bought Dude," Freeman said, "Jerald wanted to take him to some local shows. I didn't feel like that was necessary, so he stayed home. It turned out to be the wrong decision, and I didn't get hardly any mares booked to him in 1961."

Fort Worth, 1962

By June of 1961, Freeman had seen the light, and Jerald and Dude hit the show circuit. The pair won a few halter classes, performed well in reining, and capped the season with Dude standing grand at halter and placing third in the cutting at the Tulsa State Fair. Jerald felt that he had accomplished what he had set out to do and told his father that it was time to quit for the year.

Freeman had another plan in mind, however, and flabbergasted his son by declaring that he intended to show Dude at one more show that winter—the Southwestern Exposition and Fat Stock Show in Fort Worth.

"This was before the Congress or AQHA World Show," Freeman said. "Fort Worth was it, as far as big-time showing in the Southwest went. I had been in Fort Worth in 1941 when Wimpy was named the grand champion and given the first number in the AQHA registry. I never forgot that experience and had wanted to show a horse there ever since. I figured Blondy's Dude was the one.

"So, in January of 1962, I borrowed Jerald's truck and horse trailer and hauled Dude to Fort Worth. I didn't have any health papers on him. I had to wait an hour and a half for a local vet to inspect him before I could even get him into a stall.

"The next morning, I cleaned him up a little before the class. He was just getting over a cold, so I didn't give him a full bath. I just rinsed him off a little and then scraped him as dry as I could with a piece of broken glass I found on the ground. Then I led him into the arena for the aged stallion class.

"There were 37 horses in it," Freeman

At maturity, Blondy's Dude stood 15.1 hands and weighed an evenly distributed 1,150 to 1,300 pounds.

continued, "including proven champions like Range Boss, Colonel Frost, and Skipper's Image. I looked at all those horses and thought, 'Man, I'm out of my league here! If I can just place 10th, I'll be happy.'

"They cut off a bunch of the horses and lined them up with me at the end of the line. Then they said, 'Turn them

Mr Diamond Dude, one of the best sons of Blondy's Dude, was foaled in 1968 out of Miss Patsy Blake, who was by Dawson's Gary. A full brother to Dudes Baby Doll, Mr Diamond Dude has achieved an outstanding record as a sire. Included among his offspring is Diamonds Sparkle, the Superhorse at the 1979 AQHA World Show. Jerald Freeman is the handler.

Photo by Don Shugart

Dude Lit was also by Blondy's Dude and out of Miss Patsy Blake. A 1967 stallion, he earned an ROM in performance. The handler is Julian Bivens.

Photo by Orren Mixer, Courtesy *The Quarter Horse Journal*

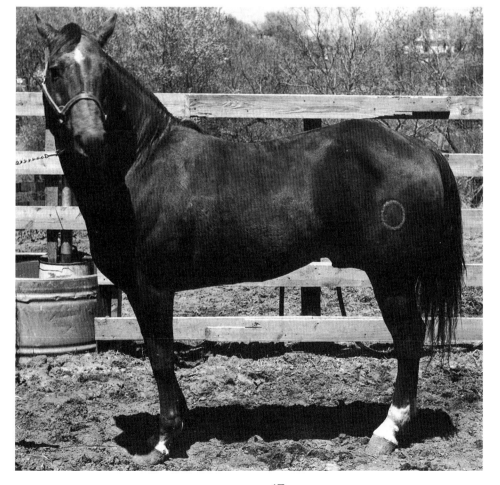

A 1967 picture of Dudes Baby Doll, who was foaled in 1965. A full sister to Mr Diamond Dude, she earned an AQHA Championship and a Superior in reining. The handler is Billy Dickerson.

Photo by D.M. McKean, Courtesy *The Quarter Horse Journal*

An undated picture of Small Town Dude, the sire of Blondy's Dude. According to AQHA records, Small Town Dude was bred by James R. Childress, Ozona, Tex., and foaled in 1943.

Photo Courtesy *The Quarter Horse Journal*

This is Dude's Dream (AQHA 244,100), who should not be confused with Dudes Dream, who was a palomino mare. By Blondy's Dude and out of Duncan Babe, Dude's Dream earned an AQHA Championship and a Superior in reining. **Photo Courtesy** *The Quarter Horse Journal*

around,' and I went from last to first. Dude won the aged stallion class over all of those great horses.

"Then they brought in the other class winners to judge for grand and reserve. Ernest Browning was judging, and he asked me to trot Dude. When I did, Dude bounced a little, so Browning asked me to trot him again, in a circle. I had never had a judge do that before or since. But I did what he asked and, when it was all over, we were named grand champion stallion at the largest Quarter Horse show up to that time. They had 795 entries at that show."

It came as no surprise that Blondy's Dude stood to a full book of mares in 1962.

After his Fort Worth victory, the Freemans showed Dude long enough to make him an AQHA Champion with 45 halter, eight reining, and four cutting points. Jerald also continued to show the big stallion in open cutting events, winning several and placing high consistently.

By 1965, the get of Blondy's Dude were beginning to make their presence felt in the halter ring. Considered one of the nation's most promising young sires, Dude followed up his 1962 halter victory at Fort Worth with a 1965 win there in the get-of-sire competition.

Back in Skiatook, the stallion had become something of a family pet and was allowed to spend considerable time grazing in the Freeman yard. It became a habit that ultimately got the stallion into some serious trouble.

"Dude used to love grazing in the yard," Freeman relates. "He'd be there waiting at the front gate when I came home from work. Then, one night in October of 1965, he managed to get a gate open to a back lot and got in with some mares. I found him the next morning with his right rear ankle shattered.

"I got the local vet out right away, and he said there was no hope. We'd have to put Dude down. I wouldn't agree to that, so we decided to fly in some specialists from Dallas to look at the ankle. They put a cast on the leg from the hock down, and strengthened it with a rigid iron brace. The whole thing weighed

This is Pale Face Dude, a 1969 gelded son of Blondy's Dude and Miss Levi, who was by Ma's Bando. Pale Face Dude earned performance ROMs in both open and youth competition. The handler is Chuck Dickens.

Photo Courtesy *The Quarter Horse Journal*

The classy Dudes Mr Kim was a sorrel foaled in 1973, by Blondy's Dude and out of Kim C Bar, by Iron Bars. Dudes Mr Kim earned a Superior in western pleasure and an AQHA Championship.

Okie Star Dude was a genuine star in timed events. He was a 1977 gelding by Blondy's Dude and out of Dainty Red Bug, by Joe Bar King. Okie Star Dude won world championships in youth barrel racing and stake racing, a Superior in open barrel racing, and many other awards. He was owned and shown by Lori Moffett.

Twenty-five of Dude's get were AQHA Champions.

more than 50 pounds, and Dude couldn't bend the leg at all.

"My heart used to go up into my throat every time that horse laid down. He'd stagger back up, losing his balance and then catching it, until he was finally up and stable—shaking and sweating. But he made a full recovery and in 1966 bred 130 mares—all live cover."

Offspring

Throughout the late 1960s, the entire 1970s, and into the 1980s, Blondy's Dude continued to enjoy widespread popularity as a sire.

Tisa Baby, a 1962 sorrel mare out of Juno Duchess, was Dude's first big show ring winner. Shown exclusively in reining, Tisa Baby earned 84 points and a Superior, and was the 1966 AQHA Reserve High-Point Reining Horse. And she would be the first in a long line of halter and performance champions by the Freeman stallion.

AQHA records reveal that Blondy's Dude sired 1,402 registered horses from 21 foal crops. Of these, 424 were performers and they amassed 3,032 halter and 7,074 performance points in the open, amateur, and youth divisions.

Twenty-five of Dude's get were AQHA Champions, and five more earned the same title in the youth division.

In halter competition, 11 sons and daughters of Blondy's Dude earned their Superiors. With 466 points to her credit, Dudes Baby Doll, a 1965 sorrel mare out of Miss Patsy Blake, was her sire's top halter point-winning get. She was followed by Superior-earning halter horses including Ada Sassy Dude, Dude's Lace, Dude's Pet, Dude's Showdown, Anita Dude, Korie Lit, Krisie Dude, He'll Go Dude, Dee Jay's Dream, and Dude's Miracle.

In performance, the get of Blondy's Dude earned 20 Superiors and 105 ROMs in the open division, 11 Superiors and 22 ROMs in youth competition, and three ROMs in the then-new amateur division.

As their sire had, Blondy's Dude horses proved to be more than capable as reining horses. In addition to the aforementioned Tisa Baby, Dude's Dream, Dude's Ada Sue, and Dudes Banjo all earned Superior awards in reining. Dude's Ada Sue, a 1964 sorrel mare out of Ada Sue Knight, was the 1971 AQHA Reserve High-Point Honor Roll Reining Horse, and Dude's Blaze, a 1965 sorrel mare by Blondy's Dude and out of Showdown Jota, was the 1968 National Reining Horse Association Futurity Champion.

In the late 1960s and 1970s, there was an abundance of great two-way halter and western pleasure horses. A number of Dude's offspring earned both their AQHA Championships as well as performance points and Superiors in western pleasure. Included in this group were Small Town Babe, a 1966 sorrel mare out of Snappy Babe; Dude's Poco Tie, a 1967 dun mare out of Miss Poco Tie; Amber Dude, a 1973 sorrel mare out of Springtime Doll; and Dudes Mr Kim, a 1973 sorrel stallion out of Kim's Bar.

In addition, four more of Dude's get— Do Tell, Ada Lady Dude, Mighty Dude McCue, and Blondys Texas Dude—earned Superiors in open western pleasure.

Like their sire, the Blondy's Dudes were versatile. Mighty Blonde, a 1970 sorrel mare out of Mighty Bee 1, was the 1977 AQHA World Champion Senior Pole Bending Horse, and earned Superiors in pole bending and barrel racing. Okie Star Dude, a 1977 chestnut gelding out of Dainty Red

Dude's Gaucho, foaled in 1966, was another good-looking son of Blondy's Dude. Dude's Gaucho was the 1974 Champion Aged Stallion of Michigan, and he also earned an AQHA Championship. He was out of Cowboy's Luxury, by Cowboy H.

Photo by Bruce Peasley, Courtesy *The Quarter Horse Journal*

Dude's Ada Sue earned a Superior in reining and an AQHA Championship. Foaled in 1964, she was by Blondy's Dude and out of Ada Sue Knight, by Bill Lawson. We believe the rider is Donna Anthony.

Photo by Frank Frasca, Courtesy *The Quarter Horse Journal*

Bug, also earned a Superior in barrel racing, and Dude's Ann, a 1971 sorrel mare out of Fanny Ann Moore, was the 1975 AQHA Honor Roll Junior Western Riding Horse.

With 128.5 performance points to his credit, Dude's Latigo, a 1972 dun stallion by Blondy's Dude and out of Poco Star Berta, was a Superior heeling horse. Both Trudy Dude, a 1973 sorrel mare out of Leo's Nelly, and Duplicate Dude, a 1975 bay stallion out of Drifting Miss, earned

Superiors in trail.

Two of Dude's get—Panzarita's Dude, a 1974 gray stallion out of Pandy Band, and Hy Fashion Blond, a 1977 sorrel mare out of Miss Hy Bonanza—earned Superiors in open hunter under saddle. And, finally, The Hifalutin Dude, a 1980 gray stallion by Blondy's Dude and out of Miss Jem Harlan, was the 1988 AQHA World Champion Senior Working Cow Horse.

In youth competition, five of Blondy's Dude's get stand out above the rest.

Okie Star Dude won four youth AQHA world championships in stake racing and barrel racing, and Krisie Dude, a 1976 sorrel mare out of Sodie McCue, was the 1976 Youth AQHA Reserve World Champion 3-year-old Mare. Dude's Poco Tie earned 375 youth points and Superiors in showmanship, western

This is Dudes Banjo, a 1977 chestnut mare by Blondy's Dude and out of Terrific Kiss, by Terrific Trouble. She earned a Superior in reining. The rider is Ray Conrad.

Photo by Michelle, Courtesy *The Quarter Horse Journal*

horsemanship, and western pleasure.

Dude's Fancy Miss, a 1971 chestnut mare out of Hawkeye Lyn, earned 301 youth points and Superiors in hunter under saddle, showmanship, western horsemanship, and western pleasure. Amber Dude, a 1973 sorrel mare out of Springtime Doll, was a youth AQHA Supreme Champion and earned a Superior in western pleasure.

In addition, both Dubie Dubie Dude and Debonair Dude were youth AQHA champions, and King Dude's Jewel earned a Superior in youth western pleasure.

Grandget

By the late 1970s, Blondy's Dude was widely regarded as one of the breed's all-time leading sires. What's more, his sons and daughters were carving out their

own niches as sires and producers.

When retired to the broodmare band, Dudes Baby Doll almost eclipsed her sparkling show career. Among others, she produced the top performance horses Corona Cody, Guru Cody, Cassandra Cody, and Silver Zulu.

A full brother to Dudes Baby Doll, Mr Diamond Dude, went on to become Jerald Freeman's senior sire. Among others, he sired Diamonds Sparkle, the 1979 AQHA World Show Superhorse.

Blondy's Dude passed on his athletic ability to his grandget as well as his get. This heading horse is Reprise Bar, by Zan Parr Bar and out of Dudey Zee, by Blondy's Dude. At the 1984 AQHA World Show, the palomino gelding won the world championship in senior heading, second in senior calf roping, and third in both senior heeling and cow horse, amassing enough points to capture the Superhorse title and its $10,000 cash award. He was ridden by Bobby Lewis for owner Carol Rose of Gainesville, Texas.

Photo by Harold Campton

Dude's Showdown, a gelding foaled in 1968, was by Blondy's Dude and out of Showdown Jota, by Showdown Wimpy. He earned a Superior in halter.

Photo Courtesy
The Quarter Horse Journal

Dimonds Ms Sparkle was another grandget of Blondy's Dude who excelled in the show ring. By Mr Diamond Dude and out of Pollyanna Rose, she was also a full sister to the great Diamonds Sparkle. She's shown here with trainer Bob Loomis aboard at the 1984 Quarter Horse Congress, where they were awarded two major NRHA trophies.

**Photo by
Harold Campton**

Diamonds Sparkle (see her chapter) also went on to become one of the most influential matrons in the history of the NRHA and AQHA.

And the list goes on and on.

In October of 1979, at the age of 22, Blondy's Dude choked on some new hay, and severe complications set in. Nursed back to health, the big stallion stood to a full book of mares in 1980. In July of that year, Dude choked again. This time there was no saving him.

Morgan Freeman said, "I took him to the front yard where he liked to be, and turned to go to the house to call the vet. This time, though, Dude didn't stay up front. He went to the back yard and just stood there. I went back and stood by him.

"Dude used to always talk to me with his ears, but this time his ears stood quiet. And his eyes told me that he'd had enough. I loved that horse like he was family, so I did what he asked me to do. I let him go."

Blondy's Dude was humanely put to sleep on July 12, 1980. He is buried in the yard that he loved to spend time in, beneath a marble stone that says, "God gives his best to those that leave the choice to him."

In the case of Blondy's Dude and Morgan Freeman, the gift seemed to be a two-way deal.

5 DIAMONDS SPARKLE

By A.J. Mangum

This world champion mare became one of the greatest producers of performance horses in the Quarter Horse breed's history.

DIAMONDS Sparkle's greatest moment in the show arena—the win that would be most associated with the palomino mare's name—almost never happened.

In 1978 trainer Sunny Jim Orr had begun showing the flashy 4-year-old mare in junior reining, winning their first outing at the National Western Stock Show in Denver. Orr continued showing Diamonds Sparkle ("Sparky"), then owned by Dick Steward of Colorado Springs, and qualified her for the World Show.

In Oklahoma City that November, Steward sat in the stands and watched as his mare, with Orr aboard, blew a pattern in a reining class he thought she could've easily won.

"We'd shown her in 20 reining classes that year," Steward said. "She won 18 times and took second twice. I fell off my chair. I knew she could've won it."

The mare's trainer and owner both were discouraged. Steward contemplated retiring her from the arena and using her as a broodmare. The mare's youthfulness, though, and the potential both Steward and Orr knew she possessed, convinced them to give her another shot.

This photo records the first time Sunny Jim Orr exhibited Diamonds Sparkle at halter. The duo finished third in the 1976 New Mexico State Fair's 2-year-old mare class.

Photo by Kay, Courtesy Dick Steward

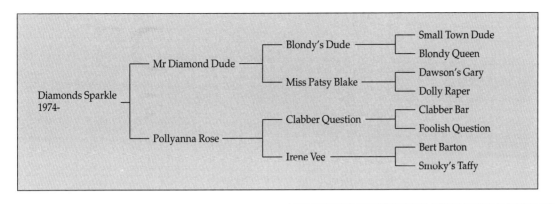

In 1979 the mare returned to the World Show as a 5-year-old, taking top-10 finishes in senior heeling and senior reining, and capping it all off with the senior heading championship.

In a sharp contrast to the previous year, the mare ranked among the top contenders for the show's coveted Superhorse title. Orr and Steward sweated out the end of the show, watching other leading horses—including Grey Lark, ridden by Oscar Crigler, and Barb A Leo, ridden by Jack Kyle—drop from contention, leaving Diamonds Sparkle by herself to claim the 1979 Superhorse award.

Orr, a reserved, quiet horseman, celebrated with an enthusiastic victory lap in the Oklahoma City arena.

"I've won lots of awards in my life," he was quoted as saying, "but nothing like this."

Steward echoed Orr's sentiment, calling the Superhorse win the "high point" of his life.

For Diamonds Sparkle, the win signaled not only the greatest achievement of her career as a show horse, but an ushering of things to come as she made the transition from performer to producer of champions.

The mare would go on to produce a series of performance winners, competitive horses with the same athleticism displayed by their dam. Through her progeny, Diamonds Sparkle would remain a dominant force on the Quarter Horse show scene for years to come.

Partnerships

Foaled in 1974, Diamonds Sparkle was sired by Mr Diamond Dude, by Blondy's Dude, and was out of Pollyanna Rose, a mare with Sir Barton, Question Mark, and

---

Halter and Performance Record: Performance Register of Merit; AQHA Champion; 1979 AQHA World Show Superhorse; 1979 AQHA Senior Heading World Champion; Superior Steer Roping; NRHA Hall of Fame.

Progeny Record: (As of September 1999)

Foal Crops: 16	Halter Registers of Merit: 1
AQHA Champions: 1	Performance Point-Earners: 11
AQHA World Champions: 4	Performance Points Earned: 2,560.5
Halter Point-Earners: 5	Performance Registers of Merit: 11
Halter Points Earned: 30.5	Superior Performance Awards: 15

Three Bars (TB) in her pedigree.

The year Diamonds Sparkle was foaled, Steward and fellow Coloradan Jerry Smith ventured to the Skiatook, Okla., farm of her breeder, Jerald Freeman. After looking at several horses Freeman had for sale, Smith asked the breeder if he had other horses hidden away, waiting for fall halter futurities.

Freeman took Smith and Steward to a barn on another ranch property and led out the palomino weanling filly he'd named Diamonds Sparkle.

"The first time I saw her I fell in love with her," Steward said. "She was outstanding. I'd never seen a more muscled weanling or a filly who could handle herself like she could."

After watching the filly work in a round pen, Steward was ready to buy

Diamonds Sparkle as a weanling with her breeder, Jerald Freeman. The filly's eye-catching looks caught the attention of Colorado horseman Dick Steward, who initially bought her from Freeman in partnership with Jerry Smith. Steward later bought out Smith's share.

Photo Courtesy Dick Steward

Moments after the presentation of the 1979 Superhorse award, Sunny Jim Orr and Dick Steward looked on as Diamonds Sparkle investigated the trophy.

Photo Courtesy Dick Steward

her. Freeman, though, wanted to ensure that Diamonds Sparkle would be shown. He had his doubts that Steward—fairly new to the horse business at the time—would put the mare into competition. Freeman agreed to the sale on the condition that Smith, a more experienced horseman, partner with Steward on the filly.

After Freeman showed Diamonds Sparkle to a second place in an Oklahoma halter futurity that fall, he shipped her to Colorado, where a new chapter in the filly's life began.

Showing Promise

Steward, after buying out Smith's half-interest in the filly, began showing Diamonds Sparkle at halter in 1975, but met with only limited success. He attributed the lackluster placings to his own inexperience in the ring.

"When I showed her as a yearling, Sunny Jim Orr was always right in front of me," Steward said. "I didn't always think he had the better horse,

but I knew he was a better showman. He agreed to help me."

Orr, a successful Pueblo, Colo., trainer, began showing Diamonds Sparkle as a 2-year-old, earning 23 points in 1976. The next winter, he started the filly under saddle and began showing her in western pleasure. She earned 31 pleasure points her first year under saddle, earning a performance ROM.

"(Diamonds Sparkle) had a lot of feel to her, a lot of flex to her body, and a nice, light nose," Orr told *Western Horseman* in 1980. "I could just touch her with the

Diamonds Sparkle and Sunny Jim Orr heeling at the 1979 Quarter Horse World Show. The mare's top-10 performance helped clinch the Superhorse title. The header is Texas trainer Gary Putman, riding Tiny Circus, another great performance horse.

Diamonds Sparkle, trainer Sunny Jim Orr, and owner Dick Steward, following the mare's win in senior heading at the 1979 AQHA World Championship Show. With additional points won in senior heeling and senior reining, Diamonds Sparkle racked up enough points to win the coveted Superhorse award.

Photo Courtesy *The Quarter Horse Journal*

Diamonds Sparkle's first foal, a daughter of Zan Parr Bar named Sparkles Rosezana, with trainer Bobby Lewis aboard, slides to a stop in the senior reining class at the 1988 Quarter Horse World Show.

Photo by Harold Campton

reins and she'd let me have her nose. Whenever I loped her in the round corral, she loped easy … wasn't trying to run off. She just wanted to do whatever I wanted her to do."

1978 was an eventful year for Diamonds Sparkle. She made her reining debut at the National Western Stock Show in Denver, earned an AQHA Championship, and, in her first appearance at the World Show, survived the flawed reining performance that would cause Steward and Orr to contemplate early retirement for the mare.

Luckily for the Quarter Horse breed, they reconsidered. Diamonds Sparkle redeemed herself the following year when she showcased her talent as a roping horse for the first time and set the stage for a series of major wins by her sons and daughters.

Transitions

In 1979 Gainesville, Tex., breeder Carol Rose was in the midst of campaigning her stallion Zan Parr Bar (see his chapter). The phenomenal roping

horse earned his second of three world halter titles that year, but the victory didn't keep Rose from taking notice of Diamonds Sparkle.

Steward, seeking a stallion to cross to his mare, the newly crowned Superhorse, was equally impressed with Zan Parr Bar.

"He was a great stallion," Steward said. "After talking to Sunny Jim and looking at other stallions, I decided I wasn't overly impressed with any of them other than Zan Parr Bar. He could

Trainer Bobby Lewis and Sparkles Rosezana won the championship in senior heading at the 1988 Quarter Horse World Show.

Photo by Harold Campton

A full sister to Sparkles Rosezana, Sparkles Suzana won many awards, including the 1992 AQHA senior calf roping world title. She's shown here with Bobby Lewis and Carol Rose.

Photo Courtesy *The Quarter Horse Journal*

do it all. He carried himself so well and had such muscle definition."

Steward sent Diamonds Sparkle to Zan Parr Bar in 1980. The transition from show mare to broodmare, Carol Rose recalls, wasn't easy.

"That first year, we didn't get her in foal," she said. "I think because of the letdown from showing, her system wasn't ready."

Veterinarians at Colorado State University confirmed that the mare needed time to make the switch from competitive horse to broodmare, and recommended some time on pasture before another attempt at breeding her.

The mare was again sent to Zan Parr Bar in 1981, this time with better results. The following spring, Diamonds Sparkle produced her first foal, Sparkles Rosezana, in stall 36 in the breeding barn at Carol Rose Quarter Horses. From then on, each of the mare's foals would be born in that very same stall at Rose's Gainesville ranch.

Sparkles Rosezana more than met Steward's expectations for Diamonds Sparkle's first foal.

"There was no question about it," he said. "It was obvious all her foals were going to be athletes from the moment they hit the ground."

Diamonds Sparkle was bred back to Zan Parr Bar in 1982 and 1984, resulting in Zans Diamond Sun and Sparkles Suzana, respectively. In 1985 Steward bred the mare to renowned reining sire Genuine Doc, another of Rose's stallions.

That summer, Carol Rose became Diamonds Sparkle's owner, also purchasing Sparkles Suzana and a half-interest in Zans Diamond Sun the same day.

After her 1986 foal, Genuine Redskin, was born, Diamonds Sparkle was bred to Zan Parr Bar in 1986 and 1987. Her 1988 foal, Sparkles La Zanna, would be among Zan Parr Bar's last, following the stallion's untimely death in the fall of 1987. Although Diamonds Sparkle would produce champions by other sires, the cross with Zan Parr Bar was something special.

Shining Spark, with trainer Tim McQuay aboard. A son of Diamonds Sparkle and the great Genuine Doc, Shining Spark won the 1993 junior reining world title, the 1994 NRHA Derby, and the 1995 NRHA Derby Saddlesmith Series. Owned by Carol Rose, Shining Spark is rapidly becoming a great sire of reining horses.

Photo by Don Shugart, Courtesy *The Quarter Horse Journal*

"I have no idea why that cross worked so well," Rose said. "I'd like to take credit for that, but I don't know if anyone can. Dick Steward picked Zan Parr Bar because he was a pretty roping horse with good conformation. That's what Diamonds Sparkle was. Zan Parr Bar happened to be in the right place at the right time. The mare is such a great producer, though, she probably could've had a great foal with any sire."

Diamonds Sparkle would go on to produce more foals by Genuine Doc, and would be crossed with Doc O'Lena, as well as Zan Parr Bar sons Zans Last Light and Zan Parr Express.

Her status as a broodmare, though, was beginning to reach new heights, fueled by her sons' and daughters' performances in the arena.

Offspring

In 1985 Sparkles Rosezana, then a 3-year-old, won the NRHA Futurity, following up by capturing the junior reining title at the 1986 Quarter Horse World Show. Trainer Craig Johnson rode her to both wins.

In 1987, Zans Diamond Sun followed in his older sister's footsteps by placing

One in four Diamonds Sparkle foals have won at least one AQHA world title.

Top 10 finishes in roping events and working cow horse gave Spark O Lena, by Doc O'Lena and out of Diamonds Sparkle, the reserve Superhorse title at the 1996 World Show. Spark O Lena and Carol Rose were joined in the arena by past AQHA President Don Burt and trainers Bobby Lewis and Bob Avila, who showed the mare.

Photo Courtesy *The Quarter Horse Journal*

third in the NRHA Futurity. That same year he won the Lazy E Classic (now called the National Reining Breeders Classic) and the junior reining at the AQHA World Show.

In 1988 Sparkles Rosezana took the senior heading world title and became the reserve world champion senior working cow horse, racking up multiple high-point awards and two Superiors in roping along the way.

Sparkles Rosezana and Zans Diamond Sun continued to make a mark for Diamonds Sparkle in 1989. Sparkles Rosezana won the reserve world title in senior reining, while Zans Diamond Sun took home four high-point awards in roping events, earned three Superior awards, and was named the 1989 AQHA year-end all-around high-point stallion and reserve all-around high-point senior horse.

Then, they passed the torch to their younger siblings, including:

- Sparkles Suzana (1985 mare by Zan Parr Bar), 1989 NRHA Derby champion.
- Genuine Redskin (1986 stallion by Genuine Doc), 1990 NRHA Derby champion.
- Shining Spark (1989 stallion by Genuine Doc), 1993 junior reining world champion, 1994 NRHA Derby winner, and 1995 NRHA Derby Saddlesmith Series winner.
- Spark O Lena (1990 gelding by Doc O'Lena), 1996 reserve Superhorse.
- Zans Light Sparkles (1991 mare by Zans Last Light), 1994 NRHA Futurity Limited Open reserve champion.

Statistics

As of September 1999, 11 foals out of Diamonds Sparkle have earned AQHA performance points, racking up a point total of more than 2,500, meaning that on average, a Diamonds Sparkle son or daughter who competes in the show ring earns well over 200 points. Greatly exceeding that average were Sparkles Suzana with 952.5 points, Zans Diamond Sun with 347.5 points, and Spark O Lena with 525.5 points.

Carrying the statistical analysis further, one in four Diamonds Sparkle foals have won at least one AQHA world title.

The NRHA honored Diamonds Sparkle in 1996, inducting the mare into their Hall of Fame in recognition of her progeny's outstanding reining performances, including major NRHA wins by Sparkles Suzana, Genuine Redskin, and Shining Spark.

Today

As of late 1999, 25-year-old Diamonds Sparkle remains a part of the broodmare band at Carol Rose Quarter Horses, and continues to produce foals through embryo transfer.

"All we've ever done with her is breed her," Rose says. "She's a fantastic mare to have around. She wants no trouble and gives you no trouble."

Steward concurs.

"She's a phenomenal mare," he said. "She did everything we ever asked her to do, and loved every minute of it. She got after cattle like you couldn't believe. She had a lot of heart, was easy to be around, had a great disposition. She caught your eye and was focused when she went in the ring. She knew the drill."

Despite, or perhaps because of, her long history with the mare, Rose is reluctant to name a favorite foal of Diamonds Sparkle.

"They're all beautiful," she says. "One of my dreams is to get Orren Mixer to paint her and all her foals in one image. I have four of her daughters in my broodmare band, two geldings— Spark O Lena and Cinco Spark—one 2-year-old stallion, one yearling filly, and of course, Sparkin Express and Shining Spark. I've always wanted to get a photo of all of them together."

When asked if Diamonds Sparkle is the broodmare equivalent of her late stallion Zan Parr Bar, Rose ranks the mare higher than the influential sire.

"She's so much more. She's one of the leading dams of all time when it comes to reining horses, roping horses, performance horses, or world champions," Rose said. "I don't think anyone can touch her. She's just superior to most any stallion or most any other mare as far as being a producer."

6 MISS PRINCESS AKA WOVEN WEB (TB)

By Diane Ciarloni

A straight Thoroughbred, she also raced as a Quarter Horse.

WOVEN WEB hit the ground in 1943. Bred by Robert J. Kleberg Jr. of the famed King Ranch in Kingsville, Tex., the dainty-looking filly was small when she was foaled. She didn't change much in terms of size, standing no more than 14.2 and never weighing more than 950 pounds at full maturity. Her small stature, however, didn't stop Kleberg from assessing her as "a hell of a mare."

By breeding, Woven Web was straight Thoroughbred, but she also raced as a Quarter Horse. Her sire was Bold Venture, who was unbeaten as a 3-year-old and who won the Kentucky Derby and the Preakness in 1936. Her dam was Bruja, by Livery. Before Woven Web's racing career was over, however, whether she was Thoroughbred or Quarter Horse would depend on where she was racing and how far she was running. If the distances were shorter and if she were competing against Quarter Horses, her name was Miss Princess. If the distances were

Woven Web raced under her given name against Thoroughbreds and under the name of Miss Princess against Quarter Horses. The man in the photo is identified as Doc Northway. That would be Dr. J.K. Northway, King Ranch veterinarian for many years.

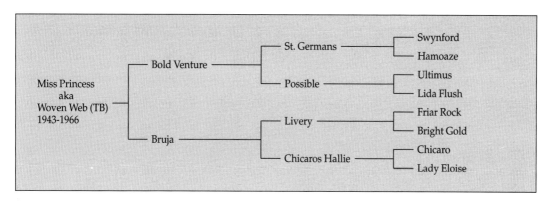

			Swynford
		St. Germans	
	Bold Venture		Hamoaze
			Ultimus
Miss Princess		Possible	
aka			Lida Flush
Woven Web (TB)			Friar Rock
1943-1966		Livery	
			Bright Gold
	Bruja		Chicaro
		Chicaros Hallie	
			Lady Eloise

longer and if the other horses filling the starting gate were Thoroughbreds, her name was Woven Web. Either way, either name, she was a hell of a mare.

Kleberg owned both Bold Venture and Bruja. He also owned Assault, who won the Thoroughbred Triple Crown and Horse of the Year honors in 1946. And Kleberg's King Ranch also owned thousands upon thousands of acres of land, filled with some of the finest cattle and horses in Texas.

One of those horses was named Nobody's Friend, and in 1941 at Tucson, Nobody's Friend was soundly beaten by a filly named Shue Fly. Kleberg didn't like losing, and he was determined to have his day against Shue Fly.

Kleberg would have to wait two years for Woven Web. In the meantime, everywhere he turned he heard racing enthusiasts singing the praises of Shue Fly (her story is in *Legends, Vol. 1*). There was no one who could touch her or stop her. She was the world champion in 1941-42, and stayed at the top throughout the next two seasons. For several years Kleberg had to listen to people throughout the country say she was the fastest Quarter Horse to ever set foot on a track.

There was no way Kleberg could avoid hearing about Shue Fly. Although the mare didn't run in recognized competitions in 1944-45, there was no one else good enough to take the world title from her. In the 1945-46 season, Shue Fly lost a 350-yard match to Miss Bank, but came back and won the Quarter Mile

Halter and Performance Record: Racing Register of Merit; 1946, 1947, 1948 World Champion Quarter Running Horse; 1946, 1947, 1948 World Champion Quarter Running Mare.

Progeny Record:

Foal Crops: 3

Foals Registered: 3

Race Starters: 2

Leading Race Money-Earner: Baloma ($324)

Race Money Earned: $324

Race Registers of Merit: 1

Championship Stake at Rillito. Her owners, the Hepler Brothers of New Mexico, arranged a rematch at 440 yards, but Shue Fly was fouled and injured.

Once again, Shue Fly was out of the competition. A clubfooted mare named Queenie (see *Legends, Vol. 1*) entered the picture. Despite her handicap, she raced her way to stardom, beating Miss Bank twice and setting a world record when she clocked :22.5 over 440 yards while carrying 127 pounds.

To the Track

It was the summer of 1945, and Kleberg's attention was on his little filly named Woven Web.

She went into training, but just as it was time for her to debut, the tracks in the United States pulled the curtain

Miss Princess set seven track records during her racing career. In this win photo, owner Bob Kleberg (far left) stands by trainer Ernest Lane, jockey Pat Castille is up, and Miss Helenita Kleberg holds the mare's bridle.

Photo Courtesy *The Quarter Horse Journal*

Kleberg was proud of his chestnut mare, but he couldn't relax until he'd beaten Shue Fly.

until the end of World War II. When that happened, owners and breeders began shipping their horses to the Hippodromo in Mexico City. Woven Web was among those going south of the border, and began her career there in March 1945. She started six times in Mexico, winning four and finishing second twice. She could compete and win at distances from 440 yards to five furlongs. She equaled the world record for 2½ furlongs when she clocked :27.2.

Kleberg was proud of his chestnut mare, but he couldn't relax until he'd beaten Shue Fly.

Woven Web returned to the United States in 1946. She was still a small filly, marked with a star on her forehead. She didn't look extremely powerful, but she was smooth-muscled and charged with energy. She was also affectionate, and openly asked for attention. Kleberg studied her from all angles, and decided to call Ernest Lane of Odom, Texas.

Lane and Kleberg had a long-standing deal whereby Lane leased Kleberg's short-running horses for the brush tracks. Lane made the trip to the King Ranch, looked at Woven Web, and agreed with Kleberg that this could very well be the mare who would give Shue Fly her payback for defeating Nobodies Friend in 1941.

Lane took the filly and turned her over to Paul Simar of Louisiana. On October 27, 1946, Simar took her to Texas where she won the Eagle Pass Championship. Now she was Miss Princess, and Kleberg was ready for Shue Fly.

Racing writer Nelson Nye long ago wrote the following account of what happened when Miss Princess arrived at Del Rio, Texas.

"Back again at Del Rio in April of 1947, Miss Princess switched flies while the rest of the equine gathering gave

*In this early match race
Miss Princess (No. 2)
beat Miss Bank at the
Del Rio Race Meet
on May 9, 1943. The
time was :22.1.*

Photo Courtesy *The
Quarter Horse Journal*

her all the room she wanted to do it in.
Mr. Lane loafed around in the genial
manner of the cat after a trip to the
goldfish bowl, and dropped a few
thoughts where they would do the most
good. After about two weeks of these
goings-on, the Heplers got Shue Fly up
out of the pasture and came along over
to see what was cooking.

"Shue Fly was 10 years old at the time
and had been meeting all competition for
the past seven years, whereas the young
and dashing Princess was a filly in her
prime. But the Heplers weren't the ones
to let that stand in their way—and
neither was Shue Fly. Perhaps there was
in this a touch of noblesse oblige."

The Heplers knew the age difference
between Shue Fly and Miss Princess, but
Shue Fly didn't. Kleberg and Odom
drummed up a $30,000 winner-take-all

match. It was the largest pot of gold to
date. The time was set for May 3, 1947.

The Match Race

Probably the best chronicle existing
of that famous day in the dusty south
Texas town of Del Rio came from Carl
Guys. He was a trainer back then, and
later became the sports editor for
Del Rio's *News-Herald*. In the January
2, 1982, issue of the *News-Herald*, Guys
wrote about the event, and it was
reprinted in the April 1991 issue of *The
Quarter Racing Journal*.

"Fans from New Mexico came by

W O R L D ' S   C H A M P I O N

Photo
by J. H.
Dodd

"MISS PRINCESS"

The **"QUEEN"** of the Quarter Tracks has the most impressive record of any Quarter Running Horse since organized Quarter Racing first started. The Lane mare from the King Ranch has showed her superior class to the whole world by taking on all comers.

In her nine starts on recognized tracks she has never been defeated. During her racing career she established two new **WORLD'S RECORDS** and equaled a third. In addition she set a three-year-old record for 330 yards and equaled the three-year-old filly record for 440 yards.

RACING RECORD

Date — Dist. — Wt. — Time	Date — Dist. — Wt. — Time
10-23-46 330—110—:17.4g	10-27-46 440—110—:22.6g
6-15-47 350— 83—:18.5g	5- 3-47 440—111—:22.3 f
10-26-47 350—115—:18.0 f	10-26-47 440—115—:22.2 f
5 -9-48 350—119—:17.8 f	2-15-48 440—124—:22.3 f
2- 1-48 400—120—:20.6 f	4-30-48 440—115—:22.0 f
	5- 9-48 440—119—:22.1 f

ERNEST H. LANE   **ODOM, TEXAS**

A description of Miss Princess in The Quarter Running Horse
1948 *referred to her as the "Queen of the Quarter tracks with the most impressive record of any Quarter running horse since organized Quarter racing first started."*
                                                        Photo by J.H. Dodd

air and in fast cars, while fans from Louisiana arrived in yellow school buses marked Calcasieu Parish from the Rayne area. And the folks from New Mexico came with bulging wallets while the Louisianans arrived with little black bags, also straining at the seams. Money was wagered on the 440-yard race at the 200, 250, 300, 350, 400, and finish marks, and one side was as sure as the other that their mare would win.

"Miss Princess pranced up the track and circled in front of the packed grandstand in the post parade. Shue Fly … strode with confidence under the talented hands of the California jockey. Pat Castille, the top jock around Louisiana, had some problems making weight and had to spend two sessions in a sweat box at Garza Shop in San Felipe here. Earl Souther (Shue Fly's jockey) was on the money at the weigh-in, and Castile was a shade on the lighter side of the weight agreed on."

Shue Fly drew the one-hole. Miss Princess was in the two. Guys continued his narrative.

"Fans who had lined the rail from the starting gate to the finish line and the spectators in the grandstand grew fidgety as the New Mexico mare caused a long delay of about 20 minutes. Finally, both were loaded into their chutes and in a moment the gates flew open. The Texas mare bolted to the front with the New Mexico mare a wink behind. Castile flicked his bat one time and Southern flashed his whip several times as the mares settled into their strides."

The race was taken, at all marked distances, by Miss Princess. Shue Fly finally got her payback, and Kleberg felt the world—at least his portion of it—was in much better shape. Miss Princess' final time was :22.3 with a 1½-length margin.

There were those loyal Shue Fly supporters who insisted there was nothing fair or sporting about the match. They cited the big gap between the

Another photo of the famous Miss Princess.

two mares' ages. They reminded everyone that Shue Fly had, basically, been jerked out of pasture for the race, weighing at least 1,200 pounds with a large percentage of it being out-of-condition fat. And, last, she was suffering from arthritis in her shoulder. All that was true, but. …

Kleberg kept Miss Princess at Del Rio, and she won every time she and Castile saw the inside of the starting gate. She proved she was no piker by defeating such accomplished names as Barbra B, Stella Moore, Lightfoot, Miss Bank, and Mae West. In 1946, '47, and '48, Miss Princess was named World Champion Quarter Running Horse. Finally, there was nothing left for Miss Princess to accomplish.

The chestnut mare was turned out at the end of the 1948 race season. The following year, she was bred to Depth Charge (TB) and in 1950 she produced Baloma, a chestnut mare who earned a race Register of Merit. Her last two foals were not successful on the track. They were Furolle, a 1951 chestnut mare sired by Cientifico (TB), and Chisera, a 1955 chestnut mare sired by On The Mark (TB).

Miss Princess, aka Woven Web, died in 1966 at the age of 23.

7 MISS BANK

By Diane Ciarloni

She was long and good-looking with a beautifully shaped head.

MISS BANK was one of the toughest competitors to ever hit the Quarter Horse racetracks. Bred by Joe O'Keefe of Sierra Blanca, Tex., she was foaled in June 1940.

She began running as a 3-year-old. Although she ran most of her races when few official records were kept, she is reputed to have competed in 300 races during an 11-year time span, winning 80 percent of them.

At one time or another she held or equaled track or world records at 220, 300, 330, 350, and 440 yards.

Miss Bank was sired by a Thoroughbred Remount stallion, Captains Courageous, and was out of an unregistered Quarter-type mare named Apron Strings. According to one story, Apron Strings, who was a top-notch polo mount, was by Brown Joe, by Joe Hancock. However, AQHA records do not list a sire and dam for her.

Miss Bank passed through the hands of a number of owners during the first few years of her life. She turned up at an Alamogordo, N.M., brush-track meet

Miss Bank equaled or held track records at five distances. This photo was taken at Rillito in 1945 when she covered 440 yards in 23 flat. The jockey is Frank Figueroa and the owner, L. Gillespie.

Photo Courtesy *The Quarter Horse Journal*

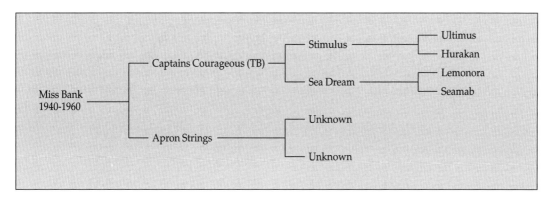

```
                                       ┌─ Stimulus ──────────┬─ Ultimus
                    ┌─ Captains Courageous (TB) ─┤            └─ Hurakan
                    │                  └─ Sea Dream ──────────┬─ Lemonora
Miss Bank           │                                         └─ Seamab
1940-1960 ──────────┤
                    │                  ┌─ Unknown
                    └─ Apron Strings ──┤
                                       └─ Unknown
```

as a young mare, under the ownership of Leon Gillespie of El Paso.

At this time, she had not even been named. When Gillespie was told by track officials that she couldn't run unless she had a name, Gillespie reportedly said, "Just call her Miss Bank." He apparently took the name from one of his business enterprises called the Old Bank Club.

Pete Reynolds of Alabama can still remember Captains Courageous, Miss Bank's sire. "He was one of the top Thoroughbred Remount stallions in the area," Reynolds recalled. "Those stallions were put out by the government to various ranches, and the O'Keefes happened to get Captains Courageous."

In addition to Miss Bank, Captains Courageous also sired the good Quarter Horse stallion Rey. Rey sired such good broodmares as Frontera Sugar, the dam of Sugar Bars, and Reina Rey, the dam of AQHA Supreme Champion Lightning Rey.

Captains Courageous also sired the Register of Merit race horses Bo Cue Blanc and CB.

Some reports say Miss Bank was bred by Ross Perner of Sierra Blanca, Tex., and bought as a yearling by Plunk Fields. According to AQHA records, however, she was bred by Joe O'Keefe. This would make sense, since Reynolds attests to Captains Courageous standing at the O'Keefe ranch.

When Miss Bank was five, Gillespie turned her training over to a couple of teenagers, his son and nephew, Bob Gillespie and Chuck Ward. The mare started 17 times for them, winning all the races. Ward, who weighed 150 pounds, rode Miss Bank to most of these wins.

Miss Bank raced against the toughest runners of her time and defeated most of

Halter and Performance Record: Race Register of Merit.

Progeny Record:

Foal Crops: 5	Race Starters: 3
Foals Registered: 5	Race Money Earned: $8,049
Halter Point-Earners: 2	Race Registers of Merit: 3
Halter Points Earned: 6	
Leading Race Money-Earner: Fantasy ($5,591)	

A photograph of Miss Bank as a broodmare that was printed in the June 1953 Arizona Stockman. *It was part of an article describing her sale to Art Pollard for $7,500, a price Pollard believed to be a record paid for a broodmare at the time.*

73

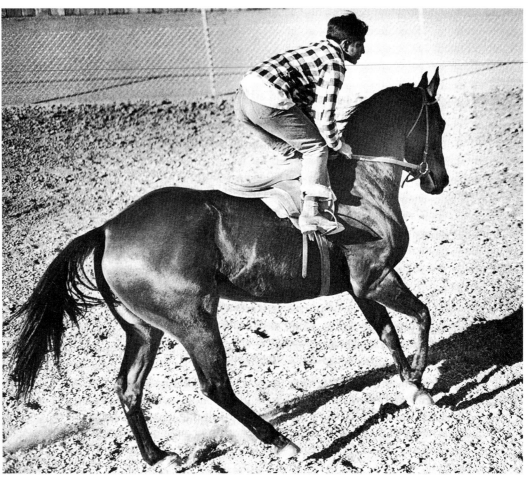

Incredibly, Miss Bank raced for 11 years, ran 300 races, and won 80 percent of them. This photo of the great mare is from Nelson Nye's book Great Moments in Quarter Racing History, *now out of print.*

A photo of Miss Bank taken during the 1948 racing season and printed in the January 1949 issue of Western Horseman.

them at one time or another.

Included among the headliners she beat were Queenie, Piggin String (TB), Miss Panama, Senor Bill, B Seven, Prissy, Vandy, Tonta Gal, Barbra B, Hard Twist, Lady Lee, Squaw H, and Shue Fly.

The Thoroughbred breeding in Miss Bank was obvious. She was long and good-looking with a beautifully shaped head. She was fine-boned, but tremendously powerful, with a solid reach that could eat up a track.

As an example of how durable Miss Bank was, she was once matched at El Paso in a 350-yard race against a horse owned by Roy Rice of Fabens, Texas. Miss Bank won by a quarter of a length. Forty-five minutes later, she ran against the same horse at the same distance, winning by daylight. Apparently Rice thought he could wear out Miss Bank because he matched his horse at her for a third time, just 30 minutes later. Miss Bank won again, by an even greater margin.

On October 5, 1946, Miss Bank won the 440-yard world championship at

Fantasy, Miss Bank's 1955 daughter by Lightning Bar, earned her ROM in racing and was Miss Bank's top money-earner. The photo was taken at Los Alamitos in April 1957.

Photo by Jack Stribling, Courtesy *The Quarter Horse Journal*

Art Pollard paid $7,500 to add Miss Bank to his broodmare band.

Albuquerque over Squaw H, Tonta Gal, and Vandy.

On December 1, 1946, at Tucson, she ran in yet another 440-yard race, also billed as the world championship, emerging the victor over Barbra B, Tonta Gal, and Hard Twist.

On December 13, 1946, at Tucson, Miss Bank was matched at two distances, 320 and 350 yards, against Shue Fly, daylighting the great world champion both times.

One of Miss Bank's greatest races took place at Albuquerque on October 4, 1947. Billed as the New Mexico Championship Quarter, it was the most important race run in New Mexico up to that time.

With Frankie Figueroa in the irons, Miss Bank carried 129 pounds, four to nine pounds more than any of her 11 rivals. The field included some of the top sprinters of the day, such as B Seven, Squaw H, Lucky Manners, Shu Baby, Bay Annie, and Byglo.

B Seven grabbed the early lead, but at the end it was Miss Bank on top by a neck. Her announced time of 22 seconds flat for the 440 set a world record.

Shortly after this race, Gillespie sold Miss Bank to D.V. Land, also of El Paso. Land continued to campaign her for several years and then sold her to Jim Derrick of Carlsbad, New Mexico.

By the early 1950s, Miss Bank's racing career was nearing its end. Art Pollard, the astute young race horse breeder from Tucson, was just beginning to assemble his famed broodmare band at this time, and he paid Derrick $7,500 for the privilege of adding Miss Bank to it.

"I believe that was a record price paid for a Quarter Horse broodmare in the early 1950s," said Pollard. "I intended to add her to my broodmare band. I never

Fantacia was a AAA race mare who became an AQHA Champion. This picture was taken in 1968 at the Texas State Fair when the pretty mare went grand, shown by Jerry Wells. Her owner was Hoss Inman. The back of the photo states that this granddaughter of Miss Bank won almost $50,000 on the track and was champion halter mare at nearly every major show.

Photo by Johnny Johnston, Courtesy *The Quarter Horse Journal*

really cared that much for racing. Oh, I love to watch it, but I was far more interested in breeding great individuals than I was in running them.

"Miss Bank was a pretty mare. She was a light bay and, overall, she reminded me of a Saddlebred. She was long and rangy, but well-balanced with a soft eye. She was a fine individual," Pollard concluded.

Miss Bank's first foal was Bankette,

a bay filly sired by Worryman, by Red Man, by Joe Hancock. Due to her foaling date of December 29, 1952, Bankette never went to the track.

As a broodmare, however, Bankette produced six Register of Merit running horses, including: Bank A Lot, SI 93; Miss Vanny, AAAT; Topette, AAA; and Rebel Cause, AAAT.

Rebel Cause, by Top Deck (TB), was the 1961 World Champion Quarter Running 3-Year-Old Colt and the 1962 World Champion Quarter Running Aged Stallion. He also went on to sire 355 Register of Merit race horses who earned $2,795,406.

Miss Bank's second foal was Desertette, a chestnut filly foaled in

This 1966 photo from the Juarez Race Track shows Fantacia after she set a track record of :22.4 for 440 yards. She was ridden by Larry Dyers, owned by Hoss Inman, and trained by Clarence Jay. Fantacia, foaled in 1963, was Miss Bank's granddaughter, out of Fantasy and by Ridge Butler.

Photo Courtesy *The Quarter Horse Journal*

1953, by Texon Boy (TB). A Register of Merit race horse, Desertette produced three ROM race horses.

Fantasy, the third foal of Miss Bank, and the first sired by Pollard's famous Lightning Bar, was foaled in 1955. Fantasy achieved a speed index of 95 and produced Fandalita, AAA; Fantacia, AAAT and AQHA Champion; Fantalisa, AAA; and Mr Fantastic, AAA.

Lightning Bank, a full brother of Fantasy, was foaled in 1958 and earned his ROM in racing.

Manor Orphan, foaled in 1960 and also sired by Lightning Bar, was Miss Bank's fifth and final foal. Although unraced, he did earn three halter points.

Miss Bank died in 1960, the victim of an outbreak of colitis-x that raged through Art Pollard's entire band of horses. It killed not only Miss Bank, but Lightning Bar, Hula Girl P, Chinchilla, and Little Nellie Bars, as well.

Pollard, one of the leading breeders of Quarter race horses at the time, never fully recovered from the devastation of the tragedy.

"Even now, I still feel the sadness of losing them all," he reflects. "But I'm proud to know Miss Bank is buried at my old ranch."

One of Pollard's memories from the glory years of his Lightning A Ranch that he treasures the most is of Miss Bank daylighting Shue Fly.

"There weren't a lot of horses who could do that to Shue Fly," he smiled. "But then, Miss Bank was a shade better than a lot of horses."

REBEL CAUSE

By Jim Goodhue

**He was a
great race
horse and sire.**

THE YEARS 1960 and 1961 might be called vintage years in Quarter Horse racing. They were among those rare years when two really outstanding runners appeared on the racing scene at the same time. Those were the years Rebel Cause and Tonto Bars Hank met head on in race after race. If one of the two had not been around, the other would have

won everything in sight and completely dominated the racing season. But with both of them in competition, Quarter Horse racing enjoyed a series of sprinting duels that made history.

At 2, Tonto Bars Hank (see his chapter in this book) seemed to have the smallest possible edge, even though he was defeated twice by Rebel Cause. For example,

Rebel Cause, one of the most respected Quarter race horses of the early 1960s, earned even greater fame as a speed sire. His get earned $2.9 million on the track and 1,146.5 points in the show ring. Orren Mixer painted this conformation study for Rebel Cause's final owner, Wes Mickle, in front of the Mickle family's Scottsdale, Ariz., ranch.

Painting by Orren Mixer

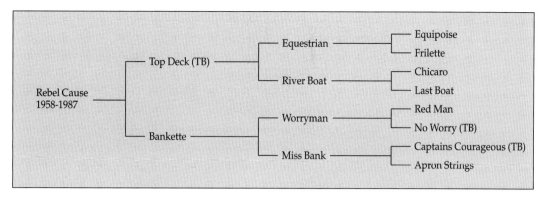

Rebel Cause set two 2-year-old colt records that season, only to have Tonto Bars Hank lower both of them later in the year. Rebel Cause actually had equaled the world record for stallions of all ages when he ran 350 yards in :17.8. His other short-lived record was 400 yards in :20.3. After much debate, AQHA awarded Tonto Bars Hank the titles of champion 2-year-old colt and champion stallion over males of all ages.

Financially, however, 1960 would have to be reckoned as a successful campaign for Rebel Cause. By the end of that year, the elegant bay colt had jumped into 17th place among the all-time leading money-earners in Quarter Horse racing.

Race Career

At Los Alamitos in 1960, Rebel Cause was victorious in both the Juvenile Championship and the Los Ninos Handicap, took second money in the Kindergarten Futurity and the Newport Dunes Stakes, and placed third in the Thanksgiving Stakes. At Ruidoso that season, he took second money for the Ruidoso Futurity and third for the All American Futurity (won by Tonto Bars Hank).

Both of the titans returned to the battle in 1961. Rebel Cause drew first blood by finishing a neck ahead of Tonto Bars Hank in the Pacific Coast QHRA Derby. The excitement of this race built because each won his trial in the identical time of :21.9 for 440 yards. Each also won his qualifying round by a full length.

Moving to Ruidoso, Rebel Cause won the Ruidoso Quarter Horse Derby on a sloppy track. Tonto Bars Hank, though, was not in the race.

Rebel Cause then returned to California to win the Pomona Quarter Horse Championship. Again, Tonto Bars Hank

Halter and Performance Record: Racing Register of Merit; 1961 World Champion Quarter Running 3-Year-Old Colt; 1962 World Champion Quarter Running Aged Stallion; Race Earnings, $85,586.

Progeny Record:

Foal Crops: 26	Performance Points Earned: 927.5
Foals Registered: 796	Performance Registers of Merit: 17
AQHA Champions: 3	Race Starters: 549
Racing World Champions: 1	Race Money Earned: $2,913,244
Halter Point-Earners: 21	Race Registers of Merit: 361
Halter Points Earned: 219	Superior Race Awards: 27
Performance Point-Earners: 52	
Leading Race Money-Earner: Turf's Best ($171,377)	

was not in the field, but No Butt was. This very capable mare, who would be named the world champion Quarter running horse the very next season, set a torrid pace. Rebel Cause's come-from-behind style brought him to the front just in time to win by a head.

Then, at Los Alamitos, Tonto Bars Hank met them both. In the 400-yard Go Man Go Stakes, the big chestnut raced into an early lead and managed to hold on as Rebel Cause and No Butt made determined efforts to head him. Rebel Cause finished a neck behind the winner and a nose ahead of the mare.

Los Alamitos' 440-yard Autumn Championship was contested the next

Rebel Cause ran a speed index of 100 at the track, where he won 13 of 35 starts and earned $85,586. The bay stallion was the 1961 World Co-Champion Quarter Running 3-Year-Old Colt and 1962 World Champion Quarter Running Aged Stallion.

Early in his career, Rebel Cause went on the list of the leading money-earners of all time.

weekend. The racing world debated about whether the additional 40 yards would move the half-Thoroughbred Rebel Cause ahead of his nemesis. Tonto Bars Hank's trademark lunge out of the gate gave him a better- than-usual start, however, and a daylight finish seemed possible. Rebel Cause fought gamely to decrease the margin. Yardage ran out with half a length's difference between the winning Tonto Bars Hank and the second-place Rebel Cause.

From 10 starts in 1961, Rebel Cause racked up seven wins, two seconds, and one third. He added a comfortable $39,027 to his bankroll.

This time, it was too close to call. The AQHA honored both Rebel Cause and Tonto Bars Hank as co-champion Quarter running 3-year-old colts.

At 4, Rebel Cause still was running among the top stakes competition, although he did not get into the win-

ner's circle for any major race. He accounted for second-place money in three 1962 Los Alamitos' stakes races: the Hard Twist Stakes, the Josie's Bar Handicap, and the Go Man Go Handicap. In the Go Man Go, he beat all but Caprideck, who was named champion running gelding for that year.

Rebel Cause also recorded two third places in added money events—the Pomona Championship and the Clabbertown G Handicap, which was won by the very prominent Alamitos Bar.

That year, AQHA created new year-end titles. One went to Rebel Cause: the 1962 Champion Quarter Running Aged Stallion.

Early in his career, Rebel Cause went on the list of the leading money-earners of all time. He remained on the list through 1969 with total earnings of $85,586.

Royal Racing Folks

Rebel Cause's successful career was no fluke. His pedigree showed him to be the product of racing royalty.

Top Deck, his sire, was one of the most successful Thoroughbred stallions ever used as a progenitor of Quarter Horse runners. His famous offspring include such speedsters as Go Man Go, Moon Deck, Decketta, Top Lady Bug, and Miss Top Flame. Descendants of the unraced Top Deck have continued to make sprinting history. His complete story can be found in the first edition of *Legends*.

Rebel Cause was bred by Haymaker Farms of Yukon, Okla., owned by television star Dale Robertson and his brother Chet. They selected a good young mare named Bankette to go to Top Deck. In addition to Rebel Cause, she produced the ROM racers Miss Vanny (Top AAA), Topette (AAA), Bank A Lot (AAA), Rebel's Sis, and Spotted Bullet.

Bankette was sired by Worryman, a solid ROM runner in the 1940s. Racing for Melville Haskell's Rincon Stock Farm, Worryman won seven of 10 starts as a 2-year-old in 1947, at distances from 220 yards to 440 yards. He set 2-year-old colt records at 300, 350, and 440 yards.

Worryman was a son of Red Man, who earned his ROM in the earliest days of recognized Quarter Horse racing. Among Red Man's other outstanding running offspring were Wampus Kitty and John Red. Red Man was sired by the great running stallion Joe Hancock, who was famous for throwing both speed and roping ability. The dam of Red Man was a roan mare from the Burnett Ranches.

Worryman's dam was a Thoroughbred mare named No Worry. She was a daughter of Eternal, a stallion highly successful in getting foals who demonstrated tremendous speed in short distance races.

Among Worryman's top runners were Dos Pesos (AAA and AAA producer) and Roan Man (AAA stakes winner). Roan Man will be remembered as the sire of Dariman (1963 Champion Quarter Running Gelding), Dari Star (1964 Champion Quarter Running Gelding), Dari Maid (Top AAA stakes winner), and many other ROM qualifiers.

Rebel Cause's second dam was the famous Miss Bank. The 1949 *AQRA Year Book* states that Miss Bank ran 60 races in four years of official starts to that date and won 25 of them. It further notes that her record was unusual in that "from the beginning she has competed with the tops." Among her many victories was one in which she equaled the world record of :15.8 for 300 yards. She accumulated fast

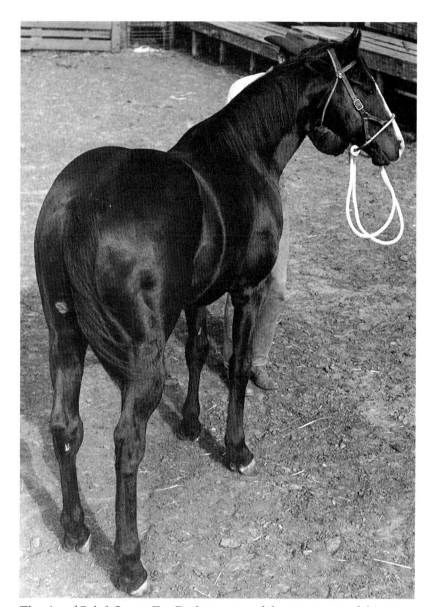

The sire of Rebel Cause, Top Deck, was one of the most successful Thoroughbred stallions ever used as a progenitor of Quarter Horse runners. His get include Go Man Go, Decketta, and Moon Deck. Top Deck's story is told in the first Legends *book.*

Photo Courtesy *The Quarter Horse Journal*

times from 220 yards to 440 yards. She is featured elsewhere in this book.

Breeding Career

The first foals from Rebel Cause arrived in 1963. They included such diversely talented horses as the track-record-setting

The striking Johnny Boone, a son of Rebel Cause out of Me Bright, by Leo, earned a speed index of 100 at the track. He later sired runners with earnings of $1.9 million and show performers with 224 points.

Photo by Orren Mixer, Courtesy Frank Holmes

A total of $2,913,244 earned by his offspring kept Rebel Cause on the all-time list for sires of money-earners through 1995.

Easy Reb and the AQHA Champion and ROM working horse Rebel Rocket.

These 1963 foals resulted from Rebel Cause standing at stud part of the year and racing part of the season. At the end of this dual-purpose year, Rebel Cause was purchased from the Robertsons by Charles W. and Wesley J. Mickle's Valley View Ranch. At the time, this ranch was located in Scottsdale, Ariz., and Rebel Cause stood there for about 10 years. Then, the Mickles moved the ranch operation and Rebel Cause to Weatherford, Texas.

When his first crop reached two years of age in 1965, Rebel Cause was among the leading sires of money-earners for the year. By 1967, he was on the all-time list

for sires of money-earners. A total of $2,913,244 earned by his offspring kept him on that list through 1995.

From Rebel Cause's 796 registered foals, 549 were starters and 369 were winners. His 32 stakes winners won 55 stakes races. And 27 of his foals were officially designated by the AQHA as Superior race horses.

Through 1996, Rebel Cause stood 34th on the list of all-time leading sires of racing ROM qualifiers. His 361 ROM foals put him in that position and kept him on the list for many years.

The leading money-earner sired by Rebel Cause was Turf's Best, who earned $171,377 in 78 starts. A 1965 black colt, Turf's Best was out of Turf Parade, a running ROM daughter of Super Charge, rated Top AAA and the 1953 Champion Quarter Running 2-Year-Old Colt.

Turf's Best won both the Rainbow and Lost Valley Downs futurities and was named the 1967 Champion Quarter Running 2-Year-Old Colt. At 3, he won the Rainbow Derby, Raton Derby, and

Turf's Best was Rebel Cause's leading money earner, with $171,377. Out of Turf Parade, by Super Charge, the black stallion was the 1967 Champion Quarter Running 2-Year-Old Colt and won six stakes in his 10-year career. Shown after winning the '67 Rainbow Futurity, Turf's Best is flanked by owner T.H. Baker (holding trophy) and trainer Morris V. Marshall (holding reins).   **Photo Courtesy** *The Quarter Horse Journal*

From Rebel Cause's first foal crop, Easy Reb was out of the mare Easy Arrive, by Arrive (TB). The 1963 roan stallion set a track record and helped establish Rebel Cause's reputation as a sire of runners.

Photo by Variety Photographic Industries Inc.

Also foaled in 1963, Rebel Rocket, out of Mary Minnick, by Norfleet, earned both racing and performance ROMs and his AQHA Championship. Shown here winning grand champion stallion at the 1969 Minnesota Quarter Horse Show, the bay stallion was owned at that time by Tony Sitzmann of E. Glacier, Montana.

Photo by Bobbie, Courtesy *The Quarter Horse Journal*

At stud, Turf's Best continued his winning ways.

Ruidoso Championship Stakes. He also set a Ruidoso track record of :21.77 for 440 yards. These accomplishments led to his selection as 1968 Champion Quarter Running 3-Year-Old Colt. After a couple of stakes placings in 1969, Turf's Best stretched out to win the 870-yard Brigand Handicap in 1970.

At stud, Turf's Best continued his winning ways. His AAA runners included Best Baby (SI 101), Miss Ataturf, O'Lonesome Me, Turf's Banker, and Turf's Reb.

Another successful Rebel Cause son, Barney O Toole, won four stakes, six other races, and $40,216. His dam was Irish Imp, a AAA daughter of Alamitos Bar.

Many of Rebel Cause's good sons were gelded and proved to be hard-knocking race horses. Prominent among these was Cause Im Fair. He won 31 of his 126 starts, was second 27 times (including the Jet Deck Stakes at the New Mexico State Fair), and took 16 third places. He totaled $110,602 in purse money.

The gelding Whittle Rebel won two futurities and two other stakes on the Arizona racing circuit. Sissys Rebel, another gelding by Rebel Cause, won the National Invitational Championship Maturity at Manor Downs, the Trinity Meadows March Maturity, and Ruidoso's Jet Deck Handicap. He placed in other stakes from 350 to 550 yards and earned $39,047. Sissys Rebel also gave Manor Downs a record of :21.66 for 440 yards.

Other stakes-winning geldings sired by Rebel Cause were Sea Rebel (Northwest Montana Fair Futurity and Derby) and Mr Rebel Cowboy (South Dakota Bred Derby). Good money-earners among his gelded sons also include Rebel Charlie ($51,955), Lifestyle ($30,987), Scottish Rite ($27,934), Bruce N Reb ($26,668), and Willie Nelson ($26,311). Willie Nelson also found time to earn 21 working points and a performance ROM.

Daughters of Rebel Cause

Rebel Cause also was represented by many notable money-earning daughters. Among them we find Rebel Killoqua. She won the Blue Ribbon Futurity and the Mid American Derby. A second in

ALL AMERICAN FUTURITY

ALL AMERICAN FUTURITY
1ST CONSOLATION
1978
RUIDOSO DOWNS

"GEEPER CREEPER"
AUSTIN MILLSPAUGH, OWNER   SAM HEAD,   TR
440 yds. 22.22 SEPTEMBER 3, 1978 W.YOUNG,   UP
MOONVIEW (2nd)   CHERISHED LADY (3rd)
FIRST CONSOLATION   PURSE $145,000.00
        RUIDOSO DOWNS, N.M.

A 1976 daughter of Rebel Cause out of Pecos Banker, by Bank Night, Geeper Creeper earned $77,902 at the racetrack. The bay filly won the Florida QHA Futurity and the first consolation of the 1978 All American Futurity, where this photo was taken.

Photo Courtesy *The Quarter Horse Journal*

The Rebel Cause daughter Mighty Michelle, out of a Bear Hug mare, showed her talents in the show ring. The 1971 mare earned both youth and open performance ROMs, placed in hunter under saddle at the open World Show and the Youth World, and was the 1980 youth reserve world champion in hunt seat equitation with rider Nancy Ruth Best.

Photo by Don Trout, Courtesy *The Quarter Horse Journal*

the Rocky Mountain Quarter Horse Association Futurity also helped to bring her earnings to $100,647.

Geeper Creeper accounted for $77,902, primarily by winning the Florida Quarter Horse Association Futurity, as well as placing in stakes at Los Alamitos, Sunland Park, and the California State Fair.

Another outstanding filly was the AAA Rebel Della, with earnings of $74,400. Although she won six of her 23

starts, her big moment in the spotlight came when she won Los Alamitos' El Primero Del Ano Derby.

Two of Rebel Cause's good stakes-winning fillies were out of the famous producer Vandy's Lass (dam of 1975 Champion 3-Year-Old Quarter Running Colt Maskeo Lad). These were Masked Lass ($59,788) and Masked Rebel ($38,269). Masked Lass, winner of the Pompano Park Futurity and the Gateway Downs Derby, gave Gateway Downs a track record of :19.84 for 400 yards. Masked Rebel won the Goliad Futurity and placed second in both the Miss America Futurity and the All American Congress Futurity.

Rebel Rainbow, although stakes-placed at other tracks, tallied all four of her stakes wins at Delta Downs. At 3, this daughter of Rebel Cause won the 330-yard division of the Silver Cup Series. At 4, she was victorious in the Speedster Handicap, as well as both the 400-yard division and the 440-yard division of the Gulf Coast Silver Cup Series. In all, she accumulated $62,268 in earnings.

Miss Flicka Reb, by Rebel Cause, totaled $61,128. This was accomplished largely by wins in the Yakima Meadow Futurity, Centennial's Lassie Stakes, the Capitol City Futurity, and Los Alamitos' Independence Day Handicap. Along the way, she set 350-yard records at both Yakima Meadows and Helena Downs.

Another Rebel Cause filly, Rebelucy, also won the Yakima Meadow and Capitol City futurities. She set the Helena Downs record for 350 yards that was lowered by her half-sister, Miss Flicka Reb. Rebelucy's earnings came to $25,451.

Show Ring Offspring

Speed is not the only claim to fame among Rebel Cause's offspring. He sired three AQHA Champions, 16 performance ROM qualifiers, and 19 halter point-earners. He also sired one Superior halter horse and three Superior performance horses.

The three AQHA Champions are Rebel Kitten, Rebel Robert, and Iron Rebel. Rebel Kitten qualified for both the racing ROM (with a speed index of 100) and the performance ROM en route

A maternal grand-daughter of Rebel Cause, Denim N Diamonds earned $731,118 at the track and was the 1981 Champion Aged Mare, 1981 Champion Aged Horse, and 1982 Champion Aged Horse. Here, the daughter of '75 champion aged stallion Timeto Thinkrich and Bachelor's Dream is escorted to the winner's circle after her victory in the 1981 Champion of Champions. That's famed jockey Jerry Nicodemus up.

Photo Courtesy *The Quarter Horse Journal*

Rebel Cause's daughters have placed him among the most noted sires of broodmares.

to her AQHA title.

Iron Rebel, a Superior western pleasure horse, has become a prominent sire of using horses. His Son Of A Rebel earned more than 2,500 AQHA points. He was a world champion in junior western pleasure and a reserve world champion in senior western pleasure. In AJQHA events he was a reserve high-point western pleasure horse and reserve high-point in horsemanship. He has Superior awards in seven performance events and was twice a youth champion.

Another versatile daughter of Rebel Cause was Rebel Kitten. First, she qualified for the racing ROM with a speed index of 100, and then she earned enough points to become a working ROM qualifier. Then she earned sufficient halter points to become an AQHA Champion. Finally, she produced foals of diverse abilities. Among them was the AAA Some Kinda Rebel, who placed

second in two futurities and one derby. Her filly, Lady Sandy Riker, turned her talents to the show arena. In youth events, she gained the rank of AQHA Champion and Superior in showmanship. Lady Sandy Riker also qualified for the youth ROM twice. In open events, she was named a working ROM performer and Superior halter horse.

Mighty Michelle, a Rebel Cause mare, also knew her way around a show arena. A reserve world champion in hunt seat equitation in youth competition, she was among the top 10 finishers in both the 1980

In 1962, the year Rebel Cause was the Champion Quarter Running Aged Stallion, Orren Mixer painted this portrait for television star Dale Robertson, the horse's breeder and owner during his race career. Ruidoso Downs serves as the backdrop for the painting.

Painting by Orren Mixer

youth and the 1975 open world shows in hunter under saddle competition.

Broodmare Sire

Rebel Cause's daughters have placed him among the most noted sires of broodmares. At the end of 1998, he was 18th on the list of all-time maternal grandsires of money-earners, and 14th on the list of all-time broodmare sires of ROM qualifiers.

The maternal grandget of Rebel Cause, through 1998, have earned more than $7.4 million (an average of more than $6,400 per starter). Among them are 41 stakes winners, 38 Superior race horses, and 704 racing ROM qualifiers (340 with speed indexes of 90 or higher). They include one world champion, Denim N Diamonds,

who won three year-end titles.

Winner of $731,118 in purses, Denim N Diamonds was out of the Rebel Cause daughter Bachelor's Dream and by Timeto Thinkrich, world champion aged stallion in 1975. After qualifying for her racing Register of Merit at 2, Denim N Diamonds began to run in earnest as a 3-year-old. That year, she won the Sunland Park Fall Derby, was second in the Kansas Derby, and third in the Rainbow Derby.

At 4, Denim N Diamonds flew to the winner's circle in the Champion Of Champions, the Los Alamitos Invitational Championship, the Peninsula Championship, the Vessels Maturity, the Shue Fly Handicap, and the Miss Peninsula Handicap. She was voted 1981 Champion Aged Marc and 1981 Champion Aged Horse.

As a 5-year-old in 1982, Denim N Diamonds made the wire first in the Go Man Go Handicap, the Horsemen's QHRA Championship, and the second division of the Go Together Handicap. She took second money in the World's Championship Classic and third in the Champion Of Champions. Again, she was selected champion aged mare.

All seven of the foals out of Bachelor's

Dream who raced were ROM qualifiers. Three were AAA, including the stakes-placed runners Cause I Dream (SI 102) and Jet Travelor.

Rebel Cause's stakes-winning Masked Rebel added more to her reputation when she was put into the broodmare band. She was the dam of 10 ROM race horses out of 12 starters.

Possibly the most consistent producer sired by Rebel Cause was the lightly raced Twayna. She won two of her four starts and earned a speed index of 95 before finding her niche as a broodmare. With nine starters, she tallied nine ROM foals. Seven of them were AAA.

Twayna's most successful runner was Casady Casanova, a son of Top Moon, who ran out $157,173 at the track. As a 2-year-old, he won three stakes at Los Alamitos—the Juvenile Invitational Handicap, the Cypress Stakes, and the Los Ninos Handicap—and placed second in the Ed Burke Memorial Futurity. The next year the bay stallion took second money in the El Primero Del Ano Derby before siring money-earners of $6.4 million.

The blood of Rebel Cause made itself felt in Mexico, too, when Thermal Express was named the 1986 Champion Aged Horse of Mexico. Thermal Express was out of Jet Bankette, a race-winning daughter of Rebel Cause.

Conclusion

Wes Mickle reports that Rebel Cause died at 29, which would have been in 1987. He is buried under an appropriate marker on the ranch at Weatherford. Nearby is the grave of his dam, Bankette, who lived to be 31.

Mickle remembers not only Rebel Cause's notable successes as a race horse and sire, but also his kind disposition. Rebel Cause commanded respect for many fine traits. All in all, he was the kind of a horse who could be, as Mickle says, "the last horse I was emotionally involved with."

Rebel Cause daughter Masked Lass earned $59,788 at the track and set a track record at Gateway Downs of :19.84 for 400 yards. The mare was out of Vandy's Lass, by Feast (TB), who also produced Masked Rebel (earner of $38,269) with Rebel Cause, and Maskeo Lad (1975 World Champion 3-Year-Old Colt) with Three Oh's.

9 TONTO BARS HANK

By Frank Holmes

He was known as "The Flying Boxcar" during his racing career.

TONTO BARS Hank's life would eventually become fast-paced, but it got off to a rather slow start. To begin with, hardly anyone was interested in C.G. and Milo Whitcomb's Quarter Horse colt when he was offered for sale as a weanling. Nor did very many people pay attention to the race- and working-bred youngster when he was again put on the market as a yearling. However, when he was a 2-year-old, the whole Quarter Horse world learned to pay attention to the big, sorrel stallion who would come to be known as "The Flying Boxcar."

Tonto Bars Hank was bred by C.G. Whitcomb and his son, Milo, and was foaled on April 12, 1958, on their ranch near Sterling, Colorado.

Tonto Bars Hank, the first Quarter running horse to win $100,000, was shown at halter after he was retired from the track. This picture was taken in January 1963 when he was named reserve champion stallion at Denver. The handler is Walter Merrick.

Photo by Darol Dickinson

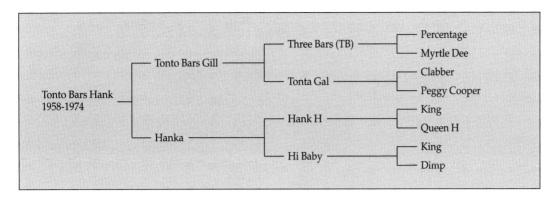

The Whitcombs had purchased Hanka, his dam, from Jack Smith of Indiahoma, Okla., in 1952. A Register of Merit race horse, she was sired by Hank H by King, and was out of Hi Baby by King.

In 1956 the Whitcombs bred Hanka to Three Bars (TB) when he was standing at Walter Merrick's 14 Ranch in Crawford, Oklahoma. She failed to settle, and the following year they decided to breed her to Tonto Bars Gill, a AAA-rated son of Three Bars (TB) who was standing in nearby Wray, Colorado. Tonto Bars Hank was the resulting foal.

Shortly after "Hank" was foaled, C.G. Whitcomb was badly injured in an automobile accident, and the decision was made to partially disperse the horses. Hanka, with 6-week-old Hank at her side, was consigned to a May 26, 1958, auction at Grand Island, Nebraska.

The Colt Nobody Wanted

On sale day the Whitcombs announced that if the buyer of their consignment was not satisfied with the colt at weaning time, they would buy him back for $900. With that guarantee in the bank, Jack McGrew of Stuart, Neb., submitted the winning bid of $1,650.

Although he would go on to become one of the industry's leading sires, Tonto Bars Gill was not yet a household name in racing circles. And Hanka, despite her record as a race horse, was an unproven producer from a working horse line. With such a mixed pedigree, Tonto Bars Hank was not considered well-bred, and his buyer chose to hold the Whitcombs to their sale-day guarantee. At six months of age, Hank reverted back to the breeders.

When Hank was foaled on their

Halter and Performance Record: AQHA Champion; Racing Register of Merit; Superior Race Horse; World Champion Quarter Running 2-Year-Old Colt and World Champion Quarter Running Stallion, 1960; and World Co-Champion 3-Year-Old Quarter Running Colt, 1961.

Progeny Record:

Foal Crops: 12	Performance Points Earned: 2,097
Foals Registered: 465	Performance Registers of Merit: 40
AQHA Champions: 8	Superior Performance Awards: 13
Supreme Champions: 1	Race Starters: 212
World Champions: 1	Race Money Earned: $478,902
Halter Point-Earners: 43	Race Registers of Merit: 95
Halter Points Earned: 1,096	Superior Race Awards: 6
Superior Halter Awards: 6	Racing World Champions: 1
Performance Point-Earners: 57	
Leading Race Money-Earner: Gigantus ($43,499)	

northeast Colorado ranch, the Whitcombs had been in the Quarter Horse business for more than 15 years. The owners of arena champions Frog W, Yucca W, King Flit, and Whitcomb's Frogette, they had always subscribed to the belief that speed was an essential quality in any horse.

"Frog W, our first great Quarter Horse," Milo Whitcomb said, "was bred by Jack Casement and carried his famous Triangle Bar brand on his left shoulder. Frog was a many-times grand champion halter horse, an accomplished reining horse, and a Certificate of Achievement-earner in the National Cutting Horse Association. But he was also a horse who possessed a lot of speed. We raced him as a 2-year-old and he won 11 races. We've always bred for speed."

In Tonto Bars Hank, the Whitcombs got what they bred for, and then some.

"After Hank was weaned," Whitcomb said, "we turned him out and let him grow up naturally. By the time he was a yearling, one of his paternal half-sisters, Miss Louton, was tearing up the tracks. So we put Hank up for sale again. This time we hung a $10,000 price tag on him.

"Ad Coors, of the Coors brewing family, did send a man to look Hank over," he continued. "But when he found out what we were asking for him, he reportedly said that there was no way he'd ever give that much money for a damn draft horse.

"Hank was always big for his age."

Having once again failed to sell him, the Whitcombs decided to run Tonto Bars Hank themselves.

"In the spring of his 2-year-old year," Whitcomb said, "I broke Hank to ride in a little pen behind the house. He was so laid-back and easygoing that, after I'd ridden him for a couple of weeks, I put my 11-year-old daughter, Celie, on him. She got along fine with him."

Once he was well-started under saddle, the Whitcombs turned Hank over to Pat Simpson for race training. A 40-year veteran of Thoroughbred racing, Simpson had just completed a sensational two years as the trainer of Miss Louton. Under Simpson's guidance, the 1956 daughter of Tonto Bars Gill and Miss Lou Dandy had been named the 1958 Champion Quarter Running 2-Year-Old Filly, the 1959 Champion Quarter Running 3-Year-Old Filly, and the 1959 Champion Quarter Running Mare.

"We had known Pat for a number of years before he came to work for us," Whitcomb said. "Based on that, and his success with Miss Louton, we felt he was the ideal person to train Hank."

To begin with, Simpson did not agree.

"We brought Pat on board as Hank's trainer in June of 1960," Whitcomb said, "and promptly shipped both of them off to Ruidoso Downs in New Mexico. After they'd been down there a while, Pat called and said he didn't think Hank

Tonto Bars Hank was not only an exceptional race horse; he also had exceptional conformation.   **Photo by Darol Dickinson**

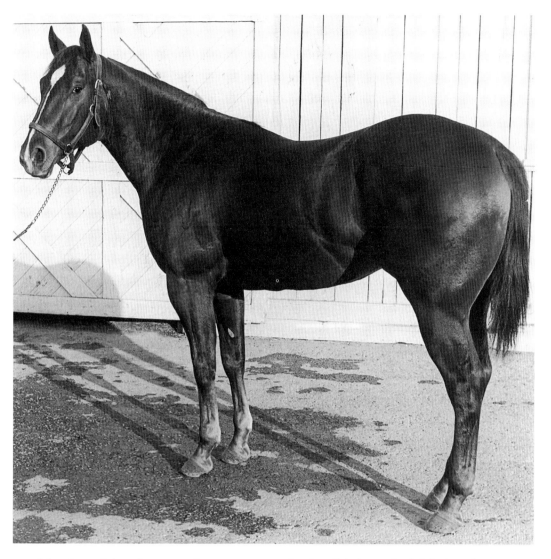

This photograph of Hank was taken when he was racing in California.

Photo by Jack Stribling

"It was the only race during his whole career that he didn't run in AAA time."

would get anything done as a 2-year-old. He said he was having a hard time getting him to even gallop during his workouts, and we would be better off bringing him home and trying him again the following year.

"We were paying Pat by the month, so we told him to stay down there, get Hank into a race, and we'd make a decision after that."

To the Track

"Hank made his first official start on July 1, 1960, in a 350-yard allowance race at Ruidoso," said Whitcomb. "He broke quickly and got a two-length jump on the field. Then he saw the grandstand and got so scared he almost stopped. Three horses passed him before he took off again, but he caught them and won the race by a half-length in AA+ time. It was the only race during his whole career

that he didn't run in AAA time."

Based on this performance, it was decided to keep Tonto Bars Hank in training.

On July 16, he was entered in another 350-yard allowance race. This time, the grandstand didn't bother him, and he covered the distance in the time of :17.9 seconds, which equaled the 2-year-old-colt record.

Hank's next start was in the Kansas Futurity trials on July 23. Failing to break well, he finished second to Heavenly Flower. In the finals on July 31, however, he broke alertly and led the race from whether their juvenile star could handle the added distance, that fear was quickly dispelled when he scored a two-length victory and established a 2-year-old-colt record time of :20.2 in the process.

Next came the big one—the 1960 All American Futurity. Scheduled to run on Labor Day, it boasted a then-unheard-of gross purse of $130,244.

In his qualifying trial heat, Hank got his first look at Rebel Cause. Owned by Chet and Dale Robertson's Haymaker Farms of Yukon, Okla., this bay son of Top Deck (TB) would be Hank's chief rival for the remainder of his racing career.

Rebel Cause came out on top in the pair's first duel, besting Hank by three-quarters of a length. But Hank's second-place time of :20.9 for the 400-yard distance was still fast enough to qualify him for the finals.

The track was fast for the All American Futurity finals on September 5. Hank broke sharply from the number six slot and led the race from wire to wire. He bested Three Deep by two lengths and Rebel Cause by an additional neck; his time of :20.2 equaled his own 2-year-old colt record set in the Kansas Futurity.

The $65,122 purse increased Hank's earnings to $76,466 and positioned him third on the list of all-time money-winning Quarter race horses.

After the All American, Hank and Simpson stopped off in Albuquerque long enough to notch another victory in a 350-yard allowance race and equal the 2-year-old-colt record in the process. Then it was on to the West Coast.

California-Bound

"All we heard while we had Hank at Ruidoso," Whitcomb said, "was just wait until he hits California. Then he'll see what real competition is. It seems that there was a 2-year-old colt by the name of Rock Bar out there that those Californians thought was unbeatable."

Tonto Bars Hank wasted little time in proving the Rock Bar fans wrong.

"On the opening day of the Los Alamitos race meet, we had Hank entered in the $5,000 Bardella," said Whitcomb. "Rock Bar was in the race, as was Rebel Cause. Hank won it by a length and a quarter over Rock Bar, with Rebel Cause finishing

Milo Whitcomb said that Hank was so laid-back and easygoing, even during his racing career, that his young daughter, Celie, could ride him with no problem.

Photo by Jack Stribling

wire to wire. His winning time of 17 flat for the 330-yard dash equaled the 2-year-old-colt mark for that distance, and the victory was worth $8,785.

On August 14, Hank was entered in the 400-yard Carl Mercer Allowance. If the Whitcombs were worried about

Tonto Bars Gill, a AAA-rated son of Three Bars (TB), was the sire of Tonto Bars Hank.

Photo by Ralph Morgan, Courtesy *The Quarter Horse Journal*

"We didn't hear too much from the Rock Bar camp from that point on."

fourth. Hank's time of :17.6 for the 350 yards set a stallion and 2-year-old-colt record and was just .1 of a second off the world mark that had been set earlier in the year by Vandy's Flash.

"We didn't hear too much from the Rock Bar camp from that point on," Whitcomb smiled.

By this time, not only the Rock Bar fans, but also the betting public and the race handicappers were convinced that Tonto Bars Hank was for real.

Entered in the 350-yard Los Ninos Handicap on November 30, Hank was bet down to 40 cents on the dollar, and assigned the top handicapped weight of 126 pounds. On a muddy track, the big sorrel colt finished second by a head to Rebel Cause, who had been asked to carry only 115 pounds. In third place, a length behind Hank, was Rock Bar.

Two weeks later, on December 14, Hank and Rebel Cause met again. The occasion was the 350-yard Newport Dunes Stakes and, in it, Rebel Cause was asked to pack the top weight of 125 pounds. At the wire, it was Hank in front by three-quarters of a length over Rebel Cause, with Sonoitan placing third.

To finish out his juvenile campaign, Hank went to the post on December 21 in the $15,000 Kindergarten Futurity. He had also been invited to compete in Los Alamitos' prestigious Autumn Championship, but that would have meant locking horns with the best-seasoned campaigners on the West Coast. It was

Tonto Bars Hank was dubbed "The Flying Boxcar" during his racing career.

Photo by Jack Stribling

Hank's year-end total stood at $93,862, and that was enough to overtake Go Man Go as the world's richest Quarter Horse.

decided by his owners and trainer to keep him within his own age division.

Like the Newport Dunes, the Kindergarten Futurity covered 350 yards and boasted a field that included Rebel Cause, Rock Bar, and Sonoitan. At the break, Rebel Cause got away on top and held on to his lead until the 330-yard mark. At that point, "The Flying Boxcar," as Hank had been affectionately dubbed by the West Coast press, went flying by the Haymaker Farms entry to win going away by a neck. Sonoitan again placed third.

With his first-place earnings of $8,250 in this race, Hank's year-end total stood at $93,862, and that was enough to overtake Go Man Go as the world's richest Quarter Horse.

Not bad for a "draft horse."

In 12 starts as a 2-year-old, Hank had won nine and placed second three times. In eight of his races, he had set or equaled world records. In recognition of these accomplishments, the big sorrel was named the 1960 Champion Quarter Running 2-Year-Old-Colt and the Champion Quarter Running Stallion.

An impressive record for sure, but the one-horse wrecking ball from northeast Colorado wasn't through yet.

Back for More

After a four-month layoff, Hank returned to the track on April 10, 1961. Entered in the Shue Fly Stakes at Los Alamitos, he finished third behind two older horses, Pap and Breeze Bar.

Five days later, he went to the post in the Pacific Coast Quarter Horse Racing Association Derby trials. This would mark Hank's first try at a full quarter-mile, and his first meeting of the year with Rebel Cause.

Hank and Rebel drew into different

trial heats, and both won their races in the identical time of :21.9. The stage was set for an exciting Derby finals.

The big event, held on April 22, lived up to all of the pre-race hype. As the gates banged open, Hank lunged into the air and broke a full length and a half behind Rebel Cause. Unleashing one of his of patented stretch drives, the Whitcomb entry began rapidly to make up the ground he had given away. Pulling even with Rebel Cause as they neared the finish line, Hank tired and was beaten by a neck.

The two colorful rivals had now tested each other's mettle on the track six times. They had each emerged victorious three times.

As consolation for his second-place finish in the Derby, Tonto Bars Hank's $5,737 share of the purse was enough to make him the first Quarter Horse to earn more than $100,000 on the track.

Hank's next start came just a week later, in the 400-yard Chicado V Handicap. Pitted against Vandy's Flash, the 1960 World Champion Quarter Running Horse, and Breeze Bar, who would be named the 1961 Champion Quarter Running Stallion, Hank was still the betting favorite of the fans.

Breaking on top when the gates opened, Hank maintained a short lead over Breeze Bar to the halfway point. The two battled head-to-head down the stretch and, at the wire, it was Breeze Bar by a head over Hank, with Vandy's Flash another three-quarters of a length to the rear.

Brilliant even in defeat, Tonto Bars Hank's time of 20 seconds flat for 400 yards established a 3-year-old-colt record, and Breeze Bar's time of :19.9—with Hank pushing him every step—set a world record and a record stallion's mark.

On May 6, Hank was at it again. This

Hank H, the maternal grandsire of Tonto Bars Hank. Foaled in 1942, Hank H was by King P-234 and out of Queen H, who was by Dan, a son of Old Joe Bailey. The back of this old photo has no ID for the jockey and others shown.

Photo by J. Leinenkugel, Courtesy *The Quarter Horse Journal*

Before they bred and raised Tonto Bars Hank, the Whitcombs' best horse was Frog W, featured in this Whitcomb ad, circa late 1950s.

time, in a 440-yard affair open to all ages, he was bested by Pap, who would be named the 1961 World Champion Quarter Running Horse, and by Breeze Bar. Finishing behind Hank in the race was No Butt, who would become the 1962 World Champion Quarter Running Horse.

May 20 found Hank back in Ruidoso for the 350-yard Mr Bar None Stakes. Bet down to 60 cents on the dollar, the big son of Tonto Bars Gill responded with a full-length victory over First Call, Antler's Trade, and Fly Straw.

On June 25, Hank finished third in a 400-yard handicap and followed that performance with a seventh-place finish in a 400-yard dash on July 9. The latter placing marked the worst performance of Hank's career, and the only time he

failed to finish in the money.

It was decided to rest him until the fall meet at Los Alamitos.

Back in California for the November 25 running of the 350-yard Hard Twist Stakes, Hank sported a new trainer, Tomey Wieburg, and a new lease on life. On a sloppy track, and running into an 8-mph headwind, Hank pulled off a decisive victory over Pap and Breeze Bar.

In his final two races of his sophomore year, Hank was pitted against his old nemesis Rebel Cause. Their first meeting took place in the 400-yard Go Man Go Stakes, held on December 9. In it, Hank held off a closing rush by Rebel Cause to win by a neck, with No Butt in the place position.

On the following weekend, in the $25,000 Autumn Championship, Hank increased his margin of victory, covering the full quarter of a mile distance in :22.2, and finishing ahead of second-place Rebel Cause by half a length, with Aunt Judy another three-quarters of a length back. Such stellar sprinters as Pap, Breeze Bar, and Table Tennis rounded out the beaten field.

Hank's bankroll now stood at $128,901. He had started 11 times as a 3-year-old and had notched five firsts, two seconds, and three thirds. Along with Rebel Cause, he was named the 1961 Co-Champion Quarter Running 3-Year-Old Colt.

Hank stood at stud the 1962 breeding season at Walter Merrick's ranch in Oklahoma. After breeding a full book of mares, the big 4-year-old—standing 15.2 and weighing 1,400 pounds—returned to the track with Merrick as his trainer.

On September 1, 1962, at Ruidoso, Hank captured the 400-yard Lightning Bar Memorial Handicap. Two weeks later, he won a 400-yard allowance race at Albuquerque. In covering the distance in a sizzling time of :19.9, Hank set a track record and equaled the current world and stallion marks.

Just three days later, Hank was bested by Straw Flight in the Shue Fly Stakes. This was followed by an October 13 date at Centennial Race Track in Denver. There, in the 440-yard Colorado Wonderland Handicap, Hank finished second to Jack Casement's great 3-year-old filly She Kitty.

Back on the West Coast for his final three races, Hank could muster no better than a third in any of them. Rebel Cause

ALL AMERICAN
FUTURITY   HORSE *Tonto Bars Hank*   PURSE *$130,244.30*
OWNER *Milo & C.G. Whitcomb* DISTANCE *400 yds*
TRAINER *Pat Simpson*   TIME *:20.2 N.W.R.* DATE *9-5-60*
                                    Trans-Photo Lab
JOCKEY *Curtis Perner*   RUIDOSO DOWNS, RUIDOSO, N. M.

was in the field in each of these races, and although he did not win any of them, he finished ahead of Hank in all of them.

The Whitcombs decided to retire their star.

The final numbers on Tonto Bars Hank's 3-year racing career were impressive. From a total of 30 starts, Hank turned in 29 AAA performances. Over the course of his 3-year racing career, he won 16 races, finished second seven times and third four times, and earned $133,918. In eight of his races he either set or equaled world records.

The Flying Boxcar had earned his retirement to stud.

Breeding Career

"For the 1963 breeding season," Milo Whitcomb said, "we chose to let Hank stand at stud at a fellow's place in Tulsa, Oklahoma. In 1964, we sold Hank to a syndicate for $125,000. He stood in New Mexico for several years, and then we moved to Missouri. Even after we sold him, we retained breedings to him, and used them as best we could."

As a sire, Hank enjoyed a moderately successful career. From 12 foal crops, he sired 465 foals. Of these, 212 went to the track and amassed 95 ROMs, six Superiors, and $478,902 in earnings.

As a halter and performance sire, Hank has 100 performers to his credit; they have accumulated one Supreme Cham-

The winner's circle photo after Hank won the 1960 All American Futurity at Ruidoso Downs. Left to right are Milo Whitcomb, C.G. Whitcomb, trainer Pat Simpson, jockey Curtis Perner, and movie star Audie Murphy, who owned Quarter Horses.

Fair Lady Tonto, a 1963 daughter of Tonto Bars Hank, was out of Whitcomb's Frogette. Fair Lady Tonto earned her ROM in racing and $1,965.

pionship, eight AQHA Championships, 19 Superiors, 40 ROMs, and 3,193 points.

Here are several of his offspring who did well in the show ring:

- Tonto Bar Angel, foaled in 1971 out of Miss Denny King, won a Superior in both open and youth western pleasure, and placed seventh in senior pleasure at the 1977 AQHA World Show.
- Oakabar Hank, foaled in 1969 out of Lomella Trouble, earned an AQHA Championship, a performance ROM, and a Superior in western pleasure.
- Do Do Chick, foaled in 1970 out of Triple Flit, earned a Superior in halter and was the 1974 Reserve World Champion Aged Stallion.
- Bee Bar Bingo, foaled in 1968 out of Bee Girl Betsy, had a Superior in open halter, a Superior in youth halter, and an AQHA Championship in both open and youth competition.

- Hank Will, foaled in 1966 out of Mine Will (TB), was an AQHA Supreme Champion and the 1972 High-Point Steer Roping (dally team roping) Stallion.
- Lucky 14, foaled in 1964 out of Heart 55, earned Superiors in western pleasure and halter (both youth and open) and was an AQHA Champion.
- Hank's leading money-earning off-spring was Gigantus, a sorrel stallion foaled in 1972 out of the mare Fan Jet, by Fly Man Fly. Bred by John S. Hamilton Jr. of Tyrone, N.M., Gigantus earned $43,499.
- Another Hank son, Rocky Beach Hank, earned $42,212 and a Superior in racing. Foaled in 1965, he was out of Waiki Ki Beach, who was by J B King and out of Naples Beach (TB).

Conclusion

Tonto Bars Hank, the horse who started life as a colt nobody wanted and went on to become the first Quarter Horse to earn $100,000 on the tracks, died from complications of colic on July 13, 1974, at the age of 16.

"Hank was a once-in-a-lifetime horse

"HANK'S DIAL DOLL"
"FOURTH DIVISION OF THE RATON QUARTER HORSE DERBY TRIALS"
LA MESA PARK, N.M.   AUG. 29, 1969   P. WALKER, UP
DIXIE MAN (2nd)   400 Yds 19.89   WAE MACHINE (3rd)
HAROLD SAUERESSIG & C.G. & MILO WHICOMB   OWNERS
          PATRICK H. SIMPSON, TRAINER

Hank's Dial Doll was one of Tonto Bars Hank's best racing off-spring. Foaled in 1966, she was out of Maggie Dial, by Johnny Dial. She had total winnings of $32,063, won a Superior in racing, and was the 1969 World Champion Quarter Running 3-Year-Old Filly.

for us," Milo Whitcomb recalled. "Conformation-wise, he was as close to perfect as any horse I've ever seen. We showed him at halter and made him an AQHA Champion, and one year, he even stood reserve champion at halter at the National Western Stock Show in Denver. How many other world champion race horses have done that?

"And Hank was the best-dispositioned stud who ever lived. If he hadn't been so fast, he would have made a helluva pony horse, because he was as steady as the Rock of Gibraltar.

"You know, we never were rich folks. If we had been, I'm sure Hank would have had more opportunities than he did, as both a race horse and a sire.

"When it's all said and done, though, he did all right. He was big and he was fast and, coming down that straightaway, he really did look just like a flying boxcar."

101

10

HARLAN

By Susan
Scarberry

**Harlan
passed
along color,
conformation,
and athletic
ability to
his offspring,
siring 17
AQHA
Champions.**

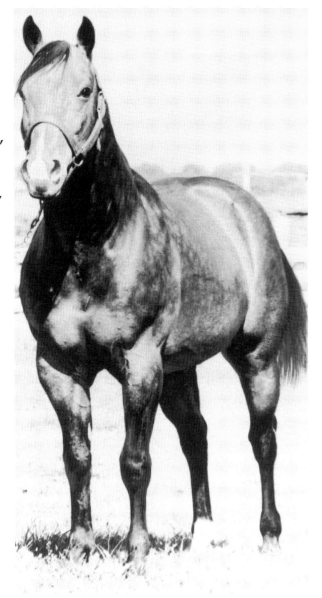

Harlan was a striking buckskin who became an exceptional sire.

Photo Courtesy *The Quarter Horse Journal*

A FABULOUS sire of performance horses, Harlan's career was nearly over before it ever began. When his 21-year-old dam couldn't provide adequate milk for Harlan, her final foal, their owners had to raise the foal on milk from a bucket.

A buckskin stallion foaled in 1951, Harlan was sired by Hank H and was out of the dun Beetch'syellowjacket daughter Dixie Beach. Hank H's owners, Paul and Jack Smith of Indiahoma, Okla., had purchased 20-year-old Dixie Beach in April 1950 at a sale held by Hank Wilson and Walter Merrick.

In November 1954 Bob and Joan Robey of Edmond, Okla., were looking for a stallion prospect sired by Hank H. As part of that search, they wrote to the Smiths. Paul Smith's return letter described a 3-year-old buckskin stallion who had been loaned to Harlan Beetch, the son of Mike Beetch and the man for whom Harlan was named, for breeding purposes. Evidently the foals, if any, resulting from those breedings were not registered with AQHA. In fact, the only registered foal sired by Harlan at that time was Hi Hank, a dun gelding who subsequently earned a performance ROM. The Saturday after they received that letter, Bob, Joan, and Joan's father drove to Indiahoma to see Harlan.

What they saw was an independent-natured, shaggy, 14.2-hand, 1,100-pound colt. As they observed feeding time, he finished his grain and then proceeded from stall to stall, finishing the grain for everyone else. Great admirers of the King P-234 bloodlines and fans of Squaw

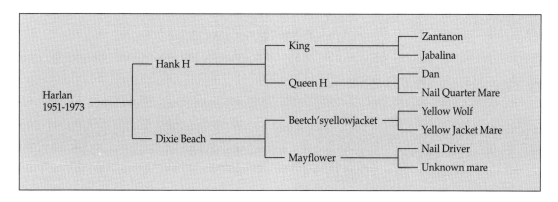

Harlan 1951-1973	Hank H	King	Zantanon
			Jabalina
		Queen H	Dan
			Nail Quarter Mare
	Dixie Beach	Beetch'syellowjacket	Yellow Wolf
			Yellow Jacket Mare
		Mayflower	Nail Driver
			Unknown mare

H, the full sister of Hank H, the Robeys decided to overlook Harlan's initial appearance and made an offer for the colt.

The asking price was $300; Bob Robey offered $200. When no compromise could be reached, he got back into his truck and drove away with Joan and her father. To this day Robey maintains that their departure was a negotiating tactic; Joan Robey maintains that she and her father talked him into returning for Harlan. Regardless of the circumstances, the Robeys purchased Harlan for $250, and with that purchase obtained one of the best all-around sires who ever lived.

Background

According to Bob and Joan, they were counting on the Hank H bloodlines when they purchased Harlan. An own son of King P-234 and out of Queen H by Dan, Hank H's race record in 10 starts included two wins, one second, three thirds, and a AA rating. In addition to his performance record, he was also an outstanding sire, with his get including 14 race ROM-earners, one AQHA high-point horse, an AQHA Champion, a Superior-earning halter horse, and eight show ROM-earners. His record as a sire is truly remarkable when you consider that Hank H died in 1952 at the age of 10, a victim of dust pneumonia caused by drought conditions in western Oklahoma.

At that time the Robeys did not know the background of Harlan's dam, Dixie Beach. She was out of Mayflower, and was a full sister to Lady Coolidge, the dam of Bert.

Based on information given in the article, "Mayflower—Granddam of Bert and Matriarch of the Breed," written by Franklin Reynolds for the October 1957 *Quarter Horse Journal*, Mayflower was

Halter and Performance Record: None.

Progeny Record:

Foal Crops: 21	Performance Point-Earners: 114
Foals Registered: 403	Performance Points Earned: 1,873
AQHA Champions: 17	Performance Registers of Merit: 51
World Champions: 1	Superior Performance Awards: 8
Halter Point-Earners: 71	Race Starters: 6
Halter Points Earned: 1,123	Race Money Earned: $1,155
Superior Halter Awards: 5	
Leading Race Money-Earner: Bradley's Hank ($328)	

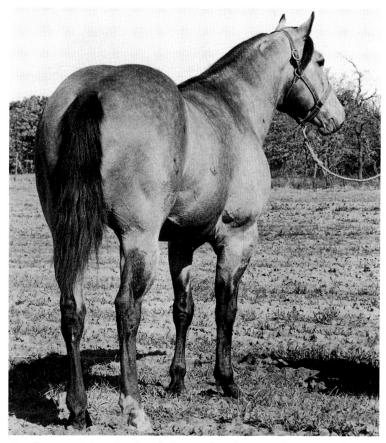

An all-around sire of racing, halter, and performance horses, Harlan put his own tremendous speed and big stop to use as owner Bob Robey's calf roping mount. **Photo Courtesy** *The Quarter Horse Journal*

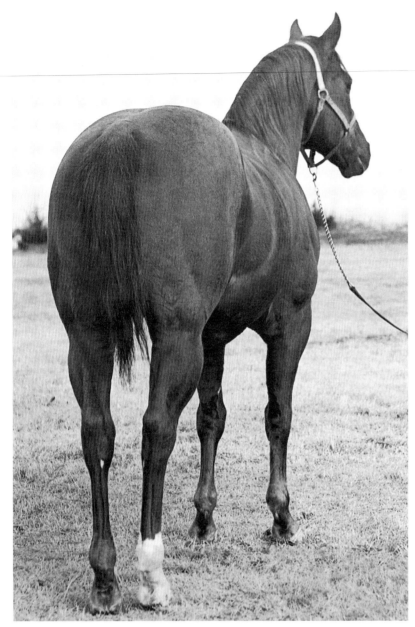

Hank H, the sire of Harlan. A son of King P-234, Hank H earned a AA rating on the racetrack, sired race and show Register of Merit-earners and an AQHA Champion, and died of dust pneumonia in 1952, at age 10. Two years later, Bob and Joan Robey purchased 3-year-old Harlan solely on the merits of his sire. **Photo Courtesy Bob Robey**

an unattractive mare with an obscure pedigree. However, she could run and, based on the appearance of her daughters, could produce conformation.

According to Reynolds, the late Mike Beetch recognized Mayflower's performance ability, purchased her, and raced her for a number of years. After she received a crippling injury, the Beetches placed her in the broodmare band. When bred to Beetch'syellowjacket (also spelled Beach's Yellow Jacket in AQHA Stud Book Vol. 3), Mayflower produced Dixie Beach and Lady Coolidge. Both of these mares were duns with black manes and tails, and both mares were subsequently raced against each other by the Beetches. When it came to speed, Lady Coolidge sizzled up to an eighth of a mile, but Dixie Beach could outrun her sister at distances longer than one-eighth.

Reynolds reports that Bert Benear, a critical judge of conformation and performance, came to look at Lady Coolidge. When Lady Coolidge passed his inspection, he purchased her for $185 and a gold watch. Over the next few years he sold her foals for a total of $10,000, and as an aged mare she brought $2,900 at the eventual Benear-Scarborough dispersal sale.

In fact, Lady Coolidge was such a success that Benear returned to the Beetches' ranch and purchased Dixie Beach. Dixie Beach, when bred to Tommy Clegg, produced Tom Benear, Bailarina, Little Dixie Beach, Dixie Ann B, and M's Tom Benear. Little Dixie Beach in turn produced Paul A, by Star Deck. Paul A became an AQHA Champion and the sire of 11 AQHA Champions. As proof that her producing ability was not linked to one stallion, Dixie Beach then produced Little Jodie, by Little Joe Springer; San Siemon's Dixie and Little Mayflower, by San Siemon; Bay Pee Wee, by Little Mike; and Harlan, by Hank H.

Performance

When the Robeys purchased Harlan, Bob Robey was roping calves at area rodeos. It was only natural that he broke

Harlan stood about 14.3 hands and retained his powerful performer's physique throughout his life. Shown here at age 21 or 22 with Harold Hudspeth, a syndicate co-owner who stood the stallion during his later years, Harlan suffered a stroke in 1973 and was buried at the Robeys' ranch in Perkins, Oklahoma.

Photo Courtesy Harold Hudspeth

Not long on looks, Dixie Beach was the 1930 dun daughter of a running mare and a foundation stallion. She produced 13 quality foals, the most famous of whom was Harlan, her final foal and her only cross with Hank H. Dixie Beach's Tommy Clegg daughter, Little Dixie Beach, produced AQHA Champion Paul A.

Photo Courtesy American Quarter Horse Heritage Center & Musuem

Bob and Joan Robey with a 1957 Harlan filly.

Harlaquita, a 1960 daughter of Harlan who became an AQHA Champion, was out of the Robeys' good mare Oklahoma Rosie, by Billy Van W. Harlaquita's handler here is Burl Holmes, an automobile dealer from Oklahoma City who acquired the mare when Bob Robey traded her as a yearling for a new station wagon.

Photo by Spencer Studio

Harlan and then proceeded to train him for calf roping. According to Robey, Harlan had tremendous speed. "I used to not hold onto the horn, but I did with him. All he had in his mind was getting out there and burying that tail and getting back on the end of that rope. That's all he had on his mind."

Robey remembers Ralph Stone, one of the best ropers in the area at that time, saying, "Man, what kind of motor you got in that horse? He don't stop—he just quits running!"

In a short time, Harlan was getting 30 to 40 mares each breeding season. During the week, Robey roped a few calves on him, bred mares to him, and then rodeoed with him on the weekends. Eventually he began to have problems settling mares. The vet examined Harlan, and then asked Robey what he did with the stallion other than breeding him. After hearing Robey's description, the vet suggested that Harlan either be used as a roping mount or a breeding stallion—but not both. That ended Harlan's roping career.

Based on his breeding success, the Robeys certainly made the right choice. Of 403 registered AQHA foals, Harlan contributed offspring to rodeo arenas, reining and cutting competitions, and the show arena. Of his 152 AQHA performers, 17 were AQHA Champions (16 open, one youth) and 51 earned ROMs (46 open, one amateur, four youth). Seven of his offspring earned performance Superiors and five earned halter Superiors. In 1965

From Harlan's first breeding season with the Robeys came the dun mare Harlene. She earned an AQHA performance ROM and a Superior in cutting. Here, she's showing off with Margaret Hudspeth in the saddle.

Photo by Jack Strayhorn

Considered by the Robeys to be Harlan's best all-around son, Harlan's Tyree earned an AQHA Championship, a halter Superior, and AQHA's 1970 High-Point Western Pleasure Stallion title. Foaled in 1963, the buckskin stallion out of Sandsarita, by Sanddrift, sired the earners of 308 halter points and 1,282 performance points from just six foal crops. **Photo by Joe Murphy**

and 1966 Harlan was the AQHA get of sire winner, and as recently as April 1999, he was still on the list of all-time leading sires of AQHA Champions.

As recently as April 1999, Harlan was still on the list of all-time leading sires of AQHA Champions.

Offspring

In Harlan's first breeding season with the Robeys, he sired Badger Blaze, who earned an AQHA performance Register of Merit, and Harlene, a dun mare who earned an AQHA performance Register of Merit and a Superior in cutting.

The following foal crops built on

that strong beginning and established Harlan's reputation as an outstanding sire. In 1958 he sired Bradley's Hank, a bay stallion who became an AQHA Champion and earned both racing and performance ROMs. According to Robey, Bradley's Hank had tremendous speed and athletic ability, and you could do anything on him that could be done horseback.

In 1959 Harlan sired Harlady, an AQHA Champion with a Superior in halter, and Bay Ting A Ling, another AQHA Champion. From the following year's crop came Harlan Dooley, an AQHA Champion with a Superior in cutting, and Harlaquita, an AQHA Champion who was leading the nation in reining when she died.

Harlaquita was out of the Robeys'

great mare Oklahoma Rosie. Robey said he had several opportunities to sell "Rose," but the mare was such a favorite with Joan that he couldn't afford the divorce that would result from such a sale. But Robey obviously felt the same way as Joan did, because he also said, "If the good Lord came to the door right now, said that I could be 25 again, and asked me which horse I wanted—Harlan or Rose—I don't know what I would say."

Jim Harlan, an AQHA Champion with a Superior in halter, was foaled in 1960. Joan Robey believes that Jim Harlan was the best halter horse sired by Harlan. The stallion sired 78 registered AQHA foals who earned 1,546 halter points and 2,151.5 performance points. Four became AQHA Champions, and four others were youth AQHA Champions.

In 1961 Harlan sired Slash J Harletta, an AQHA Champion who later took her owner, Celie Whitcomb-Ray, to the WPRA finals in barrel racing. The same foal crop produced Harlan's Pistol, a gelding out of a Nowata Star mare who went to the PRCA finals at least twice in calf roping.

The 1963 foal crop yielded what the Robeys feel was Harlan's best all-around son—Harlan's Tyree. This buckskin stallion was an AQHA Champion with a Superior in halter and a performance Register of Merit, and was the AQHA high-point western pleasure stallion in 1970. Harlan's Tyree also proved to be a tremendous sire. Although he died at the age of 7, his offspring earned 308 halter points and 1,282 performance points. Master breeder Howard Pitzer liked the Harlan's Tyree horses well enough to use that bloodline extensively in his broodmare band.

In 1965 Harlan sired Miss Harlacue. A buckskin mare with a Superior in calf roping, she was high-point calf roping horse in 1976 and went to the AQHA World Show in calf roping at least four times.

Harlan's 1970 son Harlan's Patches placed seventh at the World Show in

This bay stallion is the Harlan son Bradley's Hank, foaled in 1958. He ran AA on the racetrack and became an AQHA Champion before siring racing, halter, and performance winners. Bob Robey once said that anything that could be done horseback could be done on Bradley's Hank.

Harlan Okmulgee also passed along his sire's qualities to his own offspring, siring a calf roping world champion, OSU Miss Tom Harlan. The buckskin stallion packed his longtime owner, Harold "Huddy" Hudspeth, through 13 years of working in the arena at the AQHA World Show. Hudspeth, who called Harlan Okmulgee his own "Super-horse," donated the stallion to Oklahoma State University's breeding program at age 16.

Photo Courtesy Harold Hudspeth

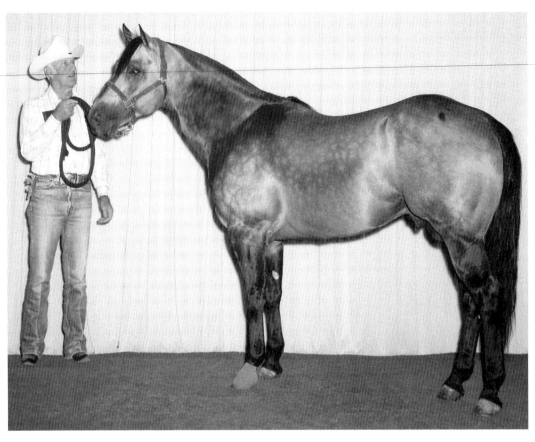

A May 1999 picture of Bob and Joan Robey at the Foundation Quarter Horse Breeders Reunion in Bartlesville, Oklahoma.

Photo by Susan Scarberry

senior reining in 1975 and was reserve world champion in that event the next year. Harlan's Trouble, foaled that same year, had an outstanding show record in team roping and breakaway roping.

Harlander

Harlander, a 1957 bay stallion, had a history that read much like his sire's. As a colt, his mother did not give enough milk for him, and his owner, H.L. (Harold) Carpenter, felt that the horse's growth was somewhat stunted. He matured to stand 14.2 hands and weigh around 1,250 pounds.

Harlander was shown at area cuttings, but he left his true legacy as a sire. Of 303 registered AQHA foals, Harlander's offspring earned 149 halter points and 812.5 performance points. Moe's Barney, a 1963 gelding by Harlander and out of Dinamo Queen, had 225 open performance, 39 open halter, 302 youth performance, and 15 youth halter points.

In addition, many of Harlander's descendants went to the rodeo arena. PRCA world champion calf roper Joe

Deb's Smokey Joe, a 1967 gelding by the Harlan son Harlander, earned a performance ROM and acclaim as a calf roping horse, ridden by Dick Foreman.
Photo by Abrahamsen, Courtesy Debby Foreman

Beaver rode Boogers Bad Boy ("Touch-down") and eventually sold him to fellow roper Trevor Brazile. Boogers Bad Boy was by Cee Booger Red and out of Reba's Good Girl, a Harlander mare.

Another product of another Cee Booger Red-Harlander mare cross was Boogers Sargeant. "Sarge" had 89.5 AQHA open points and 108.5 AQHA amateur points before entering the professional rodeo arena. Deb's Smokey Joe, a 1967 black gelding by Harlander, was a great calf roping horse ridden by Dick Foreman.

Debby Foreman of Copan, Okla., owns Cee Booger Red. According to Debby, Harlander was one of the greatest sires standing in her area. She obtained many of her Harlander broodmares from Carpenter and crossed them on Cee Booger Red; those offspring continue to set arena records in roping and barrel racing events.

Grandget

Many other Harlan sons and daughters also proved to be outstanding breeders.

Harlan Okmulgee, with only 90

registered AQHA foals, sired the earners of 365 performance points, as well as the 1992 World Champion Junior Calf Roping horse, OSU Miss Tom Harlan. The 1972 buckskin stallion was by Harlan and out of Quarter Mulgee, a granddaughter of the stallions Bert (who was out of Lady Coolidge) and Little Jodie (who was out of Dixie Beach). That gave Harlan Okmulgee three crosses to those full sisters. Harlan Okmulgee was owned by Harold "Huddy" Hudspeth until a few years before his death, when he was donated to Oklahoma State University for use in their breeding program.

A top producing daughter of Harlan, Harla Q'Beaut, also demonstrated the strength of the Lady Coolidge-Dixie Beach cross. The 1970 buckskin mare was by Harlan and out of Quarter Beaut, a double-bred Bert granddaughter. Harla Q'Beaut produced seven

Harlander left his true legacy as a sire.

111

Harlan Sport, a 1973 red dun gelding, proved more than his color had been passed down from Harlan, his great-grandsire. The gelding packed Marty Wells to three American Junior Quarter Horse Association world championships: 1984 breakaway roping, 1985 calf roping, and 1987 calf roping.

Photo by Joel Smith

American Buckskin Registry Association Supreme Champions for her owner, Buck Keister of Leavenworth, Kansas. Her full brother, Harlan's Man, was the last living breeding son of Harlan. Harlan's Man, also owned by Buck Keister at the time of his death, was put down in 1998.

Slash J Harletta, whose offspring performed primarily in rodeo arenas around the country, produced numerous barrel racing standouts. In 1971 she took her owner, the late Celie Whitcomb-Ray, to the National Finals Rodeo. In 1983 Whitcomb-Ray again made the Finals aboard Free Etta, and in 1987 and 1989 she made the Finals aboard I Got Bugs.

Both horses were foals of Slash J Harletta. Whitcomb-Ray was quoted in the February 9, 1994, *ProRodeo Sports News* as saying, "Without her colts, who without exception were all winners, I would not have been able to earn a living doing what I love the most, which is barrel racing."

Syndication

Such success was not overlooked by mare owners. Although Bob and Joan Robey both worked full-time and did not extensively advertise Harlan, the performance of his offspring increased his popularity tremendously. When breeding season began to bring 50 to 60 mares to Harlan, the Robeys decided to sell him to Bud and Evelyn Breeding in September 1962. The Breedings owned Harlan for three years and stood him at the nearby farm of Bob Robey's brother, Dick Robey.

This 1985 buckskin gelding, Harlan Crocker, is by a Wimpy-bred stallion and out of a Harlan daughter, Harla Q'Beaut. Harla Q'Beaut's dam was double-bred to Bert, who was out of Dixie Beach's full sister, Lady Coolidge. Harla Q'Beaut produced several American Buck-skin Registry Associa-tion supreme champi-ons, including Harlan Crocker, shown here with Buck Keister.

Photo by K.C. Montgomery, Courtesy Buck Keister

At the end of that three years, Bob and Joan Robey formed the Harlan Syndicate with Harold Hudspeth, Jim Nance, and Carl Mills and negotiated the repurchase of Harlan. Because the Robeys still did not want to manage a stallion with Harlan's popularity, part of the agreement was that Harlan would stand at the farm of Huddy Hudspeth in Collinsville, Oklahoma.

That arrangement continued until early May 1973, when Harlan suffered a stroke. The syndicate agreed that he should go home to Bob and Joan Robey, at that time living in Perkins, Oklahoma. After he died, he was buried there on the ranch, reunited with the two people who gave a shaggy little buckskin a chance.

In 1997 the Robeys received a certificate from AQHA marking their 40th year as Quarter Horse breeders. In addition, Bob was an AQHA judge for almost 20 years and served as director, committee chairman, and youth director of the Oklahoma Quarter Horse Association. Over the years the Robeys have raised or seen some of the all-time great horses. In their opinion Harlan was one of the best, and his record as a sire seems to justify their belief.

In a quote from the August 1987 *Eastern/Western Quarter Horse Journal*, Bob Robey summed up his feelings for Harlan in this way: "I was a poor man when I bought him and don't look on myself as much more than that now. But if it came down to it, and the only way I could make some money was to sell the head portrait (Orren) Mixer did of Harlan, we'd all starve."

11

LADY BUG'S MOON

By Alan Gold

He is one of the greatest sires of Quarter running horses.

IF THE superstition that a lady bug brings good fortune holds true, then Marvin Barnes must be the luckiest man in the world. A plain-spoken horseman from Ada, Okla., Barnes and his wife, Lela, raised and raced Lady Bug's Moon, a sprinter who carved himself a reputation as one of the fastest horses—and most popular stallions—of his day.

But Barnes' lady bug infestation began long before the blaze-faced sorrel hit the ground in 1964. You can trace it back to 1958, the year that a diminutive mare named FL Lady Bug came to Ada for the first time.

Barnes, an avid roper and a small-town

Lady Bug's Moon was a sensation on the track, winning $191,536 in the years when purses were much smaller than they are today.

Photo Courtesy *The Quarter Racing Journal*

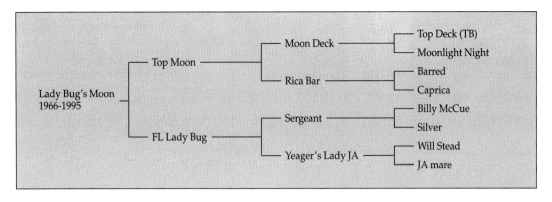

Lady Bug's Moon 1966-1995
- Top Moon
  - Moon Deck
    - Top Deck (TB)
    - Moonlight Night
  - Rica Bar
    - Barred
    - Caprica
- FL Lady Bug
  - Sergeant
    - Billy McCue
    - Silver
  - Yeager's Lady JA
    - Will Stead
    - JA mare

used car dealer, called on the experiences of both fields in his dealings with FL Lady Bug as he bought and sold her several times in the following years.

"I was trading in horses back then," Barnes said. "I'd buy her, get a deal on her, make a hundred on her, and sell her." Once he finally decided to hold on to her, he began to add about three zeroes to the profits she brought him.

Oklahomans are sometimes called "Boomers" in reference to the land rush, and the post-war generation came to be known as "baby boomers." With a double dose of that heritage, FL Lady Bug, a 1945 foal, engineered her own one-mare baby boom.

Bred by W.A. Yeager of Woodward, Okla., she was by Sergeant, an unraced son of Billy McCue, and out of Yeager's Lady JA, who was by Will Stead, who was a full brother to Sergeant. In those early days of the AQHA, Sergeant and Will Stead were each credited with siring only one Register of Merit runner. But FL Lady Bug's pedigree meant that she was just four times removed on her top side, and five times on her bottom, from Peter McCue. His one-time owner, Milo Burlingame, had said you could breed Peter McCue to a lumber wagon and get a race horse.

FL Lady Bug took her initials from the Flying L Ranch, one of her early owners.

"She was raised on a ranch and they just used her for a cow horse and things. They really didn't think about her producing a runner," Barnes said. "When I bought her, people would come by and they'd be looking for a mare to raise a roping horse. If I'd mention she might be a race horse producer, they just turned her down.

"But after her babies started running, then everybody wanted her."

Possibly because of her ranch horse ori-

Halter and Performance Record: Superior Race Horse; Register of Merit; Winner of 1968 Kansas Futurity and 1969 Rainbow Derby; 2nd in the 1968 All American Futurity and Rainbow Futurity; 3rd in the 1968 Oklahoma Futurity.

Progeny Record:

Foal Crops: 15	Performance Points Earned: 1,167
Foals Registered: 966	Performance Registers of Merit: 18
AQHA Champions: 3	Superior Performance Awards: 6
Racing World Champions: 1	Race Starters: 770
Halter Point-Earners: 7	Race Money Earned: $4,025,213
Halter Points Earned: 136	Race Registers of Merit: 502
Superior Halter Awards: 1	Superior Race Awards: 51
Performance Point-Earners: 46	

Leading Race Money-Earner: Shawne Bug ($277,023)

gins, FL Lady Bug was very protective of her foals. "We just let her foal out in the pasture, because she didn't want anybody to mess with her," Barnes recalled. "They said her mother, Yeager's Lady JA, was terribly bad that way. If she had a baby, she didn't want you to come around. FL was that way a long time. We just had to be easy with her. She was good-natured, but she just didn't want to be fooled with when she had a baby."

Like many of his would-be customers, Barnes had no interest in the racetrack at first.

"We both roped calves," said Barnes' stepson, Jerry Vaughn Whittle. "Marvin

Lady Bug's Moon as a 2-year-old in 1968 when he stood for a $1,000 stud fee. About eight years later he was syndicated for over $1 million.

Photo Courtesy *The Quarter Racing Journal*

Marvin and Lela Barnes with Lady Bug's Moon after he won the 1969 Ruidoso Rainbow Derby.

Photo Courtesy *The Quarter Racing Journal*

In July 1969 Lady Bug's Moon, with Boyd Morris in the irons, won a 350-yard race at Ruidoso Downs.

Photo Courtesy *The Quarter Racing Journal*

HORSE **LADY BUG'S MOON**
OWNER **M.L. & LELA BARNES** DISTANCE **350 YARDS** 2ND. **YANKEE Rob**
TRAINER **M.L. BARNES** TIME **17.65** DATE **7-5-69** 3RD. **KAWEAH Equa Bar**
JOCKEY **Boyd MORRIS** RUIDOSO DOWNS, RUIDOSO DOWNS, N.M. BY TIL THOMPSON

**"He was just a little bit ornery to break,"
Barnes admitted.**

knew someone who would rope off of one of FL Lady Bug's sons, Rocky Bert, on Saturday nights, and run him at the racetrack on Sundays.

"Of course, Marvin's the biggest optimist in the world and he said, 'This mare could have babies by anything and they might run.' I remember thinking that's probably the craziest thing I ever heard anybody say. But sure enough, he was right."

In 1959 Barnes bred FL Lady Bug to Olee San—a stallion of little renown in the racing world—and got Leo's Showman, a horse who showed the way of the future.

"Everyone thought we were insane to run that colt," admitted Lela Barnes. "They told us, 'You'll never get a race horse out of that mare.' And Leo's Showman was a late colt, foaled in July. But we

would not be discouraged. Marvin broke the colt, we wrapped his legs in gunny sacks, and took him to the race track."

Leo's Showman wound up tying the track record for 350 yards at Sunland Park.

"That was the first one I tried out of her, and he just went to running like mad," Marvin said. "I'd sold a few of her babies off, so I tried to get all of them back—which I did—and all of them started running. That's how I got started."

Barnes bought FL Lady Bug's '59 and

'61 babies, Lady Lasan and Lady Bug Leo. The former had a foal at her side, but he put her in training and gave her a try at Midway Downs.

"We just milked her out and ran her anyway," Barnes said. "She won by three lengths of daylight."

As a newcomer to the racing game, Barnes sometimes took an unconventional approach, and he was never afraid to admit that he was still learning. But what Marvin and Lela lacked in experience, they made up for in enthusiasm and dedication.

"We watched, we read, and we learned through trial and error," Lela said. "And we lived with them. At Ruidoso, when we had a real good one running, we would back our camper up by the front of the stall at night. When Marvin wasn't looking out the window, I was."

They finally got the chance to buy FL

Top Moon, the sire of Lady Bug's Moon, was a classy individual.

Photo Courtesy *The Quarter Racing Journal*

Lady Bug back when she missed getting in foal for the last man Barnes had sold her to, Art Beal.

Up to that time, the mare's foals who went to the track ran well although she had been bred to stallions who weren't outstanding race horses. Barnes changed tactics by sending her to Top Deck (TB), one of the hottest sires of the day.

The result was Top Ladybug, the champion 2-year-old filly of 1966, who earned $195,000. In 1965 FL Lady Bug produced Barne's Ladybug by another top sire, Mr Bar None. That filly also racked up six-figure earnings.

Lady Bug's Moon, by the Top Deck (TB) grandson Top Moon, was foaled May 15, 1966, the same day that Top Ladybug won the Oklahoma Futurity. Before his freshman season was over, he would make his dam the first Quarter Horse mare ever to produce three runners with earnings of more than $100,000 each.

"We were pretty fortunate to have FL Lady Bug," Barnes said. "Even after she was 21, she had three babies who won $550,000. It was just unbelievable what that mare could do."

As a Youngster

When Lady Bug's Moon was a baby, he may have picked up some ideas about

119

Leo's Showman, foaled in 1960, was the first of FL Lady Bug's offspring to hit the track and prove that his dam had the ability to produce speed. Rated AAAT, he sired a number of offspring who earned their ROMs in racing.

Photo by Guy Kassal, Courtesy *The Quarter Horse Journal*

Shawne Bug, foaled in 1974, was by Lady Bug's Moon and out of Shawne Win. Shawne Win was by Lewin, by Direct Win (TB), and out of Shawne (TB). Shawne Bug became his sire's top money-winner with earnings of $277,023.

Photo Courtesy *The Quarter Horse Journal*

"I don't know what he did, but when Harley brought him back, he just kept running after that and never did try to pull up."

"personal space" from his mama.

"He was just a little bit ornery to break," Barnes admitted. "Jerry Vaughn Whittle, our son, said, 'I've walked back to the house more than I've rode.'"

Whittle recalled, "It wasn't because he'd buck me off—he'd jump out from under me, he was so quick."

Barnes, still a relative novice at training for the track, realized pretty quickly that he had something special at hand. "I was doing my own training, and I found out in a hurry he could run. He'd just run off and leave them."

But his precociousness also caused problems. In brush track schooling races as a yearling, the colt opened up on his rivals right out of the gate. With a big lead in one 220-yard race, jockey Boyd Morris was not inclined to push the youngster, since he (Boyd) had injured his wrist. That's where the trouble began.

"Boyd couldn't use the whip that day," Whittle recalled. "So Lady Bug's Moon got out about five lengths in front and started slowing down. That was his first race ever, and he formed a bad habit then of getting in front and slowing down."

Barnes credited jockey Harley Crosby with correcting the problem. "I don't know what he did, but when Harley brought him back, he just kept running after that and never did try to pull up."

Lady Bug's Moon began his official career in January 1968 in the trials for the Blue Ribbon Futurity. He finished in a dead heat for first with Bonita Mujura, and lost to the same horse by a nose in the second consolation of the Futurity.

That marked the beginning of an odyssey that took Lady Bug's Moon to

121

Miss Mighty Bug, a 1971 mare by Lady Bug's Moon and out of Miss Hianmighty, won $130,204. In this picture she's in the winner's circle for the Oklahoma Derby Consolation at La Mesa Park, Raton, New Mexico. Also shown, from left: trainer Bob Schultz, jockey Roy Brooks, and assistant trainer Tim Richardson. **Photo Courtesy** *The Quarter Horse Journal*

six tracks in three states during the first half of his freshman season. By the time he lined up for the trials of his first big race, the Kansas Futurity at Ruidoso Downs in New Mexico on June 7, he'd already run nine official races.

He ran second by three-quarters of a length as the favorite to Jet Deck Junior in the Kansas trials. That caused his odds to leap to 14 to 1 in the finals. He bore out slightly at the start, but he was never

more than a neck off the pace. During the last 50 yards, he shoved his nose in front of Parr's Request, with Jet Deck Junior a neck farther back in third. That was worth $40,048.

After that, Lady Bug's Moon was trailered up the state to La Mesa Park, where he ran second in the trials and third in the finals of the Oklahoma Futurity. Jet Deck Junior prevailed in the finals.

Back at Ruidoso, Lady Bug's Moon won his Rainbow Futurity trial by three lengths, then stumbled badly coming out of the gate in the finals. He gathered himself up to run second by a head to Joada Bux.

"He got to the front," Whittle recalled, "but he'd used up all his gas to do it."

The stallion had developed chips in both knees, probably in one of his early season races. He still managed to run with the best 2-year-olds in the world,

Mr Hay Bug was a 1971 sorrel stallion by Lady Bug's Moon and out of Miss Hay Day. He won $182,330, and is shown here in the winner's circle for the 1974 West Texas Derby at Sunland Park.

Photo Courtesy *The Quarter Racing Journal*

"He was very easy to get along with," Whittle remarked.

but the problem was gaining on him.

"I remember at the All American Futurity, I was leading him to the track, and it had come a big rain," Barnes said. "He couldn't step over the water—I'd have to lead him around it—he was so sore. But once he got on the track, that completely left him; he didn't pay any attention to that."

As the second favorite in the All American, Lady Bug's Moon went to the front, but got nipped at the wire by a hard-charging Three Oh's.

"I remember the jockey just set there on him with the stick up," Barnes recalled. "He thought he had it won easy, and he just coasted. But here comes Jerry Nicode-mus riding Three Oh's and just nosed him out about two or three inches."

Chasing Lady Bug's Moon were Top Bug and Ralph's Lady Bug. That meant that the second, third, and fourth horses in the All American Futurity were out of FL Lady Bug or one of her daughters.

Following the 1968 All American, Barnes took Lady Bug's Moon to a veterinarian in Kentucky who removed chips from both knees. After the horse recovered, he was bred to 67 mares the following spring.

"He was very easy to get along with," Whittle remarked. "That was kind of a trademark of the Lady Bug breeding. I'd gallop him, cool him out, load him in the trailer, and take him to the breeding barn a couple of miles from where we lived."

After minimal training, the stallion

OSO. DOWNS

In 1974 Rose Bug (#9) won the All American Derby Consolation. She was by Lady Bug's Moon and out of Casco Rose. Her career earnings totaled $57,398.

Photo Courtesy *The Quarter Horse Journal*

came back to win his 3-year-old debut in the Ruidoso Invitational Handicap on July 5, 1969, running :17.65 for 350 yards.

A two-length win in the Rainbow Derby trials got him into the finals, where he beat his old rival Jet Deck Junior by a nose on a muddy track. Lady Bug's Moon closed out his career by finishing fourth in the Sunland Fall Derby.

"He was an extremely good gate horse," Whittle said. "Of course, the Lady Bug breeding, that kind of came with the whole group, not just Lady Bug's Moon. They would stand in the paddock like they weren't going to run at all. There wasn't a lot of nonsense. They won a lot of races because of how smart they were."

Offspring

In the following years, Lady Bug's Moon stood to as many as 300 mares in a season. His breeding career got a tremendous boost when Chicory Moon emerged from his first crop to win $177,000 and be named 1973 World Champion 3-Year-Old Gelding.

Chicory Moon led an army of 86 Lady Bug's Moon stakes horses over the years, including Shawne Bug, Mr Hay Bug, Miss Mighty Bug, Jerry's Bug, Glittering Moon, Miss Hay Bug, Lilie Bug, Solid Gold San, Carols She Kitty, My Afton Bug, His Gallant Bug, and Ladybugs Model.

In 1976 Marvin and Lela Barnes sold Lady Bug's Moon to George Middleton of St. Louis for what was reportedly a record price of $1,276,000. However, a couple of years later, Barnes bought the horse back to give him more exposure to

Mr Master Bug won the 1982 All American Futurity over a field that included his sister, Miss Squaw Hand, who ran second. Both horses were by Master Hand (TB) and out of Lady Bug's Moon daughters. Mr Master Bug went on to earn $1.7 million at the track and six racing world championship titles.

Photo Courtesy *The Quarter Horse Journal*

southwestern breeders.

Lady Bug's Moon sired 966 foals; his 770 starters combined to win 1,568 races and earn $4,025,213. But he may have left an even more important mark as a broodmare sire. Two of his daughters produced Mr Master Bug and Miss Squaw Hand, the horses who accomplished the unique feat of running first and second in the All American Futurity in 1982. Both were bred and owned by Marvin and Lela Barnes.

Lady Bug's Moon daughters also produced Dashing Phoebe, 1985 2-Year-Old World Champion Filly and 1986 3-Year-Old World Champion Filly, and First Prize Rose, the dam of world champion and leading sire First Down Dash.

"The Lady Bugs were just an outstanding family who made the owners and the trainers look good," reflected Whittle.

"We didn't know what we were doing, especially in the early years. There were people who knew a lot more about racing and training race horses that we were outrunning just because we had a better horse, a faster horse. They made us look good, they sure did."

Lady Bug's Moon died April 12, 1995.

12 DASH FOR CASH

By Sally Harrison

Phenomenal as a race horse, he became equally phenomenal as a sire.

Dash For Cash revolutionized the Quarter Horse racing industry. He is still the all-time leading sire of racing Quarter Horses, with earners of more than $39 million. His son, First Down Dash, is the second-leading sire, with offspring earning over $28 million, so far.

Photo by Sally Harrison

IN THREE words, his name captured the spirit of the sport. And in the opinion of many observers, he was the last word in Quarter Horse racing.

Dash For Cash aced his first start in a 300-yard futurity trial and never looked back. During a career spanning three years and 25 starts, he won 21 races. He placed second three times. He was the first horse to win the Champion of Champions back-to-back and the first horse in two decades to be named world champion in consecutive years.

Nine of his victories came in major stakes. His track record in the 440-yard Champion of Champions at Los Alamitos—where, in the words of his trainer C.W.

"Bubba" Cascio, "He beat good horses bad"—endures as one of the sport's classic moments. Yet, Dash For Cash's brilliant career on the track was eventually over-shadowed by his career as a sire.

The handsome sorrel colt resulted from a partnership between B.F. Phillips Jr. of Frisco, Tex., and the legendary King Ranch of south Texas.

King Ranch had already been raising Quarter Horses and Thoroughbreds for almost a century when Phillips purchased his first registered Quarter Horse, Cadillac Dave, in 1951. Sired by Royal King, Cadillac Dave was trained as a cutting horse and, following his purchase, Phillips plunged into showing with ardent commitment. A

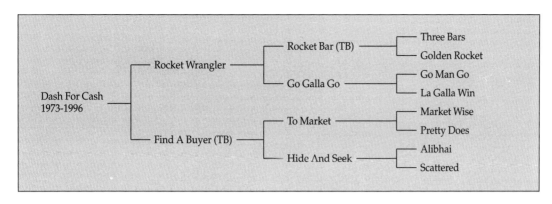

```
                                         ┌─ Three Bars
                        ┌─ Rocket Bar (TB) ─┤
                        │                 └─ Golden Rocket
          ┌─ Rocket Wrangler ─┤
          │             │                 ┌─ Go Man Go
          │             └─ Go Galla Go ───┤
Dash For Cash ─┤                          └─ La Galla Win
1973-1996     │
          │                               ┌─ Market Wise
          │             ┌─ To Market ─────┤
          │             │                 └─ Pretty Does
          └─ Find A Buyer (TB) ─┤
                        │                 ┌─ Alibhai
                        └─ Hide And Seek ─┤
                                          └─ Scattered
```

whole stable of show mounts followed Cadillac Dave, and at one point Phillips Ranch show horses were top-ranked in halter, cutting, reining, and roping.

Phillips owned Steel Bars, the sire of AQHA Champion Aledo Bar, and in the mid-1960s, Phillips won the National Cutting Horse Association's non-pro world championship twice in a row on Gin Echols. But in 1966, Phillips held a record-breaking dispersal of 230 show horses and turned his attention to racing. Within a few years, Phillips Ranch had emerged as one of the nation's premier racing facilities, home to prominent stallions such as Double Bid, Rocket Wrangler, Raise Your Glass (TB), St Bar, Some Kinda Man, Dividend (TB), and later, Streakin Six, Mr. Crimson Ruler (TB)—and Dash For Cash.

Every year, beginning in the late 1960s, in an arrangement struck with the King Ranch, Phillips selected a few King Ranch Thoroughbred mares to breed on a foal-sharing basis. In 1972, one of his choices was Find A Buyer (TB), a daughter of To Market (TB), winner of both the 1950 Arlington and Washington Park futurities. Since early speed, evidenced by a successful 2-year-old career, is an important criterion for Quarter Horse breeders, To Market's accomplishments made Find A Buyer a sound choice. Although he was not especially impressed with her plain appearance, Phillips felt confident that Rocket Wrangler would lend polish to Find A Buyer's foal.

Although he would have looked at home in a halter class, Rocket Wrangler's forte was the racetrack. His sire, Rocket Bar, by Three Bars (TB), was a leading race and broodmare sire; his dam was stakes winner Go Galla Go, by the great "Roan Rogue," Go Man Go.

Rocket Wrangler was the first horse to win both the All American and Rainbow futurities at Ruidoso Downs, and

Halter and Performance Record: Race Register of Merit; 1976 World Champion Quarter Running 3-Year-Old Colt, World Champion Quarter Running 3-Year-Old, and World Champion Quarter Running Horse; 1977 World Champion Quarter Running Aged Stallion, World Champion Quarter Running Aged Horse, and World Champion Quarter Running Horse; AQHA Hall of Fame Horse; Race Earnings, $507,688.

Progeny Record: (As of September 1999)

Foal Crops: 19	Performance Points Earned: 364.5
Foals Registered: 1,369	Performance Registers of Merit: 10
AQHA Champions: 1	Superior Performance Awards: 2
Supreme Champions: 1	Race Starters: 1,154
Racing World Champions: 16	Race Money Earned: $39,271,989
Halter Point-Earners: 2	Race Registers of Merit: 956
Halter Points Earned: 17.5	Superior Race Awards: 122
Performance Point-Earners: 17	
Leading Race Money-Earner: Dashingly ($1,754,323)	

Artist Jim Reno compared Dash For Cash to Secretariat (TB): "They both had what old horsemen call 'the look of eagles.' They looked like they could see 100 miles away."

Photo by Sally Harrison

A grandson of both Three Bars (TB) and Go Man Go, Rocket Wrangler was the first horse to win both the All American and Rainbow futurities and was named the 1970 World Champion Quarter Running 2-Year-Old.

Photo by Bill McNabb Jr., Courtesy *The Quarter Racing Journal*

Although considered somewhat homely, Find A Buyer (TB) passed on the speed of her sire, To Market, to her best son, Dash For Cash. It's been said that Dash For Cash's conformation was almost a direct composite of Find A Buyer and Rocket Wrangler.

Photo by Richard Chamberlain, Courtesy *The Quarter Racing Journal*

Dash For Cash paraded in the sale ring before the Phillips Ranch and Dash For Cash Futurity Sale on July 20, 1984. Much to the disappointment of buyers, the famed stallion was not for sale.

Photo by Sally Harrison

was named 1970 World Champion Quarter Running 2-Year-Old for his victories. Later, he ranked among the nation's top 10 sires and broodmare sires.

But Rocket Wrangler had something in addition to good looks and early foot to hand down to his foals.

"Rocket Wrangler and Dash For Cash both had good heads on them, and real good dispositions," said jockey Jerry Nicodemus, who rode both stallions to the winner's circle. "You'd just show Dash For Cash something one time and he'd catch on. Training or running, we never had a problem with him. I think not making any mistakes is what made him really great."

Although Find A Buyer produced 13 Quarter Horse foals for Phillips and King Ranch, none of them came close to Dash For Cash's record. However, her daughter by Truckle Feature, Rose Among Thorns, is the dam of I Hear A Symphony, 1994 World Champion Quarter Running 3-Year-Old and winner of the All American Derby.

Sparkling like a diamond next to his homely dam, Dash For Cash exceeded Phillips' expectations right from the start. By the time the colt was a long yearling, Phillips knew he had something special. "I was helping Bubba (Cascio) break him in Texas," remembered Jerry Nicodemus, "and he showed some run right off. We had

Dash For Cash with his breeder and owner, B.F. Phillips Jr., in 1987.
Photo by Sally Harrison

a whole barnful of babies and he was my pick. He just felt so good, and real athletic."

To the Track

Trainer Bubba Cascio reported Dash For Cash's stride to be 32 feet, among the longest ever measured. Equine artist Jim

Bubba Cascio trained and Jerry Nicodemus rode Rocket Wrangler, shown here, to his 2-year-old victories. Later the pair would take Dash For Cash to the winner's circle, as well.

Photo Courtesy *The Quarter Horse Journal*

Dash For Cash with trainer Bubba Cascio.   **Photo by Alan Gold**

Reno, whose monumental bronze statues of Dash For Cash, with Nicodemus aboard, stand in front of the AQHA Heritage Center and Museum in Amarillo and at the 6666 Ranch in Guthrie, Tex., said that the precocious colt had the same physical proportions as the great Thoroughbred champion Secretariat.

"Both Dash For Cash and Secretariat stood 16.2 as 3-year-olds, and they had identical measurements," noted Reno, who also measured Secretariat for a statue that stands at the Kentucky Horse Park in Lexington and a smaller one at the National Museum of Racing in Saratoga, New York. "And they both had what old horsemen call 'the look of eagles.' They looked like they could see 100 miles away. They were awesome."

Dash For Cash qualified for the Lubbock Downs (Tex.) Futurity in his career debut, and set a new track record for 300 yards while winning the finals. Next on his agenda was the 350-yard Sun Country Futurity in Sunland Park, N.M., where he set a stakes record. He continued his unblemished streak at Ruidoso Downs in New Mexico, where he racked up

several allowance wins in preparation for the All American Futurity time trials.

Although Dash For Cash won his All American Futurity trial by daylight, his relatively slow time qualified him for the second consolation rather than the main event. As it turned out, the All American paled in comparison to his next race—a race with the Grim Reaper.

Shortly after the All American Futurity trials, Dash For Cash colicked, and his life was barely saved by a blood transfusion from Rocket Wrangler, who was standing at Buena Suerte Ranch in Roswell, N.M., 60 miles from Ruidoso. A few weeks later, however, the seemingly undefeatable runner was back on his feet in the winner's circle for the Jet Deck Stakes at Albuquerque. It was his eighth consecutive win.

Dash For Cash's incredible win streak came to an end in El Paso, when he finished sixth to Bugs Alive In 75 in the Sunland Fall Futurity. It was to be the only time in his career that he finished worse than second. After nine months of strenuous campaigning, it seemed he was ready for a well-deserved rest.

Following a five-month layoff, he went back to Ruidoso, where he won his trial for the Kansas Derby. Just as in the All American Futurity trials, however, his time missed the cutoff for the finals. Ironically, because he won with such ease and without being pressed by his opponents, there was little to motivate him to run faster.

With six weeks remaining until the Rainbow Derby trials, Phillips and Cascio decided to send Dash For Cash to California for a shot at the rich Los Alamitos Derby. Since Cascio still had a barnful of runners

at Ruidoso Downs, he called on D. Wayne Lukas, who at the time trained Quarter Horses at Los Alamitos Race Course, to run the colt there. Dash For Cash responded with the first stakes win of his 3-year-old season and the fourth of his career.

Upon his return to Ruidoso, the big sorrel cruised to a four-length win in the Rainbow Derby trials. He was the odds-on favorite in the finals, but left the starting gates in what had become his usual come-from-behind fashion, and spotted a half-length to the winner, I'm Gorgeous, when she crossed the wire. While the All American Derby trial was another easy victory, two weeks later Dash For Cash got caught in traffic in the finals and placed second to Mito Wise Dancer.

The Legend Begins

Dash For Cash's next win came in the New Mexico State Fair Handicap, which proved to be a warmup for the biggest race of his career. In the prestigious Champion of Champions at Los Alamitos, Dash For Cash once again met Mito Wise Dancer and I'm Gorgeous. This time, however, he seemed to sense the need for a change of strategy, and breaking smartly from the gates, nailed the contentious field going 440 yards in the record time of :21.17.

"It was the easiest stakes win I've

Dash For Cash won the 1976 Champion of Champions at Los Alamitos by 1½ lengths, a feat in a Quarter Horse race comparable to the Thoroughbred Secretariat's 31-length victory in the Belmont Stakes. Dash For Cash's :21.17 track record at 440 yards still stands.

Photo by Milt Martinez, Courtesy *The Quarter Racing Journal*

Bubba Cascio told Jerry Nicodemus that Dash was sure to win the '76 Champion of Champions and suggested that the jockey stand up and glance over his shoulder after they crossed the finish line. Nicodemus did, creating the quintessential photo of two-time world champion Dash For Cash in full stride.

Photo by Milt Martinez, Courtesy *The Quarter Racing Journal*

Jerry Nicodemus was known as the "Ice Man," for the icewater in his veins and his ability to think and nerve his horses through impossible situations. This shot of Nicodemus and Dash For Cash after the '76 Champion of Champions was the model for Jim Reno's famous bronze.

Photo by Milt Martinez, Courtesy *The Quarter Horse Journal*

ever had," said Nicodemus. "I was kind of looking around to see how far we were in front, because he felt like he was really putting everything together. It felt like a fast race."

His spectacular Champion of Champions victory sealed the ballot for 1976 championship honors. Dash For Cash was named 1976 World Champion Quarter Running 3-Year-Old Colt, World Champion Quarter Running 3-Year-Old, and, more importantly, World Champion Quarter Running Horse (a title known in racing circles as, simply, *the* world champion). In 1977, with wins in the Vessels Maturity, the Los Alamitos Invitational Championship, and once again, the Champion of Champions, Dash For Cash reclaimed world championship honors.

When he retired at the end of his 4-year-old season, he was the first Quarter Horse to earn $500,000 without the benefit of wins in the rich All American Futurity or Derby. "I wish he would have run some more," said Nicodemus. "But he proved everything he needed to prove. He had so much class; it just stuck out all over him."

Syndication

Dash For Cash's racing success marked just the first phase of a brilliant career. Under a syndicate arrangement managed by Phillips, he soon claimed the top spot on leading sire lists.

In 1977, flooded with breeding in-

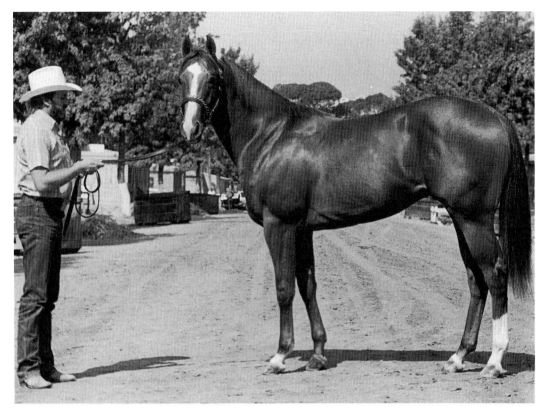

By far the best son of Dash For Cash ever foaled, First Down Dash (shown here as a 2-year-old with trainer Mike Robbins) won the Kindergarten and Dash For Cash futurities in 1986. The following year, the 3-year-old sorrel stallion won the Champion of Champions by 1¾ lengths and was named world champion. Now a prepotent sire, First Down Dash has had 116 stakes winners and the earners of $28 million, from only nine foal crops (as of 1999).

Photo Courtesy *The Quarter Racing Journal*

From Dash's second foal crop, the refined and elegant filly Justanold Love won the 1982 All American Derby at 10 to 1 odds, beating the previous and the following year's world champions in the process. The race was the only time 1981 world champ Special Effort was outrun. Justanold Love also won the 1982 Champion of Champions.

Photo Courtesy *The Quarter Racing Journal*

Cash Rate, foaled in 1980, proved that Dash For Cash could sire sons as well as daughters, but only after Cash Rate was taken out of training as B.F. Phillips' next team roping horse and taken to the track. The gutty gelding won the 1985 Champion of Champions by 1¼ lengths with jockey James Lackey, shown here, who has said Cash Rate was his favorite horse.

Photo Courtesy *The Quarter Racing Journal*

By 1983 single breeding shares to Dash For Cash were selling for as much as $500,000.

quiries, Phillips formulated a ground-breaking $2.5 million syndication for his famous runner. Forty shares were sold for $62,500 each, with two breedings per year allotted each share.

"Dash For Cash ran under the name of B.F. Phillips Jr. and King Ranch," said Mike Carter, a long-time financial advisor to Phillips and executor of the Phillips estate. "Part of the reason for the syndication was to raise money to buy out King Ranch."

Phillips looked to the Thoroughbred industry for a model for the syndicate. "If we can't learn something from the Thoroughbred people who have been in the business for 200 years, we've got our eyes closed," he once said. "You've got to pattern after success."

Although he bred a few mares in the spring of 1977, Dash For Cash officially began his stud career in 1978 at the Phillips Ranch in Frisco. He remained there until the ranch dispersal in 1993, five years after B.F. Phillips' death. His last home was the historic Four Sixes

Ranch in Guthrie, Tex., owned by Phillips' former wife, Anne Burnett Marion.

Offspring

Dash For Cash's first small crop of foals, which earned more than $1.2 million, included the fillies Baby Hold On and Queen For Cash; his second crop, with daughters Dashingly, Dash Again, and Justanold Love, won $3.1 million.

Dashingly pocketed nearly $600,000 as a 2-year-old, and ended her career with $1.75 million in earnings. By the time the millionaire mare retired in 1983, her sire had become such a hot commodity that single breeding shares were selling for as much as $500,000. According to Mike Carter, one breeder paid $750,000 for a share—12 times its original value.

Using his own shares, Phillips brought Dash For Cash a star-studded lineup of mares through a series of foal-sharing partnerships. With Minnie Rhea Wood, he bred major money-earners Flow Of Cash and Countin The Cash, along with Cash Rate, a gelding who became the world champion in 1985.

At first, Dash For Cash was pegged as a "filly sire," and even when his son Cash Rate earned more than $500,000 as

From Dash's second
crop, Dashingly came
into her own as a
4-year-old in 1983.
Outrun by her sister
Justanold Love in '82,
Dashingly won the
1983 All American
Gold Cup and was
named that year's
world champion.

**Photo by Bill Pitt Jr.,
Courtesy** *The Quarter
Racing Journal*

The feminine, classy
Dashs Dream was the
1984 World Champion
Quarter Running
Horse and a millionaire
without winning the
lucrative All American
Futurity. Under a
hand ride from jockey
Danny Cardoza,
in the irons here,
the mare covered a quarter-
mile in :21.04 in the
trials for the '84 All
American Gold Cup—
still the third-fastest
quarter-mile in history.

Photo Courtesy *The
Quarter Racing Journal*

The Dash For Cash son Miss N Cash, out of a Doc Bar mare, won the 1987 National Cutting Horse Association Derby and went on to sire NCHA Futurity Champion Dox Miss N Reno.

Photo by Pat Hall, Courtesy *The Quarter Horse Journal*

an older horse, and another son, On A High, won more than $1 million as a 2-year-old, some horsemen still doubted that a son could ever approach Dash For Cash's success.

Then Phillips and A.F. "Sonny" Stanley Jr. teamed up to breed First Down Dash, the world champion of 1987. By the close of 1998, First Down Dash had sired the earners of nearly $25 million, including four All American Futurity winners, and was rated first among leading sires, whose ranks also included four of his sons.

In another foal-share arrangement, with McRae Enterprises, the result was 1990 world champion Dash For Speed. Over the years, Phillips and Dash For Cash syndicate owners became breeders of dozens of other major stakes winners, among them five world champions.

Make Mine Cash, Dashs Dream, Floren-tine, Dash For Speed, Dashingly, and On A High each earned more than $1 million; Justanold Love, Cash Rate, First Down Dash, Meganette, Dashing Phoebe, Takin On The Cash, and Sound Dash each earned over $500,000.

The foal-sharing magic worked in the cutting arena, too, where Phillips and Dan Lufkin teamed up to breed Miss N Cash, a Dash For Cash son who won the National Cutting Horse Association Derby and went on to sire NCHA Futurity Champion Dox Miss N Reno.

While Dash For Cash's effect on the racing industry is indelible, his influence knows no boundaries. In 1996, AQHA honored Gotum Gone as the first Supreme Champion since Goldseeker Bud achieved that status 16 years earlier. The 7-year-old gelded son of Dash For Cash earned a speed rating of 90 on the track, before turning to the show arena where he won classes in halter, reining, and roping.

Later Years

As the years passed, many visitors turned up at Phillips Ranch with the sole

In 1996, Gotum Gone, a 1989 gelding by Dash and out of a Beduino (TB) and Alamitos Bar-bred mare, became the first AQHA Supreme Champion in 16 years, earning a speed index of 90 on the track and winning show points in halter, reining, and roping.

Photo Courtesy *The Quarter Horse Journal*

purpose of seeing the legendary stallion. Always the gentleman, Dash For Cash never failed to oblige by striking a pose when led from his stall.

In the fall of 1987, just weeks after the Texas legislature legalized pari-mutuel racing, something Phillips had worked tirelessly toward for decades, the famous stallion and his breeder were photographed on the lawn at Phillips Ranch for the cover of *Quarter Week* magazine. Time stood still as the two great champions of racing gazed toward the horizon.

"Come on, old pardner," Phillips said, as he led Dash For Cash back to his stable after the photo session. Two months later, Phillips suffered a fatal heart attack while delivering a congratulatory speech to members of the Texas Horse Racing Association.

On May 20, 1996, immobilized by EPM, a progressive neurological disease that had plagued him for several years, 23-year-old Dash For Cash was humanely destroyed at the Four Sixes Ranch.

"I don't think in my lifetime I'll see another Quarter Horse who will have the kind of impact that he's had on the breed," said Glenn Blodgett, D.V.M., director of horse operations for Burnett Ranches, which is headquartered at the

Four Sixes. "He's one of those rare individuals. You could tell there was something special about his foals even before they were dry."

Dash For Cash's ashes are buried at the American Quarter Horse Heritage Center & Museum in Amarillo, near the life-size bronze created by Jim Reno and donated by Anne Marion, in memory of *the* "champion of champions."

Dash For Cash's ashes are buried near his large-as-life bronze statue that stands in front of the American Quarter Horse Heritage Center & Museum in Amarillo, Texas.

Photo by Jenny Wohl-farth, Courtesy *The Quarter Horse Journal*

13

VANDY

By Jim Goodhue

He was a phenomenal race horse and sire.

FROM 1955 through 1960, there wasn't a single year when AQHA's list of racing champions didn't include one or more foals sired by the brilliant Vandy. He had become as formidable in the breeding pen as he'd been on the sprinting straightaways.

Without much of an *official* race record to boast of, Vandy gained his fame in 23 unofficial starts, crossing the finish line first 19 times. That *unofficial*

record of blazing early speed was enough to attract plenty of mare owners, and the resulting offspring burned up the tracks for the better part of a decade. Three daughters and two sons were responsible for 11 world championship titles.

Vandy's offspring have made him legendary. But the really amazing part of Vandy's story began much earlier, in 1943, with the controversy surrounding the reg-

Vandy with trainer Connie Brown and jockey Earl Southern, after setting a track record for 440 yards at Raton. Note the partially broken girth. The date on this photo is July 1957, and the owner is listed as T. Gray. Vandy's unofficial race record shows 23 starts, with 19 wins, two seconds, a third, and a fourth.

Photo by Tommy Thompson, Courtesy *The Quarter Horse Journal*

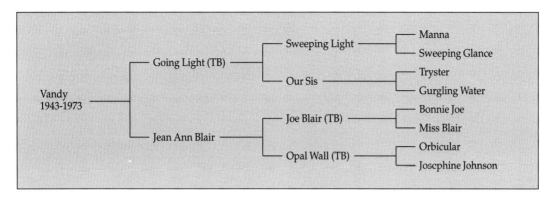

istration as a Quarter Horse of a colt with four Thoroughbred grandparents.

Background

During the Depression era, some breeders found it did not pay to register even their most blue-blooded foals with The Jockey Club, the Thoroughbred registry. It appears that the filly Jean Ann Blair was one of these. A daughter of Joe Blair (TB), the sire of Joe Reed (P-3) (see his story in the first *Legends* book), she was out of a Thoroughbred mare named Opal Wall. On both sides, she had the blood of some of the most famous speed-producing American Thoroughbred bloodlines.

Since Jean Ann Blair was not registered, her 1943 colt was ineligible for registration in The Jockey Club, even though he'd been sired by the Thoroughbred Going Light. Through this combination, the colt named Vandy traced to Bonnie Joe, Domino, Manna, *Bonnie Scotland, Leamington, Ben Brush, and Spendthrift. Thoroughbreds from these bloodlines often made their reputations for spectacular speed at relatively shorter races, rather than in distance racing.

Because these bloodlines showed no accepted Quarter Horse blood, however, Vandy was not welcomed for registration by the AQHA as it was constituted in those days. Two other registries, however, also were founded in the early 1940s. These were the American Quarter Racing Association and the National Quarter Horse Breeders Association. Vandy was enrolled in both of them.

The AQRA listed any horse of any breeding if he/she was to be campaigned in the "short-horse" races sponsored by that organization. In 1949 this group and its records were taken into the AQHA. Moved to AQHA headquarters in Ama-

Halter and Performance Record: Racing Register of Merit.

Progeny Record:

Foal Crops: 22	Performance Point-Earners: 8
Foals Registered: 309	Performance Points Earned: 60
AQHA Champions: 1	Race Starters: 207
Racing World Champions: 5	Race Money Earned: $785,156
Halter Point-Earners: 14	Race Registers of Merit: 110
Halter Points Earned: 74	Superior Race Awards: 14
Leading Race Money-Earner: Vandy's Flash ($97,348)	

A head shot of Vandy, who became legendary through the accomplishments of his get and grandget, who racked up AQHA awards. The stallion barely made it into the AQHA registry himself. Enrolled with both the American Quarter Racing Association and National Quarter Horse Breeders Association, he was added to AQHA's rolls when the other organizations joined AQHA in 1949. **Photo Courtesy The Quarter Horse Journal**

This is Garrett's Miss Pawhuska, a ROM-earning race mare who produced some of Vandy's most successful runners. Their offspring Vanetta Dee, Vannevar, and Vandy's Flash are responsible for nine of the 11 racing world championships earned by Vandy progeny. A daughter of the immortal Leo, Garrett's Miss Pawhuska is buried beside Vandy in Oklahoma.

Photo Courtesy *The Quarter Horse Journal*

rillo, the AQRA became the AQHA Performance Department. Horses in the AQRA who were not otherwise registered were to be considered the equivalent of the AQHA Appendix listing.

The NQHBA accepted horses it felt could contribute to the foundation of a Quarter Horse breed. It not only registered horses such as Vandy, with his totally Thoroughbred pedigree, but it also registered some horses who had certificates issued by The Jockey Club—such as Woven Web (aka Miss Princess—see her chapter in this book) and the well-known Piggin String (his story is told in *Legends 3*).

Then the NQHBA also was absorbed by the AQHA in 1949, with the stipulation that all horses in the NQHBA would be eligible to receive numbered (Tentative) registration certificates. The only exception was that those horses registered in both the NQHBA and The Jockey Club were left only with their Thoroughbred papers. Their foals, of course, would be eligible for Appendix certificates when the other parent had a numbered AQHA certificate.

Despite having nothing but Thoroughbred blood, Vandy was eligible for Tentative registry because he didn't have a certificate from The Jockey Club. Once in the AQHA, he quickly earned his way out of the Tentative and into the Permanent registry. He then had the registration rights of any stallion listed by the AQHA.

Noted Quarter Horse historian Nelson C. Nye accurately described Vandy as a Thoroughbred with a Quarter Horse

The Thoroughbred stallion Joe Blair with jockey Lee Burkes at his halter. Joe Blair sired Jean Ann Blair, Vandy's dam.

Photo Courtesy The Quarter Horse Journal

Vandy became particularly known for breaking hard from the start, whether it was from starting gates or in a lap-and-tap match.

number. He wasn't just talking about the long-legged stallion's conformation; he also was describing the horse's breeding.

Race Career

Vandy's official race record, which the AQHA acquired when it absorbed the American Quarter Racing Association, shows two wins and a second from three starts. It also lists a track record at La Mesa Park of :22.0 for 440 yards. Naturally, he'd qualified for a racing Register of Merit.

Nelson C. Nye, a conscientious historian of the early years of the modern Quarter Horse era, found information on 23 starts for Vandy. From these, he tallied 19 wins, two seconds, a third, and a fourth.

Vandy's breeder, Dave Ware, gave the sorrel colt his first opportunity on the track. Unfortunately, he gave him only 18 days of training before running him in the 1945 Pawhuska (Oklahoma) Open Futurity. After being carried to the extreme outside twice, Vandy was declared third from a close photo-finish.

Apparently, Ware didn't consider that good enough. That fall, he sold the colt and his dam to Tom Gray of Tulsa. Gray made a practice of accumulating good

horses. He's noted for owning the famous stallions Question Mark (see *Legends 3*) and Oil Capital (TB), among others.

According to Nye, Gray turned Vandy over to C. L. (Connie) Brown for training. The colt then began his career in earnest—running in match races more often than on recognized tracks. He became particularly known for breaking hard from the start, whether it was from starting gates or in a lap-and-tap match.

Fairly early in his racing days, Vandy became the property of Dee Garrett of Pawhuska, Oklahoma. The two formed a close-knit partnership until Vandy's death in January 1973, according to AQHA records.

One of Vandy's major races was at Del Rio, Texas. There he ran second to Miss Princess (registered with The Jockey Club as Woven Web). The quality of the horses he contested is illustrated by the fact that this spectacularly speedy mare was

Vanetta Dee was the most successful daughter from the Vandy-Garrett's Miss Pawhuska cross, earning $82,629 during her six-year racing career. The sorrel mare also earned the 1955 world champion 3-year-old filly title and was the world champion mare three years in a row, from 1956 to 1958.

Photo Courtesy *The Quarter Horse Journal*

named world champion Quarter running horse for three racing seasons.

Moving to the New Mexico State Fairgrounds in Albuquerque, Vandy ran a second to Barbra B while she was setting an AQRA record for 3-year-olds. Her time was a scorching :22.6 for 440 yards.

Vandy's poorest race was the New Mexico Championship. Running against some of the top sprinters then in training, he finished fourth. It was thought he was hampered by the altitude, and it probably didn't help that Vandy's jockey was riding with his broken right arm in a cast.

At Eagle Pass, Tex., Vandy ran his last race. Despite breaking down as he came out of the gates with his usual tremendous start, he ran courageously and won the 330-yard race over Lucky and May West Ferguson, two very classy speedsters. He was in such pain that it was

difficult to get him from the winner's circle back to his stall.

Retired from the track and allowed to recover from his injury, Vandy was quickly put to stud. His second career proved to be even more notable than his first.

Progeny

Vandy's first foal crop (1948) included two racing ROM qualifiers, Vandy Jr and the stakes-placed Lady Vandy B. The next crop included the stakes-winning Vandy's Question and the stakes-placed Lorane's Vandy. Vandy's Question, who set a Pawhuska track record of :23.0 for 440 yards, was a son of Lorane Question. Lorane's Vandy was out of Lorane, the dam of Lorane Question.

The champion Pokey Vandy, out of Beggar's Pokey, by Beggar Boy (TB), appeared in the 1951 crop. She won the Rocky Mountain Quarter Horse Futurity at 2. Though she didn't find the winner's circle in her 3-year-old campaign, she placed in stakes races.

In 1955 Pokey Vandy raced for a new owner (Hugh Huntley) and with a new trainer (Newt Keck). For these two men, who were later to win three

Vandy's 1953 son, Vannevar, was named the 1956 and '57 Champion Quarter Running Gelding.

Photo Courtesy *The Quarter Horse Journal*

runnings of the All American Futurity, Pokey Vandy provided the first taste of the big time.

Pokey Vandy was moved to Los Alamitos, where she really hit her stride. She won the 400-yard Gold Bar Stakes over Vanetta Dee, Monita, and Ridge Butler. A week later, she stretched out under the top weight of 120 pounds to win the Autumn Championship. That time she not only beat Vanetta Dee, Monita, and Ridge Butler again, but she added the likes of Gold Note, Moon Deck, and Arizonan to the defeated.

Pokey Vandy also had given Los Alamitos a record of :22.0 for 440 yards. Considering the reputations of her great competitors and the time in which she triumphed over them, it came as little surprise that she was named 1955 World Champion Quarter Running Mare.

In the same crop as Pokey Vandy was an overshadowed but capable daughter of Vandy named Vandy Reed. She won the

1953 Kansas Futurity and placed in several other stakes races.

A Magical Cross

Also in the 1951 foal crop was the first performer from the cross of Vandy on the Leo mare, Garrett's Miss Pawhuska—one of the most successful nicks in the history of the breed. Their pairings would produce three world champions responsible for nine world championships. Their first runner, a AAA filly named Vandy's Betty, won four of her 15 starts and placed second once.

The second winning sibling from this

Two-time champion running gelding Vandy's Flash was also named the 1960 World Champion Quarter Running Horse.

Photo by Jack Stribling, Courtesy *The Quarter Horse Journal*

Following her victory in the Nebraska Quarter Horse Association Futurity, Vanetta Dee was prepped for bigger things.

golden combination was foaled in 1952. She was the immortal Vanetta Dee, a force on the straightaways for six racing seasons and the champion quarter running mare three years in a row—1956-58.

Following her victory in the Nebraska Quarter Horse Association Futurity, Vanetta Dee was prepped for bigger things. Often running against older horses in 1955, Vanetta Dee won the Clabbertown G Handicap and took second money in the Hard Twist Stakes and the Gold Bar Stakes. These efforts gave her the year's title of champion 3-year-old filly.

At 4 Vanetta Dee won the Northern California Racing Association Stakes and Los Alamitos' Johnny Dial Stakes. She

ran close thirds in four more races, indicating she was the best of her sex in competition, so she earned the coveted title of world champion quarter running mare for the first time.

Vanetta Dee again was named the champion mare in 1957 when she won the Bright Eyes Stakes and placed in several other major stakes races, setting a track record at Centennial of :20.1 for 400 yards. In 1958 she also won several stellar events, and claimed the mare championship once again.

As a 7-year-old in 1959, Vanetta Dee was not ready to retire. She won two stakes at Los Alamitos—the Shue Fly Stakes and the Miss Princess Invitational Handicap—and the Howell Trailer Handicap at Pawhuska, where she set two track records for 400 yards, :20.6 and :20.5. She rounded out her career with lifetime earnings of $82,629.

There is the distinct possibility that Vanetta Dee might have won even higher honors had she not been running with the likes of Go Man Go, Mr Bar None, and her two full brothers, Vannevar and Vandy's Flash.

Vanetta Dee's 1953 brother, Vannevar, won the Pacific Coast Quarter Horse Racing Association Derby as a 3-year-old. The caliber (and gender) of the horses beating him in other races, as well as the ones who trailed him, made it appropriate for the AQHA to name him 1956 Champion Quarter Running Gelding.

As a 4-year-old the next year, Vannevar was still striding long. That season, he won Ruidoso's Blowed Toad Memorial Handicap and the Shue Fly Stakes at the New Mexico State Fair. He also had a string of seconds, and repeated as the year's champion gelding. A winner for three more years, Vannevar concluded his career with earnings of slightly more than $40,000.

Vannevar's younger brother, Vandy's Flash, was foaled in 1954. He, too, did not make an impression as a 2-year-old; but at 3 he won both the Ruidoso Derby and the New Mexico Breeders' Derby. In 1958 Vandy's Flash won the Ruidoso Maturity and ran up a string of impressive seconds in major stakes races. These were enough to give him the title of 1958 Champion Quarter Running Gelding.

Vandy's Flash never reached the winner's circle in a 1959 stakes event, but in 1960 he was better than ever. He reclaimed his champion gelding honors and was also named the 1960 World Champion Quarter Running Horse. Continuing to run through 1964, the gelding retired with earnings of $97,348.

Other Runners

Although there were to be no more champions from the matings of Garrett's Miss Pawhuska with Vandy, the stallion sired other very capable sprinters.

Aunt Judy, foaled in 1957, proved that some Vandy foals could burn up the tracks as 2-year-olds. Her dam, Aunt Amie, was another daughter of Leo, a stakes winner in her own right, and the producer of eight racing ROM qualifiers.

In 1959 Aunt Judy won the Kinder-

Although this photograph of Pokey Pat is marred, we are using it anyway to show what a good-looking horse he was. The 1955 bay stallion was by Vandy and out of Nancy Baby, by Benson's Hickorybill. Pokey Pat started 66 times on the track, earning $10,653 and a racing ROM. The information on this picture says it was taken at Indio, Calif., where he won a hackamore class.

Photo Courtesy *The Quarter Horse Journal*

Vanguard, by Vandy and out of Comet Francis, was the 1967 AQHA High-Point Steer Roping Horse and an AQHA Champion. (As has been mentioned in other chapters, steer roping was AQHA's term for dally team roping years ago.)

Photo by Serpa, Courtesy *The Quarter Horse Journal*

Many people felt in those days that Vandy's foals showed too much Thoroughbred blood.

garten Stakes at Los Alamitos and ran second in the Ruidoso Futurity. Those wins helped her claim the title of 1959 Champion Quarter Running 2-Year-Old Filly. Aunt Judy also won several major races in 1960 and 1961.

Among Vandy's 110 ROM runners were such outstanding stakes winners as Bright Bardee (New Mexico Breeders Derby), Vandelita (San Mateo Invitational Handicap), Horny Bill (Bay Meadows Handicap), Bailey's Vandy (winner of four futurities in Minnesota, Illinois, and Wisconsin), Pokey Pat (Bay Meadows' Saratoga and Santa Clara Invitational Handicap), Vanoka (Uranium Downs Derby), and Mr Walt (Colorado Wonderland Handicap).

Performance Horses

Many people felt in those days that Vandy's foals showed too much Thoroughbred blood in looks and tempera-

ment to do anything but run. They overlooked the fact that Vandy had sired three performance ROM qualifiers, plus four other working point-earners and 14 halter point-earners.

They definitely overlooked Vanguard, by Vandy and out of Comet Francis, a AAA daughter of Bill Spokane. Vanguard was the 1967 AQHA High-Point Steer Roping Horse and had the kind of conformation that helped him earn the title of AQHA Champion. A winner on the track, Vanguard was a ROM-qualifier both in racing and performance events. Vanguard passed his versatility along by siring the AQHA Champion Irish Guard, the Superior halter horse Cameo Van, and earners of both racing and performance ROMs.

Vandy Daughters

With the exception of such sons as Vanguard, Pokey Pat, Vandy II (AAA full brother to Pokey Vandy), and the injured Joe Blair, many of Vandy's top-quality male foals were gelded. This meant that a major part of the task of passing along Vandy's genes was left to his daughters.

They came through with flying colors.

From the 631 starters out of Vandy's daughters, there were 373 winners and 338 ROM runners. Their 47 stakes winners were victorious in some 80 stakes races. There were 39 others who placed in stakes, and 26 earned Superior race horse designations. Then, to top it off, three of their foals accounted for six year-end racing championships.

Not to be ignored are the six AQHA Champions, four Youth Champions, and 23 working ROM performers out of Vandy's daughters. The Vandy mares produced 36 halter point-earners, including three Superior halter horses. They also were the dams of 71 performance point-earners, who earned 5,194.5 points. One individual won the Superior title in two working events (Mr Money Cause in barrel racing and pole bending).

The biggest money-earner out of a Vandy mare was Mr Jet Moore, by Jet Deck and out of Dyna Van (SI 95). Mr Jet Moore won 21 races, including 10 stakes races, and $341,405. At 2 and 3, he also set four track records at the top straight-aways, including Los Alamitos (:19.75 for 440 yards) and Ruidoso Downs (:17.59 for 350 yards). Mr Jet Moore was the 1972 Champion 3-Year-Old Colt, Champion Stallion, and World Champion Quarter Running Horse.

Vandy's champion runner, Pokey Vandy, produced Pokey Bar, the 1961 Champion 2-Year-Old Colt and the 1962 Champion 3-Year-Old Colt. At 2 Pokey Bar won the All American Futurity, the Kindergarten Futurity, and the Los Alamitos Thanksgiving Stakes. He also equaled the 400-yard track record at Ruidoso (:19.9). At 3 Pokey Bar won stakes races including two derbies and the Los Alamitos Invitational Championship. During that season, he equaled the 440-yard track record at Los Alamitos.

Many other mares, including Vanetta Dee, added further to Vandy's tallies as a maternal grandsire. Because her racing career was so long, Vanetta Dee did not get much opportunity to excel as a producer. All three of her foals who got to the track, though, qualified for racing ROMs and two were AAA.

The Vandy daughter Vanessa Dee, herself a racing ROM earner, produced four runners who earned $37,177 and one

A phenomenal youth performance horse, Van Decka excelled in a variety of events, earning a multitude of championships and Superiors in both open and youth competition. A 1967 bay gelding, he was by Decka Center and out of Vanessa Dee, by Vandy. He was shown by youth exhibitors Kim and Cheryl Johnson, Mary Elizabeth Jones, and Tara Green; the back of this photo identifies the rider as Cheryl Johnson.

Photo by Don Trout, Courtesy *The Quarter Horse Journal*

performer who earned 4,388 show points. The performer, Van Decka, compiled one of the most impressive records in the history of AQHA youth events. Sired by Decka Center, Van Decka won the 1974 world championship in youth show-

DEE GARRETT   -VANSARITA TOO-   OWNER-Tr.
————————— MR. RUN BAR, 2nd - MISS BOLEO BAR, 3rd —————————
PURSE $15,300   400 YDS...20.91   JOCKEY, W. HUNT...
OCT. 10, 1964   HAWTHORNE   SCHULTZFOTO
    =THE CHICAGO QUARTER HORSE DERBY=

The last runner from the Vandy-Garrett's Miss Pawhuska pairing, Vansarita Too won two stakes races, one of which was the 1964 Chicago Quarter Horse Derby. The 1961 sorrel mare ran the 400-yard race in :20.91. Later, she produced 12 race starters who earned $183,408 at the track. This picture lists Dee Garrett as the mare's owner and trainer, and W. Hunt as the jockey.

Photo Courtesy *The Quarter Horse Journal*

Some of Vandy's daughters had winning offspring in working arenas as well as racetracks.

manship and placed in the top 10 at four Youth World Shows and open World Show. The gelding racked up nine youth high-point awards, two all-around youth high-point awards, and open and youth AQHA Champion designations.

Late in her lifetime, Vanessa Dee was acquired by Orbin Garrett, a nephew of Dee Garrett. When he retired from a career as a professional calf roper, Orbin began raising race horses in earnest. Naturally, he used Vandy blood in his program. Vanessa Dee produced for Orbin a mare named Miss Decka, by his popular stallion Decka Center. Although she was unraced, Miss Decka produced the stakes winner China Doll Su and the stakes placer Suwanee Jude.

Many other daughters of Vandy also produced stakes winners. An abbreviated list includes Vandy's Katsy (dam of Sweet Daddy, SI 108, a four-time stakes winner), Van Pen (dam of Vandy Hug and multiple stakes winner Twisty Van), Vandy's Candy (dam of Maggie McGowan, SI 100), Vandy Jane (Speedy Chant and Wiggle), Beggar Vanet (Top O' The Bar and Beggar's Money), Vandelita (Truly Elligant and Cheque Deck), and My Brand (Triangle Slash and Brandin' Time).

Some of Vandy's daughters, such as Vandy Whiz, My Vandy Kay, Vandoozie, Angela Liz, and Vansarita, had winning offspring in working arenas as well as racetracks.

Others had their best success with performance horses. Examples are Vandy's Jerrie (dam of Vantive, ROM performer in both open and youth contests) and Vandy's Marcia (dam of Mr Money Cause, Superior in both barrel racing and pole bending).

Today, the blood of Vandy lives on in the pedigrees of top horses. Although he died in 1973, according to AQHA records, his influence is felt among the most accomplished competitors in many events.

Orbin Garret reports, "Vandy is buried about four miles west of Pawhuska on the ranch which had been owned by the late Dee Garrett. The old horse died just after covering a mare." Fittingly, Garrett's Miss Pawhuska is buried by his side.

14 IMPRESSIVE

By A.J. Mangum

His influence changed the halter-horse world forever.

TAGGED with a one-word name that described his own appearance as well as his stature as a sire, Impressive single-handedly changed the western horse world, becoming one of the most influential halter-horse sires ever known.

At the height of his fame, though, after establishing himself as the anchor for a bloodline of champions, Impressive would be linked to a crippling genetic defect. The disorder would become as much a part of his identity as the line of outstanding horses he sired.

Foaled in Oklahoma on April 15, 1969, Impressive was sired by the Thoroughbred Lucky Bar, a Three Bars son, and was out of Glamour Bars, herself a double-bred Three Bars mare. AQHA lists Perry Cotton, one of California's pioneer breeders of registered Quarter Horses, as Impressive's breeder. Cotton, who lived in Missouri at the time, owned both Lucky Bar and Glamour Bars, but sold the mare just months before Impressive was foaled.

Impressive's first owner was Nick McNair of Pryor, Oklahoma. McNair filed

Impressive's winning halter conformation turned heads, and his ability as a sire changed the Quarter Horse breed.

Photo by Darol Dickinson, Courtesy *The Quarter Horse Journal*

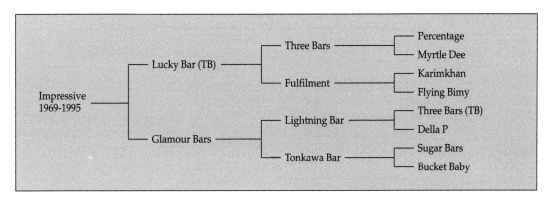

Impressive 1969-1995

- Lucky Bar (TB)
  - Three Bars
    - Percentage
    - Myrtle Dee
  - Fulfilment
    - Karimkhan
    - Flying Bimy
- Glamour Bars
  - Lightning Bar
    - Three Bars (TB)
    - Della P
  - Tonkawa Bar
    - Sugar Bars
    - Bucket Baby

a registration application with AQHA, requesting Glamour Bars' sorrel son be named Tripple Bars, indicating the preponderance of Three Bars blood in the colt. In January of 1970, though, before the registration request cleared, McNair sold the colt to Blair and Nancy Folck of Springfield, Ohio.

Even as a yearling, Impressive's conformation created a buzz within the Quarter Horse industry. Blair Folck, one of the founders of the All American Quarter Horse Congress, had heard through the grapevine about McNair's colt. At a chance meeting with McNair at the Blue Ribbon Futurity in Sallisaw, Okla., he asked about the young horse. McNair invited Folck to stop by his place and take a look.

In an interview for a 1985 *Quarter Horse Journal* feature, Folck recalled, "Sometimes you look at a colt's front end and it's really nice, then walk around behind, and it's a whole different story. But not with this colt. We'd stopped by at about midnight and Nick showed him to us under a light he had on a pole … and even then, we could see he was nice all around."

McNair asked $3,000 for the colt and after trying to negotiate, Folck finally met his price.

"Nick got to thinking about it, and then he offered me $500 to call off the deal," Folck said.

Folck had no intention of backpedaling, though. He took the colt home and expedited registration procedures, submitting several new choices for the colt's name. His first choice, Impressive, was granted.

The Beginnings of Fame

As Impressive developed into a stocky and muscled yearling with remarkable

Halter and Performance Record: 1974 AQHA World Champion Aged Stallion.

Progeny Record: (As of September 1999)

Foal Crops: 24	Superior Halter Awards: 146
Foals Registered: 2,250	Performance Point-Earners: 268
AQHA Champions: 24	Performance Points Earned: 5,624
World Champions: 29	Performance Registers of Merit: 118
Halter Point-Earners: 846	Superior Performance Awards: 32
Halter Points Earned: 19,038.5	Race Starters: 10
Halter Registers of Merit: 68	Race Money Earned: $1,653

conformation, Folck became acquainted with the colt, who was turned out with other young horses until spring.

"He was a playful colt, like they all are," Folck said. "He was a kind horse, wasn't mean at all or any more aggressive than any others, but so full of energy that he couldn't hardly hold himself. He was kind of an erratic little colt—real nervous."

Folck, then president of the Ohio Quarter Horse Association, began showing Impressive at halter, but his results,

Impressive with handler Chuck McDowell following the stallion's win in the aged stallion class at the first Quarter Horse World Show, held in 1974.

Photo Courtesy *The Quarter Horse Journal*

surprisingly, were less than stellar.

"I showed him four or five times and got him beat about as much as he won," Folck said. "It'd bug the heck out of me because I didn't think there was anything in the world that should have been over him."

Folck theorized there was nothing wrong with Impressive that a nicer halter couldn't fix. Outfitted in a new Arabian show halter, sans silver, Impressive earned his first win at a small Quarter

Horse show in Coshocton, Ohio.

At Impressive's next show, the Indiana State Fair in Indianapolis, he won the yearling halter class, and caught the eye of his next owner, Dean Landers of Des Moines, Iowa. Landers was no stranger to good horses. His stallion lineup had included Coy's Bonanza, Two Eyed Jack, and Sonny Dee Bar. The horseman paid $20,000 on the spot for the yearling.

"(I) showed him 10, 15, 20 times and never got him beat," Landers told *The Quarter Horse Journal* in 1985. "He was a nice colt, one of the most outstanding individuals there was."

From eight outings in AQHA-approved shows while under Landers' ownership, Impressive took home eight first-place trophies, a grand championship, and two reserve grand titles. At home, Landers kept Impressive isolated from other horses, keeping him fit for halter through a strict feeding and exercise regimen.

At the 1970 Quarter Horse Congress in Columbus, Ohio, Landers sold Impressive—after the horse's victory in the show's yearling stallion futurity—to Fennel Brown of Washington, Mo., who paid $40,000 for the colt. The next spring, Brown transferred ownership of Impressive to his business, Brown Quarries.

Hoping to make a race horse out of Impressive (his sire had earned $17,705 on the track, winning four of 26 starts), Brown refused offers for the horse in excess of $100,000 and sent the stallion to trainer Charlie Champion in Ardmore, Oklahoma. The trainer described Impressive as being extremely smooth, with a good stride and "nice, easy lope." The colt's future as a race horse, though, was in doubt from the start.

Champion told *The Quarter Horse Journal*, "We took our time with him because he was such a high-priced horse. We'd probably been training him three or four months before we ever took him to the gate. Impressive was extremely powerful, even as a 2-year-old. He showed some speed, a lot of early speed, when we worked him with some other horses we had there. But I don't think he could have ever gone over about 300 to 350 yards, and since he was so stout and heavy, I was afraid there was a good chance he'd hurt himself."

Thus, Brown's hope of turning Impressive into a runner came to an abrupt end. The stallion's fame, though, had yet to reach its apex.

New Heights

Eyeing Impressive's future as a breeding stallion, Brown saw the horse's Appendix registration status (denoting he was half-Thoroughbred, half-Quarter Horse) as an obstacle, preventing widespread promotion of the horse. Under

Sired by Lucky Bar, a Thoroughbred son of Three Bars, and out of the double-bred Three Bars mare Glamour Bars, Impressive had a stout, muscled look that immediately impressed halter-horse enthusiasts.

Photo Courtesy *The Quarter Horse Journal*

AQHA rules, an Appendix-registered stallion could stand only to mares with Permanent registration designation.

To advance from Appendix status, Impressive would have to earn additional AQHA points in performance events, or

Impressor, by Impressive and out of Miss Windy Spur, was among the first champions sired by Impressive. Impressor won the 1975 yearling stallion world title.

Photos by Gary Lake, Courtesy *The Quarter Horse Journal*

be approved by two AQHA inspectors. A veterinary exam showed Impressive had developed pedal osteitis—inflammation of the coffin bone—and navicular bursitis. In the attending veterinarian's opinion, Impressive couldn't compete in performance events.

Invoking AQHA's hardship clauses, Brown asked that Impressive be inspected. In the late summer of 1971, two inspectors approved the stallion's muscling, way of traveling, and conformation, green-lighting his advancement from Appendix to numbered status.

Brown continued campaigning Impressive, earning multiple firsts and a

Impressive cavorting in his paddock. One-time Impressive owner Fennel Brown put the stallion into race train-ing, hoping to capital-ize on the race breeding of his Thoroughbred sire, Lucky Bar. Trainers feared that Impressive's stout build would lead to injuries, so his race training was cut short.

Photo by Don Trout, Courtesy *The Quarter Horse Journal*

score of grand championships at shows across the Midwest. By then a seasoned halter horse, Impressive had become used to traveling and being in the unfamiliar environments of various fair-grounds. At the 1972 Congress, though, the horse's nervousness, first noted by Blair Folck, nearly ended Impressive's show career prematurely.

The stallion reared in his stall, catching a front leg in the stall screen. The leg swelled, but prompt veterinary care kept the horse from aggravating the injury. Undeterred, Brown looked toward the stal-lion's future, turning down a $150,000 offer for Impressive made by a customer of Folck's. The next year, the same prospec-tive buyer doubled the offer. Again, Brown declined, tearing up the check.

"Ain't nobody in this world got the money to buy this horse," he told Folck.

In 1974, just months after Brown's death from a heart attack, AQHA hosted

the first World Championship Quarter Horse Show in Louisville, Kentucky. Impressive became the breed's first world champion aged stallion. After another show in Lincoln, Neb., Impressive retired from the show ring with 48 halter points.

A Legend Grows

By the mid-1970s, Impressive progeny had begun building the stallion's fame as a halter-horse sire. In 1975 the stallion debuted on AQHA's list of leading sires of halter winners, ranking second behind Two Eyed Jack. The next year, he took the second position on the list of leading sires of point-earning halter horses, again

Horses like Impressive Dottie, who won the 1980 reserve yearling mare world championship and 1981 2-year-old mare world championship, helped build Impressive's early reputation as a sire of champions.

Photo by Don Shugart, Courtesy *The Quarter Horse Journal*

The growing number of wins by his get earned Impressive the top spot on AQHA's leading halter sires lists.

standing behind Two Eyed Jack.

Impressive progeny such as Impressor, Mr Impressive, and The Barn Burner were among the earliest to contribute to their sire's growing reputation. Impressor, out of Miss Windy Spur by Stormy C Moore, won the 1975 yearling stallion world championship.

Mr Impressive, out of Joak Easter Gal by Joak, earned the 1976 2-year-old stallion world title.

The Barn Burner, out of Atom Ann by Voo Doo Rocket, took the 1977

yearling stallion world title.

The growing number of wins by his get earned Impressive the top spot as AQHA's leading sire of halter winners in 1979; by the next year, he ranked first on the list of halter-horse sires as well.

In 1982 Richard Brown, Fennel's son, syndicated the horse for nearly $6 million, selling 40 percent ownership to syndicate shareholders and 60 percent interest to a Dallas-based partnership. After being syndicated, Impressive stood the 1982 season at trainer Tommy Manion's Aubrey, Tex., ranch, commanding a $25,000 stud fee.

Plans to lump Impressive into a "syndicate of champions" that included Sonny Dee Bar, Top Impressive, and Impressive Poise never materialized. Impressive was then sent to Red Gate Quarter Horses at Valley View, Tex., for the 1983 breeding season. Allen and Maurine Faulkner purchased controlling interest in the stallion that summer, and

Another of Impressive's earliest progeny, The Barn Burner, out of Atom Ann, earned the 1977 yearling stallion world championship.

Photo by Waltenberry, Courtesy *The Quarter Horse Journal*

Impressive left for the Faulkners' farm in Edmond, Oklahoma. By then, he still stood for a hefty fee—$15,000. Impressive still held the top positions on AQHA's leading sires lists, having been deposed briefly in 1981 by his own son, Mr Impressive. At the decade's end, his rankings would still remain intact.

Making His Mark

Sons or daughters of Impressive claimed championships at every Quarter Horse World Show from 1975 to 1991. In halter competition, it became a given that Impressive-bred horses would fill the card of every judge who had a chance to evaluate them. Repeat world champions weren't uncommon among the stallion's get.

Examples:
- Heza Impressive, out of Lovely Face by Bar Face, earned the 1978 weanling

stallion championship, returning in 1979 to take the reserve world title for yearling stallions.
- Impressive Dottie, out of Amac Lucky Dot by Lucky Pierre, won the 1980 reserve yearling mare championship, then came back in 1981 to claim the world 2-year-old title.
- Impress On, out of Jag On Niki by Jag On, took the 1981 yearling stallion world championship and the 1982 reserve title for 2-year-olds.
- Tardee Impressive, out of My Vandy

Sons or daughters of Impressive claimed championships at every Quarter Horse World Show from 1975 to 1991.

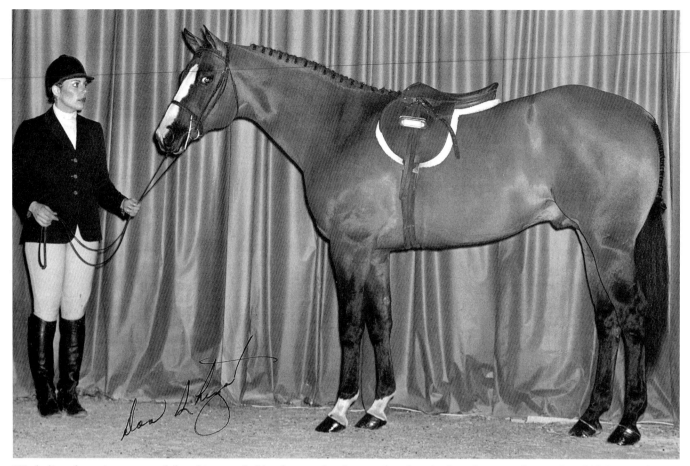

His halter champion sons and daughters made him famous, but Impressive also sired performance horses. In 1983 Impressive Chase, a 1979 stallion by Impressive and out of Josie D Chase, earned the pleasure driving world title and junior hunter under saddle reserve world title.

Photo by Don Shugart, Courtesy *The Quarter Horse Journal*

Impressive's success as a sire was so pronounced that much of his toughest competition came from his own sons.

Tardy by Tardy Too, won the 1984 world championship for 2-year-old stallions, then returned in 1988 to take the reserve aged stallion title.

- Precedence, out of Miss Snoflurry by Missle Step, earned back-to-back world championships, winning the 1987 2-year-old stallion title and 1988 3-year-old title.
- Decker Impressive was one of Impressive's most successful sons. A 1984 gelding out of Sis Roy Deck by Roy Deck, he earned no less than eight

world halter titles, including: 1986 amateur 2-year-old, 1986 open 2-year-old, 1987 youth 3-year-old, 1987 amateur 3-year-old, 1987 open 3-year-old, 1988 youth aged gelding, 1988 amateur aged gelding, and 1988 open aged gelding.

Of the stallions sired by Impressive, though, Noble Tradition, a 1987 stallion out of Magnolia Gay by Magnolia Pay, brought home the most world halter titles, winning in four age groups and taking reserve in a fifth. His resume includes: 1987 world champion weanling, 1988 world champion yearling, 1989 world champion 2-year-old, 1990 world champion 3-year-old, and 1991 reserve world champion aged stallion.

Other world champion get included Impressive Prince (1978 2-year-old stallion title), Conclusive (1981 aged stallion title),

Impress Forty Five (1978 yearling stallion title), Impressive Reward (1980 youth 3-year-old mare title), Impressive Buda (1979 yearling stallion title), Impressive Dandy (1980 2-year-old stallion title), Top Impressive (1981 3-year-old stallion title), Impressive Tardy (1980 weanling stallion title), My Impression (1981 youth yearling mare title), Zip To Impress (1983 3-year-old stallion title), Imprimis (1983 aged stallion title), and Americas Impression (1987 youth 2-year-old mare title).

In performance events, outstanding Impressive get included Impressive Chase, a 1979 stallion out of Josie D Chase by Joak. In 1983 he earned the world pleasure driving title and the reserve junior hunter under saddle world championship.

Impressive's success as a sire was so pronounced that much of his toughest competition came from his own sons. Ten years after the stallion's first appearance on AQHA's leading sires lists, seven of the top 20 leading sires of halter class winners and point-earning halter horses were sired by Impressive.

HYPP

By the early 1990s, veterinarians had begun diagnosing with increasing frequency a serious metabolic disease affecting the Quarter Horse, Paint Horse, and Appaloosa breeds. The disease: hyperkalemic periodic paralysis. Characterized by abnormal blood potassium levels, HYPP-afflicted horses can suffer periodic episodes of muscle weakness, quivering, and paralysis. In extreme cases, horses collapse or die.

Affected horses tended to have the heavily muscled conformation favored in halter competition. Both veterinarians and horsemen began noticing a pattern among the horses diagnosed. Rumors as to the disorder's origins began to spread as the number of diagnoses increased.

Studies, primarily at the University of California at Davis, concluded that HYPP was a dominant inheritable trait. HYPP couldn't be "caught"; it had to be inherited. And, researchers noted that all affected horses seemed to come

Impressive Prince, Impressive's son out of Dixie Banker (herself a Three Bars-bred mare), won the 1978 2-year-old stallion world championship.

Photo by Harold Campton, Courtesy *The Quarter Horse Journal*

from one bloodline.

Although many in the horse industry had developed what they considered a solid theory as to which bloodline was being referenced, neither AQHA nor UC Davis identified the line immediately, indicating only that it was a bloodline

Impressive Reward, by Impressive and out of Glomo, earned the 1980 youth world title for 3-year-old mares.

Photo by Dalco, Courtesy *The Quarter Horse Journal*

known for producing world champion halter horses in the three breeds mentioned. In the meantime, HYPP was transmitted to thousands of horses as of the early 1990s, according to a February 1993 *Western Horseman* article authored by Dr. Robert M. Miller.

Publicity spread through the equestrian media, even reaching mainstream publications like the *New York Times*.

Official identification of the affected bloodline didn't come until the 1992 convention of the American Association of Equine Practitioners. Speaking in Orlando, key HYPP researcher Dr. Sharon Spier identified the Impressive line as the one associated with the genetic defect that had rocked the stock horse world.

Responding to a question from the audience, Spier said, "I can tell you this: All of the horses in our test group were descendants of Impressive."

Not all Impressive-bred horses were affected, but it appeared all affected horses were Impressive-bred. With more than 100,000 horses in the extended Impressive family, a sizable—and popular—segment of the Quarter Horse breed was suddenly considered at risk from HYPP.

Horsemen were forced to reevaluate the Impressive bloodline. Some questioned whether the stock horse breeds could afford to continue incorporating horses with the HYPP defect into the registries. Owners began educating themselves on ways to manage HYPP-affected horses, using medication, exercise, and carefully monitored diets.

In the show ring, though, the Impressive line remained unhindered by the challenges facing its patriarch. The family of horses continued to set the standard in halter competition.

Legacy

Impressive progeny continue to be a powerful force in the show arena, despite widespread knowledge of the HYPP gene and its effects. Today, stallions tracing to Impressive—sons, grandsons, great-grandsons—still dominate AQHA's lists of leading halter sires.

In 1996 the AQHA Stud Book and Registration Committee officially added HYPP to the registry's list of undesirable traits and genetic defects. A definition of the disorder was added to the AQHA rulebook, and the registration papers of potentially affected foals—those tracing to Impressive—began including a notation encouraging testing to confirm the presence or absence of the HYPP gene.

In 1990 Impressive transferred to Cecil Johnson of Edmond, Okla., four years before returning to the Faulkner family. On March 20, 1995, as his last foals were hitting the ground, Impressive died at age 26, under the ownership of Maurine Faulkner. The stallion sired 2,250 foals in

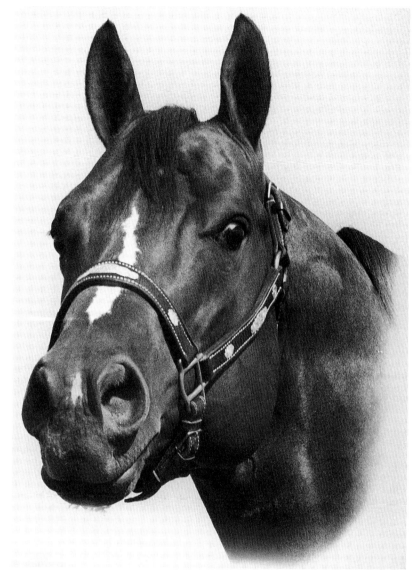

Even after being linked to the genetic defect HYPP, Impressive remains an icon in the stock-horse world. The Impressive family continues to be a dominant force in the halter arena.

Photo by Darol Dickinson, Courtesy *The Quarter Horse Journal*

24 crops. Among his get were 846 halter-point earners who claimed a total of 19,038.5 points. Though not as well known for producing saddle horses, Impressive sired 268 performance-point earners who earned a total of 5,624 performance points. The stallion sired 29 world champions who earned 38 titles.

15 FILLINIC

By Mike
Boardman

**She established
a dynasty of
cow horses.**

SHE ARRIVED at Greg Ward's modest Poplar, Calif., training facility after being purchased at auction by Basque businessman Frank Maitia. Her past was questionable.

Several owners had passed her on, each apparently unable to handle the filly's explosive energy. That energy was the first thing Ward noticed as he rode across the pasture to find the refined little mare tied to his fence and creating a minor dust storm, pawing a hole in the ground deep enough to make a gopher proud.

Even her pedigree was questionable. Several generations back there appears a mysterious mare who had wandered in off the Arizona desert and was simply known as the Fiedler Mare #33. Now that mystery mare's fourth-generation offspring stood wide-eyed and shooting sparks in Ward's yard. Her name was Fillinic.

Greg Ward and Fillinic: "The mare that made me as a trainer," said Ward. "They say it's 50 percent the horse and 50 percent the trainer, but with her it was more like Fillinic 70 percent and me 30 percent."

**Photo by
Anna Robertson**

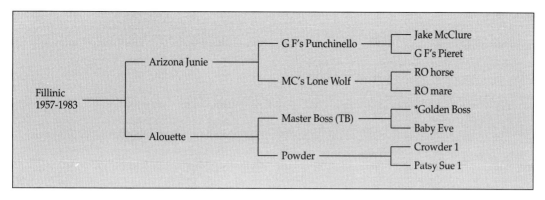

			Jake McClure
		G F's Punchinello	
			G F's Pieret
	Arizona Junie		
			RO horse
		MC's Lone Wolf	
			RO mare
Fillinic 1957-1983			
			*Golden Boss
		Master Boss (TB)	
			Baby Eve
	Alouette		
			Crowder 1
		Powder	
			Patsy Sue 1

Unusual Beginnings

Her AQHA papers indicate that K.B. McMicken of Goodyear Farms in Litchfield, Ariz., bred her. Horses from Goodyear Farms had been proving themselves with horsemen from all over the United States for many years. Records kept by McMicken show that he bred well in excess of 500 head between 1920 and 1959. Many went to the U.S. Army, while many more became polo ponies, jumpers, and show horses. Others found fame as rope horses, taking Arizona cowboys to the pay window year after year. During the Great Depression, Goodyear horses were bringing $500 and more. McMicken sold top-quality horses to top-quality horsemen. Tom Finley was a buyer, as was Fat Jones, who bought for the Hollywood movie business.

Fillinic's breeder is an interesting contributor to the Quarter Horse of today. K.B. McMicken, cousin of the then-president of Goodyear Tire and Rubber Company, had been sent to Arizona to grow cotton, desperately needed in the manufacture of tires during World War I. A tireless and dedicated worker, he soon had over 17,000 acres producing cotton and turned to other projects.

McMicken noticed, it is told, that the demand for good horses was not being met. With his typical thirst for knowledge and marked ability to study a situation and bring change, McMicken set about reading all he could on pedigrees and the genetics of horse breeding. He purchased a number of mares, sifting down to two who met his standards: Anita, a bay Standardbred pacer by Oh So, by Nut Wood, who could do the mile in 2:18; and the Fiedler Mare #33.

Rancher Herbert Meyers had caught up this mystery mare from the desert and sold her to Fred Fiedler, who gave her the name before selling her to Goodyear

Halter and Performance Record: AQHA point-earner in working cow horse; 1966 California Reined Cow Horse Association Open Bridle Champion; two-time Cow Palace Open Hackamore Champion; Cow Palace Open Bridle Champion.

Progeny Record:

Foal Crops: 10   Foals Registered: 10

Farms. McMicken believed that she was all or at least part Thoroughbred. It was the cross on the Fiedler Mare #33 that three generations later produced Fillinic's dam, Alouette, by a Thoroughbred, Master Boss, who was a son of the imported stallion, *Golden Boss. Powder, the dam of Alouette, had a pedigree that twice went to the great (King) Possum, as well as to a Morgan mare and an Arab, *Jameel, imported from the Middle East by the Turkish ambassador to the United States. It is perhaps from this exotic background that Fillinic came by her amazing energy.

Although many Quarter Horse breeders of the 1990s might look askance at Fillinic's pedigree, it should be noted that although her dam, Alouette, did not have a performance record herself, she was a full sister to Dusty Boss, who won the Arizona Cutting Horse of the Year title in 1948 with Goodyear Farms trainer Hank Alrich. McMicken's son Bob gave a reining demonstration on Dusty Boss before the Shah of Iran in a state visit to Phoenix. Alouette herself was judged Arizona Broodmare of the Year in 1950.

Alouette was bred twice to Arizona Junie, producing MC's Sky Rocket in

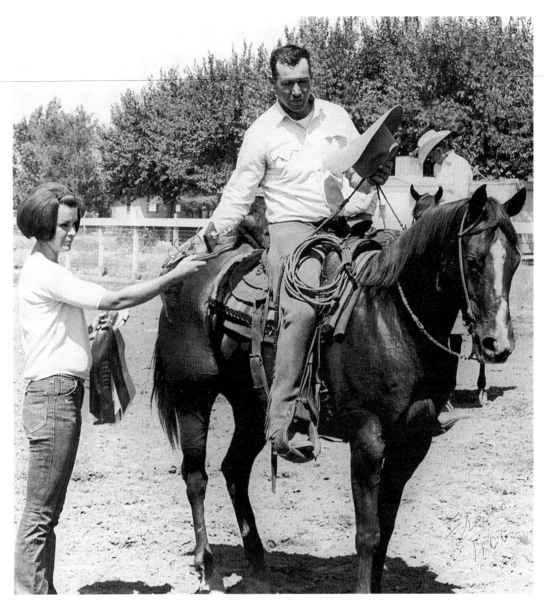

Greg Ward and Fillinic in Fresno, Calif., in 1966. Fillinic was a winner in hackamore and bridle classes, and was the 1966 California Reined Cow Horse Association Open Bridle Champion. Because of some bad cuts on her hind legs and one across her nose, Ward concluded the high-strung mare had been in some wrecks before he got her. The scar across her nose is visible in this photo, as is legendary horseman Don Dodge in the background.

Photo by Ford's Photography

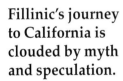

Fillinic's journey to California is clouded by myth and speculation.

1956 and Fillinic in 1957, before being sold at the Goodyear Farms dispersal in the late '50s to a rancher from Oakdale, California. She produced two more foals there, before having to be put down after breaking a leg.

Fillinic's sire, Arizona Junie, was a descendant of Anita, the other foundation broodmare for Goodyear Farms. Bob McMicken states that all Anita's foals showed a lot of speed, and he recalls match-racing several of them, especially

a bald-faced mare, Masquerade, who was to be the granddam of G F's Punchinello, the sire of Arizona Junie.

Cutting horse trainers Hank Alrich and Grady Stewart told Greg Ward they had seen G F's Punchinello cutting in an Arizona feedlot without a rider. Bearing an uncanny resemblance to his sire, Arizona Junie stamped his sons and daughters with his prepotent conformation and ability.

Fillinic's journey to California is clouded by myth and speculation, but research and AQHA records indicate that she was sold as a yearling through Glendale, Ariz., horse trader Roy Harelson to Bertha and Albert Plaster of Little Horse Thief Ranch, Summit, California. Two more owners followed in short order before Frank Maitia purchased her and tied her to Greg Ward's fence.

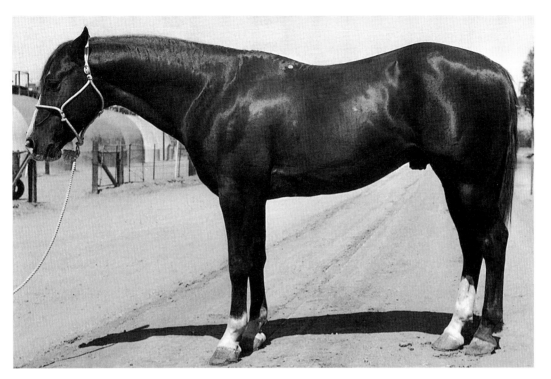

Arizona Junie, the sire of Fillinic. Arizona Junie was a descendant of Anita, one of two foundation broodmares for Goodyear Farms in Litchfield, Arizona. Goodyear Farms' other foundation broodmare was the Fiedler Mare #33, a mysterious mare of unknown origins who wandered in off the Arizona desert.

Photo Courtesy Margaret McMicken-Bartol

*Fillinic's dam, Alouette, traced to the mysterious Fiedler Mare #33, who was believed to be part or all Thoroughbred. Alouette was by the Thoroughbred stallion Master Boss, by *Golden Boss. Alouette was named Arizona Broodmare of the Year in 1950.*

Photo by Richard Schaus

Alouette's full brother Dusty Boss was Arizona Cutting Horse of the Year in 1948. In 1950, Bob McMicken and the gelding (shown here) performed a reining demonstration in a command performance for the Shah of Iran. McMicken is the son of K.B. McMicken, the mastermind behind Goodyear Farms' breeding program.

Photo Courtesy Margaret McMicken-Bartol

Fillinic was hair-trigger quick and took a lot of riding.

The Perfect Match

It was to be a perfect match—the hot little mare and the very calm, very savvy young horseman. Ward (who at the time was part-time ranch help and part-time horse trainer with just two outside horses in the barn) had been looking hard for a prospect that would put his name up there with the winning trainers of the day. Now she stood digging holes in his yard, and there was something about her that made Ward feel he had found his star.

Barely 14.3 hands, huge-hipped, short-coupled, and perhaps a bit short through the neck, Fillinic was badly cut up on her back legs and had a large cut across her nose right where a bosal would sit. She'd already been in some wrecks, Ward decided. But after only three days, he said he "knew I had something special."

Fillinic was hair-trigger quick and took a lot of riding. Ward had the time and patience to harness that energy. He was rewarded with a smooth, fluid mare who proved she had what it took to be a winner. He approached Maitia and asked to buy the mare, but was offered a partnership instead. Ward wanted to own this special mare himself. Maitia, who had no wish to sell her, priced Fillinic at $3,000, knowing Ward couldn't possibly come up with that kind of money.

They say that hunger made the monkey eat red pepper. Hunger to own Fillinic forced Greg Ward to go to his mother and ask for a loan. Mrs. Ward cashed a small annuity, believing wholeheartedly in her talented young son, and Ward proudly took ownership of the mare who would put him on the map. Could it have been that the high-strung Fillinic had proven too much of a challenge for the earlier owners, needing the sure and steady hand of the "Master," Greg Ward, the man who was to make Fillinic, just as Fillinic was to make him?

Armed with grit, determination, and a share of his mother's belief in him, Ward

Fillinic's paternal grandsire, G F's Punchinello. Cutting horse trainers Hank Alrich and Grady Stewart told Greg Ward they once saw G F's Punchinello cutting in an Arizona feedlot without a rider.

Photo Courtesy Margaret McMicken-Bartol

Sugar Vandy, a 1963 chestnut stallion by Sugar Bars and out of the Vandy daughter Vandy's Katsy, proved to be a magical cross with Fillinic. Together they produced six gifted daughters, who later passed their talents to their offspring.

Photo by Bill McNabb Jr.

Springinic, the 1970 daughter of Fillinic and Sugar Vandy, won the open hackamore division of the 1974 and 1975 Grand National at San Francisco's Cow Palace.

Photo by Fallaw, Courtesy Laura Ward

Ward rode his explosive little mare everywhere he could.

took to seriously training the refined chestnut mare. With the British Pony Club Handbook (the only book he ever read on training, according to Ward) as his only study book, he set about making the frenetic mare into a working cow horse deluxe. As much pure horseman as horse trainer, Ward prided himself on developing a horse into a responsive and willing partner. He also prided himself on never clipping bridle paths or nose whiskers on his horses. He had never been seen cleaning a saddle, and he didn't care if a horse walked off while he was mounting. He believed they had enough to think about already as youngsters. Fillinic had plenty to think about, and she took it all in. Ward rode his explosive little mare

everywhere he could, in the mountains working cattle, branding for neighbors, and roping on her with friends at night.

To the Show Pen

Always a bit wild-eyed and certainly high-strung, Fillinic, with Ward channeling her explosive energy into a controlled tornado, hit the show circuit and started to win, and win, and win some more. Legendary horseman and trainer Ronnie Richards said, "To beat them, you had better be well-mounted and then some!"

Ward kept Fillinic in the hackamore as long as possible, ever careful of her badly scarred nose. Before her hackamore days were over, Fillinic took the prestigious open hackamore championship at San Francisco's Cow Palace, the largest show on the Pacific Coast. To prove it was not a fluke, she came back and did it again a year later. The following year, well into the bridle under Ward's masterful hands, Fillinic was back at the Cow Palace to win

the open bridle championship.

Fillinic and Greg Ward were three times California Reined Cow Horse Association Top Ten finalists, and in 1966 Fillinic stood at the top of the ranks as Open Bridle Champion. In every arena, from CRCHA to AQHA, Fillinic proved to be a winner. Even after starting her career as a brood-mare, Fillinic still came to show and win when asked. But in 1968, Fillinic was per-manently retired from the show pen. She took her place at the head of what would be one of the most successful breeding programs ever established around a single broodmare. She had made Greg Ward one of the most respected young trainers in the reined cow horse business, and now she would add to his luster through Ward Ranch-bred horses for generations to come.

(*Note:* The California Reined Cow Horse Association is now the National Reined Cow Horse Association.)

Fillinic's Brood

Fillinic proved to be an easy breeder and crossed on a number of stallions, always producing foals who had her unique stamp. They were highly energetic, natu-rally athletic, and wonderful cow horses, hard-workers who were willing to learn. But most of all, they were all show horses.

Her first foal, a bay stallion named Amynic, so impressed Ward (who had bred Fillinic to Wayward Win without any real forethought) that he decided to breed

her to another hot young horse he had in training, Sugar Vandy. This nick would prove to be magical, producing one major performer after another.

• Sugarnic was first, foaled in 1969. The sorrel mare set the standard for her future siblings by winning the 1972 CRCHA Snaffle Bit Futurity. Sugarnic was the 1974 and 1975 CRCHA Reserve Champion Bridle Horse and the 1975 and 1976 CRCHA World Champion Stock Horse. When bred to Doc's Remedy, Sug-arnic produced Sugar Remedy, the high-point mare at the 1981 CRCHA Snaffle Bit Futurity. In turn, Sugar Remedy was the dam of the 1988 NRCHA SBF Reserve Champion, Peppy Remedy.

A black 1995 son of Peppy Remedy and Reminic, named Reminics Pep, was Greg Ward's partner during the 1998 NRCHA Futurity. "Magic" and Ward brought the seasoned and knowledge-able crowd to their feet as they put on the most memorable and, sadly, the final performance of Ward's long and illustrious career.

Unknown to many, Greg Ward was dying of cancer and had only a few

Sugarnic, Fillinic's first foal by her best match, Sugar Vandy, in action with Laura Ward. The 1969 sorrel mare won the 1972 CRCHA Snaf-fle Bit Futurity and was the 1975 and 1976 CRCHA World Cham-pion Stock Horse.

Photo by Anna Robertson

In 1976, Fillinic was bred to a Thoroughbred race horse, Doc Marcus. The Wards had hoped to race the resulting gelding, Bioninic, but his race career ended after he shinbucked just before his first out. Instead, Greg Ward started the horse under saddle. Here, the gelding is shown winning the ladies bridle class at a show in Bakersfield, Calif., in 1984, with Greg's daughter, Wende Ward.

Photo by Barclay Livestock Photography, Courtesy Laura Ward

short weeks left to live. He had to be lifted into the saddle to give the ride of his life, and he died a few months later.

- Springinic, second of the six daughters of Fillinic and Sugar Vandy, hit the ground in 1970 and followed her dam's lead by winning the hackamore division at the Cow Palace twice. Later part of the broodmare band, the sorrel mare produced a string of offspring who would set the standard for years to come.

- Next to come along was Wininic, a 1972 chestnut mare who made her contribution to the record books by being a semifinalist at the 1975 CRCHA Futurity. She produced another generation of stars, including Master Remedy, winner of over $177,000 and a member of the CRCHA leading sires list many times.

- Fillinic's 1974 filly by Sugar Vandy, Picinic, was shown just long enough to prove her performance ability before she, too, went to the breeding farm to uphold the prolific producing tradition of her dam and sisters.

- A full sister to Picinic, Quickinic, foaled in 1975, followed in that family tradition with a long list of performers to her credit.

- The last product of the Fillinic-Sugar Vandy cross, the 1976 sorrel mare Anuthernic, kept the legend alive by not only producing reined cow horses and reiners, but also sending one son to the 1997 AQHA World Show in heeling. A daughter of Anuthernic, the brilliant Pepinic, was reserve champion at the 1983 NCHA Futurity before producing Pepinics Dually by Dual Doc.

- Bioninic, a 1977 sorrel gelding. Greg Ward liked Thoroughbred blood in his horses, believing that the only time it hurt was when it was not there. To support his beliefs and satisfy his desire to send one of Fillinic's offspring to the track, he bred her to a Thoroughbred horse owned by long-time speed horse breeder Ed C. Allred. Doc Marcus, the stakes-winning stallion chosen by the Wards, went back to the great Man O' War twice in his pedigree, along with Blenheim II, The Tetrarch, Nearco, and Ultimis.

Bioninic resulted from this breeding and lived up to expectations. He was sent to noted race trainer and Ward family friend Blane Schvaneveldt to be made ready for some upcoming futurities. Shin-bucked just before his first race, Bioninic returned home to rest and recuperate. After Ward saw Bioninic playing in a pasture, it was decided, belatedly, to start the horse and prepare him for the CRCHA Futurity. Plagued with bad luck, Bioninic, a hot favorite for the 1980 event, jumped out of his stall the night before the finals, causing enough soreness to take him out of contention.

- The spring of 1977 saw Fillinic bred to NCHA Derby finalist, Doc's Remedy, producing Reminic, yet another Ward Ranch superstar. Reminic blazed a path across the country, earning in excess of $90,000 in the cutting pen. The bay stallion went on to be a major sire of NCHA, NRCHA, and NRHA performers, and to show up on the leading sires lists of these associations 14 times.
- The Wards bred Fillinic for the last time in 1981 to Dual Doc, a Ward-bred son of Doc's Remedy. The pretty bay filly from this match was referred to as "the Fillinic filly." Soon shortened to Fillynic, she was a Ward Ranch favorite. After a short performance career (as was the norm for Fillinic daughters) with earnings of over $50,000, she joined the numerous Fillinic daughters and granddaughters in the breeding program, where she had three foals before being found dead in her pasture of unknown causes.

Fillinic's Legacy

Bobby Cotta, a young apprentice trainer with the Wards, was out feeding early one fall morning when he found Fillinic, surrounded by other mares, down on her side and unable to rise. It was very apparent that Fillinic had a severely broken leg and would have to be euthanized.

The last of the first generation, Fillynic was originally nicknamed "the Fillinic filly." The 1982 daughter of Fillinic and Dual Doc was a Ward Ranch favorite and earned more than $50,000 before joining her dam and sisters in the broodmare band.

Photo Courtesy Laura Ward

Greg Ward openly shed tears as Fillinic was laid to rest in the front yard of the Ward Ranch, under a boulder with a plaque reflecting Greg and Laura Ward's love of this wild-eyed little mare who had given them so much. The plaque reads:

FILLINIC 1957 - 1983 … A truly incredible mare, whose heart and spirit became the foundation of the Ward Ranch. Her bright personality, sensitivity, and "quick as a deer" ability was passed down to her sons and

Wards and Fillinics have dominated snaffle bit cow horse futurities. Shown here at the 1981 Snaffle Bit Futurity are two Fillinic granddaughters, Spring Remedy, with Wende Ward, and Sugar Remedy, with Greg Ward; a Doc's Remedy stallion, Home Remedy, with John Ward; and Laura and Amy Ward, standing. Greg and Sugar Remedy, a daughter of Sugarnic, won the event; the mare later produced the 1988 NRCHA SBF Reserve Champ, Peppy Remedy. **WH Photo**

Fillinic is buried in the front yard of the Wards' Tulare, Calif., ranch.
Photo Courtesy Mike Boardman

daughters—Amynic, Sugarnic, Springinic, Wininic, Picinic, Quickinic, Anuthernic, Bioninic, Reminic and her last—Fillynic. It has continued on in her grandchildren, and will continue through the generations to come. A man is lucky to have one great horse in his lifetime—she gave us a lifetime of greatness … we will never forget her. With all our love to Fillinic. Greg and Laura Ward.

Walking through the shed-row of Ward's busy training operation today or in the quiet, verdant pastures of the beautiful breeding farm at River Ranch—surrounded by first-, second-, and on down to fifth- and now sixth-generation Fillinic progeny—one has to pause and realize that over 200 descendants of this amazing little mare have been major money-earners in NCHA, NRHA, NRCHA, and AQHA events.

This is impressive enough, but one cannot forget the many other Fillinic offspring who have given good service on ranches all across the nation. The many who have carried the Fillinic name to

Doc's Remedy (left, with Greg Ward), a 1973 son of Doc Bar and Teresa Tivio, played a key role in Greg Ward's breeding program. For example, when Fillinic was bred to Doc's Remedy, she produced the great Reminic; and when Sugarnic was bred to Doc's Remedy, she produced Sugar Remedy. Both Reminic and Sugar Remedy appear in the pedigree of Reminics Pep ("Magic"), Greg's winning mount at the 1998 SBF. This picture was taken at the 1976 NCHA Futurity where Greg and Doc's Remedy tied with Tom Lyons and Doc's Oak (right) for fourth place. Doc's Oak, by Doc Bar and out of Susie's Bay, by Poco Tivio, also went on to become a renowned sire. **Photo by Jerry Matacale**

Canada, Europe, and Australia are too numerous to count. It is doubtful that any one mare in Quarter Horse history has done so much in such a short time.

A stallion has many opportunities each year to leave his mark, yet a mare has only one. Fillinic left her mark on every one of her 10 sons and daughters, and they in turn passed along Fillinic's unique mark to each and every generation following them.

Ward had looked hopefully for more horses carrying Fillinic's pedigree, even charging Arizona horseman and longtime friend Grady Stewart with the responsibility of seeking some out for him. Ironically, they never looked in the right places. Trainer and friend Ronnie Richards had a stallion out

of a mare who was very similarly bred to Fillinic. Well-known Oregon breeder Dan Opie had a half-sister to Fillinic.

Greg, son John, and daughter Wende have absolutely dominated the snaffle bit futurities over the years, riding several generations of Fillinic's offspring. Although Greg is gone now, John, with his effervescent grin and firm belief in the Fillinic dynasty, coupled with sister Wende's support, is confidently continuing the tradition of their father and his great little mare, Fillinic.

16 ZIPPO PINE BAR

By Betsy Lynch

He produced a dynasty of horses with almost universal appeal.

ZIPPO PINE Bar was exactly the right horse at exactly the right time. As an individual, he was pretty, personable, willing, and athletic. As a sire, he passed these qualities on with such astonishing regularity that he produced a dynasty of horses with almost universal appeal.

He became known in the 1980s and '90s as the pleasure horse sire. But to label Zippo Pine Bar as simply a sire of pleasure horses would perhaps sell him short. His offspring have demonstrated a diversity of talents. They have been loved and promoted by youth, amateurs, and professionals alike, who continue to add weight and volume to a record book that is an inch thick and growing daily. Zippo Pine Bar has had such a profound impact on the Quarter Horse, Paint, and Appaloosa breeds that his story won't be complete for generations to come.

Background

Of course, he had all the elements for greatness. Foaled in 1969, Zippo Pine Bar was by AAA-running horse stallion Zippo Pat Bars and out of the AQHA Champion and four-time AQHA Champion-producing mare Dollie Pine. He was bred by

An AQHA Champion and high-point title winner in western riding, Zippo Pine Bar passed on his athleticism and disposition to his winning Quarter Horse, Appaloosa, and Paint offspring. As of September 1999, his Quarter Horse progeny had earned more than 50,000 show ring points and 50 reserve and world championships.

Photo by Don Shugart, Courtesy Bob Perry Quarter Horses Inc.

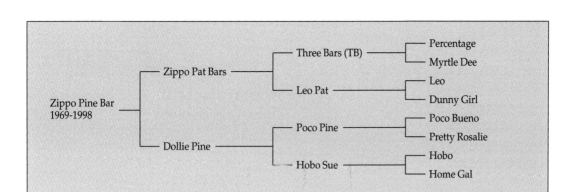

```
                                                    ┌─ Percentage
                            ┌─ Three Bars (TB) ──────┤
          ┌─ Zippo Pat Bars ┤                        └─ Myrtle Dee
          │                 │
          │                 │                        ┌─ Leo
          │                 └─ Leo Pat ──────────────┤
Zippo Pine Bar                                       └─ Dunny Girl
1969-1998 ┤
          │                                          ┌─ Poco Bueno
          │                 ┌─ Poco Pine ────────────┤
          │                 │                        └─ Pretty Rosalie
          └─ Dollie Pine ───┤
                            │                        ┌─ Hobo
                            └─ Hobo Sue ─────────────┤
                                                     └─ Home Gal
```

Lloyd Geweke of Ord, Nebraska. The horse's pedigree boasts a long line of legends, including Three Bars (TB) and Leo on his sire's side, and AQHA Champion Poco Pine, a leading sire of AQHA Champions by Poco Bueno, on his dam's side. Credit for the outstanding genetic mix belongs in large measure to Paul Curtner of Jacksboro, Tex., who bred both Zippo Pat Bars and Dollie Pine.

Nebraska farmer and rancher Norman Reynolds and his business partner, L.S. Whaley of California, acquired Zippo Pine Bar from Lloyd Geweke in the fall of 1969. Sadly, Geweke was dispersing his herd after a car crash had claimed the life of his college-aged son, a young man who had been an avid student of horse husbandry. Reynolds and Whaley attended the sale hoping to find a stallion to cross on a band of broodmares that Whaley had acquired from a business associate gone broke.

Reynolds studied the sale catalog and found two horses of particular interest. One was an older stallion by Poco Pine named Pine's Chico; the other was a weanling, Zippo Pine Bar. Whaley bought Pine's Chico, who was somewhat crippled, and the two men also partnered on Zippo Pine Bar—perhaps as a bit of insurance. Although Zippo wouldn't be old enough to breed for several years, Reynolds was struck not only by the colt's pedigree, but also his good looks and naturally friendly disposition.

Reynolds and Whaley paid $1,650 for Zippo Pine Bar that day, which Reynolds thought was plenty for a weanling when many of the foals were bringing $500-$600. Reynolds also bid on Zippo's dam, Dollie Pine, but dropped out once the bidding surpassed $2,500. He and Whaley decided that they already had enough mares.

Dollie Pine sold for over $3,000, and

Halter and Performance Record: Performance Register of Merit; AQHA Champion; 1972 High-Point Junior Western Riding Horse and High-Point Junior Western Riding Stallion; Superior in Western Pleasure; National Snaffle Bit Association Hall of Fame; American Quarter Horse Hall of Fame.

Progeny Record: (as of September 1999)

Foal Crops: 26	Halter Registers of Merit: 14
Foals Registered: 1,646	Superior Halter Awards: 5
AQHA Champions: 10	Performance Point-Earners: 1,308
World Champions: 13	Performance Points Earned: 48,788
Halter Point-Earners: 180	Performance Registers of Merit: 790
Halter Points Earned: 1,060.5	Superior Performance Awards: 274
Total Lifetime AQHA Incentive Fund Earnings: $813,896.27	

although Reynolds regretted not buying her, he eventually acquired the foal she was carrying at the time. That filly was a full sister to Zippo Pine Bar named Scarborough Fair. The mare earned her AQHA Championship and later produced the halter champions Zip To Impress and Impressive Zippo.

When Zippo Pine Bar came to live at the Reynolds farm in Lexington, Neb., he immediately became the hobby of Norman Reynolds' daughter, Linda. She fitted the colt and showed him in halter classes as a yearling. "He was a real pet," Reynolds recalled with a chuckle. He

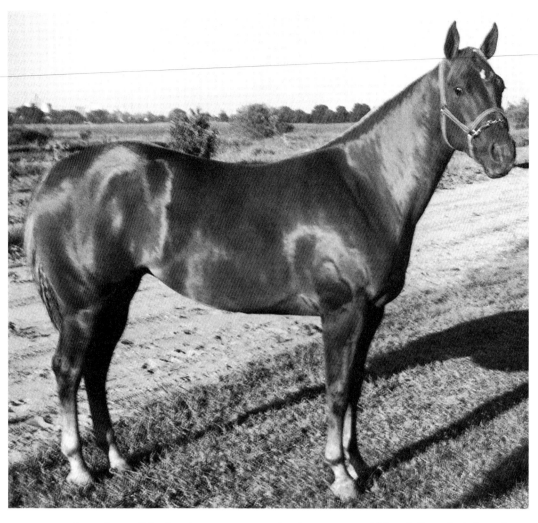

A 1960 daughter of the Poco Bueno son Poco Pine, Dollie Pine earned her own AQHA Championship before producing four AQHA Champions, one of whom was Zippo Pine Bar, her 1969 son by Zippo Pat Bars. In this photo, undated but probably taken during her show career in the mid-1960s, the sorrel mare had won the reserve champion mare title at a show in Glen Rose, Texas. She was owned at the time by B.D. Green of Gorman, Texas.

Photo Courtesy *The Quarter Horse Journal*

was so gentle and sensible that it never gave Reynolds a moment's pause that his daughter was handling and showing a young stallion.

Training and Showing

When Zippo turned 2, Reynolds asked Bill Keyser to take the colt for training. Keyser had built a good reputation training and showing horses for Howard Pitzer. He had struck out on his own and was running his training operation in Ord. As a neighbor, Keyser was very familiar with the quality of horses who

had come out of Lloyd Geweke's breeding program and was delighted to take Zippo. Keyser was the first person to put a leg over the horse and the only one to show him under saddle.

"He was a real easy horse to break," recalled Keyser, whose first goal was to prepare the 2-year-old for the Nebraska Pleasure Futurity. "He didn't ever buck. But for a long time, I told Norman that we had him entered in the wrong futurity. Zippo had quite a lot of energy and he really liked to go. He was such a long time in slowing down, I thought we needed to have him in one of the running horse futurities," he laughed. "Then all of a sudden, one day it dawned on him that I wanted him to go slow. It happened overnight, and he was really solid from then on."

When Zippo Pine Bar debuted at the Nebraska Pleasure Futurity, the colt won both go-rounds and the finals—a

"Zippo Pine Bar was almost like a ballerina when he moved," said Ann Myers, owner of the Zippo son Zips Chocolate Chip. "Zippo had that cadence-driven movement and easy lope. He didn't have to think about it or work at it. And he reproduced that."

Photo by Don Shugart, Courtesy Bob Perry Quarter Horses Inc.

primer for things to come.

"He was a really, really good mover," Keyser confirmed. "That was his prime asset. He was so smooth at a trot and lope, and really well broke. He didn't make mistakes. He had a real nice headset and traveled pretty flat, although at that time, the horses were allowed to be a little more natural, so he didn't carry his head as low as the pleasure horses do now.

"And I'll tell you what. He did spoil you. There was one period when I was showing him as a 3-year-old that he won seven big pleasure classes in a row," Keyser continued. "And when you rode Zippo, you didn't ride for second place. You went in feeling like you had a real shot at winning every class."

But there is one recollection that after more than 25 years still makes Bill Keyser laugh, and it wasn't a moment of glory. He and Zippo were at the Denver National Western Stock Show. They had won their elimination round in the western pleasure class, and the finals had been slated during the evening rodeo performance.

"I was feeling really good, and, of course, I thought we had a really good shot of winning this thing," Keyser remembered. "Zippo was fine out behind

in the warm-up area, but as soon as I rode through the gate, I felt him just kind of catch his breath. We barely touched the ground for the first three times around the arena. He was scared to death. Consequently, we didn't do well," he chuckled. "There was just something about the acoustics in the coliseum; Denver can be a spooky place for a lot of horses."

Despite this momentary lapse, Zippo Pine Bar was remarkably consistent as a show horse. Keyser also realized early on that Zippo was a exceptionally gifted athlete. For one thing, the stallion could change leads effortlessly, and Keyser knew he would make an outstanding western riding horse.

"I've been training horses for a living forever," he said. "In that time, I've had two horses who were the kind of lead changers that Zippo was—and the other was Two Eyed Jack. Zippo was just so

The back of this photo has two descriptions: "Bill Keyser and Zippo Pine Bar, high-point halter horse for Reynolds & Whaley" and "Zippo after winning the Nebraska pleasure futurity." Nebraska rancher Norman Reynolds partnered on Zippo as a weanling with Californian L.S. Whaley. Bill Keyser started Zippo as a 2-year-old, and their first competition was the Nebraska pleasure futurity. They won both go-rounds and the final.

(Note: This photo was torn at Zippo's right front leg. That's why his cannon bone looks like it has a dip in it.)

Photo by Hughes, Courtesy Bill Keyser

clean in his leads. When you asked him to change, you had both of them, just bang. And you could change leads 15 times if you wanted to and you'd still be going the same speed."

When Zippo was 3, Keyser showed him to the AQHA Honor Roll in junior western riding. He also completed his AQHA Championship. When Zippo's show career ended that year, he had earned 33 halter points, 112 performance points, a Superior in western pleasure, and the titles of 1972 High-Point Junior Western Riding Horse and High-Point Western Riding Stallion in the nation.

At the same time Keyser was campaigning Zippo Pine Bar in halter, western pleasure, and western riding, he had also begun to work the horse on cattle. He had high hopes for Zippo.

"When I first started cutting on him, he was doing things so hard, I was afraid he was going to hurt himself," recalled Keyser. "He had lots of cow and was a real physical horse. I think in my own mind, he could have been a tremendous cutting horse if we had kept going with him. But by the end of his 3-year-old year, he had already accomplished so much that Norman wanted to start breeding

Bill Keyser and 3-year-old Zippo at the 1972 All American Quarter Horse Congress. "He was a really, really good mover," said Keyser. "He didn't make mistakes. There was one period when I was showing him as a 3-year-old that he won seven big pleasure classes in a row. And when you rode Zippo, you didn't ride for second place. You went in feeling like you had a real shot at winning every class."

Photo by Harold Campton, Courtesy Norman Reynolds

mares with him," explained Keyser. "I had no trouble understanding that. I was fortunate to have had him for two years."

The Breeding Barn

When Zippo went home to Lexington, he began his career as a sire. Pine's Chico had suffered a mishap and died, so Zippo's services were needed to cover the ranch mares. Norman Reynolds also stood Zippo to outside mares for $150, and he wasn't opposed to using the stallion's services to barter for goods, services, and even livestock.

The demand for breedings wasn't great at that point, Reynolds admitted, and they weren't really doing much to promote him. The fact was, the Reynoldses were busy running a feedlot and farming operation; the horse business was a minor concern. The mares who came to his court were primarily working mares of no particular lineage, not the blue-blood show stock that would later fill his book. But friends and neighbors were certainly enjoying improvements in their ranching stock thanks to Zippo.

"I didn't really know what we had until one day, when we were rounding up cattle

with the area ranchers, I looked around and saw that just about everybody was riding a Zippo. That gave me an indication that he was doing a good job," said Reynolds. "We bred him to everything and anything. Then, when he got more popular, people started bringing good mares to him, producers."

Nevertheless, it appeared that Zippo could make the most of any match.

"I remember particularly when they brought an old King-bred mare named Poco Mary Jane. If you ever decided you didn't want to breed a mare, she would have been it. She was small and kind of homely. Yet her resulting filly, Quitabitazip, was the one who Keith Whistle won the Quarter Horse Congress Pleasure Futurity with. She won a bunch.

"I decided then that I couldn't say 'no' to any horse. I don't know who would be smart enough to know which

Bob and Ann Perry, here receiving Zippo's National Snaffle Bit Association Hall of Fame award, purchased the stallion at age 15. Norman Reynolds decided the Perrys could handle Zippo's breeding business better than his family could. The Perrys then moved Zippo to their brand-new broodmare facility in Valley View, Tex., where he lived until his death in 1998.

Photo by Pennau Photography, Courtesy *The Quarter Horse Journal*

ones not to breed," Reynolds explained with a chuckle.

Zippo's Show Offspring

While Midwestern ranchers were enjoying the smooth gaits and easy dispositions of Zippo's get, several of his offspring were also finding their way into the show ring. In 1976, Zippo's Shasta, out of Social Shasta, was Zippo's first big winner. Interestingly, she claimed her title for her beauty rather than her movement; Zippo's

Shasta was named the reserve world champion 2-year-old halter mare.

In 1977, Four L Roxzip, a gelding out of Roxie Pine, was the AQHA reserve world champion junior western pleasure horse. Then, in 1978, Zippo's Jan, trained and shown by none other than Bill Keyser, became Zippo Pine Bar's first AQHA Champion. She also earned her Superior in western pleasure.

Even with these successes, most people hadn't really started to pay close attention to pleasure horse pedigrees. Getting a good pleasure horse was mostly left to chance rather than the result of selective breeding.

But when amateur rider Lu Ann Paul began turning heads with a remarkable bay gelding named Melody Zipper, the tide began to change. In 1979, Melody Zipper was the AQHA reserve all-around high-point amateur horse and second on the Honor Roll in western pleasure and hunter under saddle. In 1980, Melody Zipper topped that by being named the high-point all-around amateur horse in the nation. Paul also won a world championship with him and was the AQHA year-end high-point winner in hunt seat equitation, western horsemanship, and hunter under saddle, and reserve high-point in western pleasure.

During the next four years, Melody Zipper won nine more world championships or reserve championships, and seven more national high-point or reserve high-point titles. In 1983, he was the World Show All-Around Amateur Horse. By the time Melody Zipper was retired from the show ring, he had accumulated 1,900 AQHA points.

In the early 1980s, people started to recognize the pattern. Zippo's offspring were winning consistently in major competition. What's more, the pleasure industry was emerging as a prestigious, popular, and lucrative segment of the show horse market. Pleasure classes had mass appeal because virtually anyone and everyone could participate. Major futurities were being organized that paid substantial cash and prizes to the winners.

When Quitabitazip won the Quarter Horse Congress 2-Year-Old Pleasure Futurity in 1983, the Zippo Pine Bar buzz began in earnest. The filly won approximately $70,000 in futurity earnings, and that got people's attention.

Mr Zippo Pine became the next phenomenon. The gelding was successfully shown by Jody Galyean for Darrell and Jan Saul of Arkansas. His reported pleasure earnings are an estimated $200,000.

Before owning a Zippo became an all-out craze, Darrell Saul was among the first to recognize their performance potential and went to Nebraska on a scouting mission. He called Norman Reynolds and showed up at the Reynoldses' on Thanksgiving Day to look at prospects. Reynolds said he wouldn't talk horses until after the football game. "Nebraska was playing Oklahoma," he said by way of explanation. So Saul watched the game, enjoyed a holiday dinner with the Reynolds family, and was finally taken on a tour of the horse pens.

Saul bought at least a dozen prospects that trip, mostly weanlings and coming 2-year-olds. Among them was his future $200,000 futurity and maturity winner Mr Zippo Pine. For a number of years, Saul returned to Nebraska each year to buy Reynolds' entire colt crop, buying eight to twelve a year. Those purchases netted a number of pleasure stars, including Zippos Mr Good Bar and Zippos Aloha, both full siblings to Mr Zippo Pine out of the King-bred mare Tamara Wess.

It wasn't long before other pleasure enthusiasts began to locate Lexington, Neb., on the map. Drenda Chappell, a well-known horse broker, went so far as to get an AQHA printout of Zippo's get, then hooked up her truck and trailer and went from farm to ranch throughout Nebraska, Iowa, and neighboring states in search of prospects to satisfy the growing demand for pleasure horses. "A lot of people really didn't know what they had standing out in their fields," remembered Chappell.

New Owners

By this time the Reynoldses were being inundated with requests for breedings. They raised the stallion's fee from $150 to $300, and then to $700. In 1985, the last year Zippo stood at the Reynolds' ranch, approximately 200 mares were booked to him.

Yet running a full-time horse breeding operation on top of managing a full-scale farming and ranching enterprise was becoming a burden, Reynolds admitted.

Zippo as an older horse. Zippo was retired from the show ring after his 3-year-old campaign and returned to the Reynolds family farm to take over ranch stallion duties. Long before his offspring made him famous in show circles, he populated neighboring ranches with intelligent, handy, good-moving ranch mounts. In fact, Norman Reynolds sometimes used Zippo himself to check pastures. **Photo Courtesy** *The Quarter Horse Journal*

"We're basically farmers," he explained. "We didn't have the facilities for all these mares, so we built some things and started breeding artificially. But still we couldn't handle that many mares. That's when we started thinking that maybe we needed to have him someplace else."

Yet until Norman Reynolds received the call from Bob Perry in California one Sunday afternoon, he hadn't thought seriously about selling Zippo Pine Bar. He certainly hadn't advertised the horse for sale, and he doesn't recall having men-

181

*Horacio Ramirez—with
sons Victor, Raul, and
Robert aboard Zippo—
groomed and cared for the
stallion daily for 12 years
until Zippo died at age 29.*

**Photo by Peri, Courtesy Bob
Perry Quarter Horses Inc.**

*Joe Jeane managed the Perrys' Valley View facility with his wife, pleasure
trainer Suzy Jeane. When visitors came to the ranch—which they did by the
hundreds each year—Joe Jeane would take Zippo out of his stall and jog up and
down the barn aisles alongside him—without a lead rope on the stallion's halter.*

Photo by Kathy Kadash-Swan

tioned to anyone that he might even consider it. Yet the farm economy was down and Reynolds was worried about the future, so when Bob Perry asked Reynolds to price the stallion, he did.

"They had a really good talk and Bob finally got around to asking whether Zippo was for sale," recalled Ann Perry. "Then I heard Bob ask, 'How much?' And I could tell by the look on his face that something was going to happen. Then he told Norman, 'I need to talk to my wife. I'll call you back in the morning.'"

The Perrys were excited by the prospect of owning the horse, but realized they couldn't get to Nebraska for several weeks to see the stallion in person. However, based on what they already knew about Zippo and his offspring, they called Reynolds back the next day and told him they would buy the 15-year-old stallion sight unseen on one contingency: that he pass a pre-purchase exam by Colorado State University veterinarians for breeding and soundness. Reynolds had a contingency of his own: He could retain four breedings a year. It was agreed.

Zips Chocolate Chip, a 1985 Zippo son out of a Custus Jaguar mare, won several pleasure futurities at 2 and was the AQHA 1989 Junior Western Pleasure World Champion under trainer Cleve Wells. The bay stallion has become a leading sire of pleasure and performance horses, often switching places with or running a close second to his famous daddy on leading sires lists.

Photo by Don Shugart

In 1985, the Perrys heard a rumor that Zippo Pine Bar might be for sale.

"We bought him in August right before the big Reno Spectacular Pleasure Futurities," recalled Ann. "When we went there and told people that we were the lucky new owners of Zippo Pine Bar, nobody could really believe it," she laughed. "It was great."

It's not that the Perrys weren't serious about the horse business. They were, and the whole family was involved. They had gone from being "backyard breeders" with a single mare to owning a number of broodmares and show horses. Eventually they bought a young stallion named Ada Two Eyed Dude, whom they promoted and stood at stud. One year the Perrys attended 78 horse shows.

Ann had become a serious student of pedigrees. At one point the Perrys had even tried to buy a Two Eyed Jack stallion out of Dollie Pine. Although

that transaction didn't work out, when Ann learned that the winning pleasure horses she was watching at all the major shows were by Zippo Pine Bar, a son of Dollie Pine, her curiosity was aroused even further.

In 1985, the Perrys heard a rumor that Zippo Pine Bar might be for sale. They asked a trainer to inquire for them. When the trainer failed to take the initiative, the Perrys decided to pursue the matter themselves. Their timing was perfect.

They had recently bought 121 acres in Valley View, Tex., as a "retirement investment" and a place to keep their broodmares. Reynolds was ready to turn was corralled outdoors with a shed to shield off the worst of the Nebraska weather, and Reynolds would ride him when needed to check pens or bring mares in from the pasture. Zippo was a beloved member of the Reynolds family, but they had always treated him like an ordinary horse. Ann Perry attributes Zippo Pine Bar's health and longevity to the Reynoldses' common sense care.

When Bob and Ann Perry met Zippo for the first time, Norman Reynolds walked up to the horse in his pen, slipped on a halter with lead rope, hopped aboard bareback, and trotted him over to the couple. They were delighted by his gentleness and his excellent physical condition—unclipped bridlepath, shaggy fetlocks, sunbleached coat, and all. He didn't have a bump or a blemish. That was remarkable in itself considering his age and how extensively he had been shown, trained, ridden, and hauled.

After one last cold Nebraska winter, he moved to Texas with eight of his daughters, mares the Perrys had purchased from Reynolds during their first visit to meet Zippo. Once he arrived at Bob Perry Quarter Horses, he never left the ranch. In fact, he always had the same stall.

For the last 10 years of his life, Zippo Pine Bar was cared for on a daily basis by Joe and Suzy Jeane, who ran the Perrys' training and breeding operation. They loved and understood Zippo as well as anyone, including the fact that the usually sociable Zippo disliked anyone watching him eat and was annoyed whenever geldings were led past his stall. When visitors came to the ranch—which they did by the hundreds each year—Joe Jeane would take Zippo out of his stall and jog up and down the barn aisles alongside him. There was no need for a lead rope; the stallion stayed right with Joe.

"He just loved showing off," said Ann Perry.

The Jeanes were with Zippo Pine Bar when he was humanely laid to rest on January 12, 1998, at age 29 following a major stroke.

Significant Offspring

When they acquired Zippo Pine Bar, the Perrys hoped for at least three or four

This 1987 daughter of Zippo, out of Miss Brio, by Brio, was bred by Bob and Ann Perry. Fancy Zippin earned open and amateur performance ROMs and an open Superior in western pleasure.
Photo by Don Shugart, Courtesy Bob Perry Quarter Horses Inc.

over Zippo's breeding and promotion to people who could give it the full attention it deserved. It was a hard decision, Reynolds admitted, but selling the stallion to the Perrys seemed like the best thing for all concerned.

While the Perrys built their facilities in Valley View, Zippo Pine Bar remained with the Reynoldses in Nebraska. "We decided that he'd done so well there for all those years, he would be better off in the environment he was used to," explained Ann.

Even with his rising celebrity status, Zippo had never been pampered. He

Zippo's first major show ring success, Melody Zipper, was a 1976 bay gelding bred by Norman Reynolds out of a King Jaguar mare. In amateur competition, Melody Zipper earned three world championships, seven reserve world championships, the 1983 World Show all-around amateur award with Lu Ann Paul, and 1,900 total AQHA show points. That's Lu Ann in the saddle, with her late husband, Don Paul, and Shirley and Norman Reynolds standing.

Photo by Harold Campton, Courtesy Norman Reynolds

strong breeding seasons with him. They were blessed with a dozen. When they brought him to Texas in 1986, he had already sired almost 600 offspring and his reputation was firmly established. Demand for breedings remained strong. They kept his book open and raised his fee to $1,750. The new owners weren't the least bit concerned about saturating the market with Zippo's get.

"There was such a demand for them and the characteristics and traits that his offspring had, we just didn't worry about

it," confirmed Ann.

But as the stallion aged, they limited his book by raising his stud fee. It went to $5,000, then to $7,500, and finally to $10,000. Breeders weren't deterred, but they did become more selective about the mares they sent to him.

"We were so fortunate because

185

Trainer Cleve Wells showed another Zippo son, Zippo Can Do, to a junior western pleasure world championship nine years after Cleve claimed the same title with Zips Chocolate Chip. Zippo Can Do, a 1994 sorrel stallion, is out of A Girl Named Jones, a race-bred mare with Jet Deck, Sugar Bars, Rebel Cause, and Joe Reed II in her pedigree.

Photo by Jennifer Barron, Courtesy *The Quarter Horse Journal*

the cream of the crop came to him," said Ann.

Yet one of the truly remarkable things is that some of Zippo Pine Bars' best sons and daughters were produced by mares without lengthy resumes.

Zips Chocolate Chip, for instance, was foaled in 1985 to Fancy Blue Chip, by Custus Jaguar. The mare was a nice individual and had an AQHA point or two,

but she had never really been promoted. Ann Myers purchased Fancy Blue Chip at a horse sale. The major attraction for Myers was that the mare was in foal to Zippo Pine Bar. Myers had been following the pleasure futurities and knew the Zippos were taking the lion's share of the winnings. Fancy Blue Chip turned out to be an exceptional broodmare when crossed on Zippo Pine Bar.

The mare produced Zip Blue Chip in 1984, and Myers liked that foal so well that she immediately took Fancy Blue Chip to Nebraska to be rebred. The next year, 1985, she produced Zips

Chocolate Chip.

When Zip Blue Chip was 2, Myers, herself an amateur rider, took the colt to the Tom Powers Futurity to market to prospective buyers. Trainer Cleve Wells saw him there and liked him so well that he bought him.

"That's when I really got to know Cleve," said Myers. "He fell in love with that colt." Unfortunately, Zip Blue Chip died before he could be shown. So when Zips Chocolate Chip came of age, Myers asked Wells to train and show him.

It turned out to be a great match. In his first futurity, Zips Chocolate Chip won both go-rounds and placed first under all five judges. Wells showed Chip in five western pleasure futurities that year, and the fancy bay colt won three of them and was second in two. Two years later, Wells piloted Chip to an AQHA world championship in junior western pleasure.

"For the high-level futurities and events, it's imperative that a horse have good cadence," observed Myers. "Zippo Pine Bar was almost like a ballerina when he moved. He was so soft, he just sort of floated. He had really good cadence. You could see it when he just played. And Zippo threw that so strongly in his foals. That was definitely a key to Chip and why he did so well. If a horse doesn't have it naturally, you can hold it together for a short time, but not all the way around the ring for a whole class. Zippo had that cadence-driven movement and easy lope. He didn't have to think about it or work at it. And he reproduced that."

The records more than bear this out. As of 1999, for more than 10 consecutive years, Zippo Pine Bar has been at the top of the AQHA Leading Performance Sires list. He's also been the National Snaffle Bit Association's leading sire, as well as the leading maternal and paternal grandsire of pleasure horses. Zippo Pine Bar entered the NSBA Hall of Fame in 1992, and will be a 2000 inductee into the American Quarter Horse Hall of Fame. In fact, so great has been Zippo Pine Bar's following and influence, he has even become a Breyer® model horse.

During his lifetime, Zippo Pine Bar sired 1,646 AQHA foals, 68 Appaloosas, and 72 Paints. The last, a colt named

Zippo sired the 1990 AQHA World Show Superhorse Zipabull. This 1986 bay stallion out of Miss Flash Bull, by Mr Flash Bull, also earned the 1990 junior hunter hack world championship and the 1989 junior western riding reserve title.

Photo by Don Shugart, Courtesy Bob Perry Quarter Horses Inc.

Zippo Finale (AQHA), was born at the Perrys' ranch in 1998. Collectively these horses have already earned well over 50,000 show points.

"People thought we were nuts to buy a 15-year-old stallion," remembered Ann Perry. "But we thought, 'This is great. Zippo is already a champion. The horse trainers are beating the door down for his colts.' We'd already gone through all that hauling with Ada Two Eyed Dude. We wanted to focus on the breeding.

187

"And when you look at the records, sure there are some horses who became famous sires relatively young—Zips Chocolate Chip is one—but for the most part, there really aren't that many whose offspring really catch on until after the stallions are at least 10 or 12."

They way they looked at it, Zippo had just hit his prime. Reynolds joked that if he had known Zippo would live to be so old, he wouldn't have sold him. Then he amended on a more serious note that he was delighted by the way the Perrys cared for and promoted the stallion over the years.

His Disposition

Although Zippo consistently passed on his athletic abilities, most Zippo Pine Bar fans agree that it was his unerring ability to pass on his quiet, cooperative disposition that led to his unprecedented success as a sire. Almost without exception, his sons and daughters seem to have his same innate desire to please.

"Sure, they've sired world and Congress champions and all that stuff," said Ann Myers. "But ultimately, the Zippos are on the leading sires lists because almost anybody can get along with them. There are a lot of youth and amateurs who ride them—they're the weekend warriors. A lot of the points come from people who show on the weekends all around the country. Disposition is the big key."

Once the Zippos were "discovered," there was no limit to their success. Half of all his offspring have made it to the show ring. In two dozen years of AQHA competition, his get amassed (as of September 1999) more than 50,000 points, 800-plus ROMs, and 50 world and reserve world championships. His AQHA Champions include Zippo's Jan, Zippo Cash Bar, Zippos Social Bar, Misters Zipper, KB Masterpiece, License To Zip, Zippos Rockin Robin, and Zippos Watch Jack.

His Appaloosa and Paint sons and daughters have made their mark as well, with 20 APHA national or world cham-

pionships, and 48 Appaloosa national and world championships or ApHC year-end high-point titles. With so many of Zippo Pine Bar's sons and daughters continuing to be shown, the final tally won't be known for years.

Although Zippo Pine Bar became known as a western pleasure horse sire, it's fun to look at other offspring.

Fast Regulation, for example, was a reserve world champion in pole bending.

Lonsum Zippo was a reserve world champion in senior working hunter and a youth world champion in working hunter and equitation over fences.

Zipabull was the 1990 AQHA World Show Superhorse, a world champion in junior hunter hack, and a reserve world champion in junior western riding. (Many of Zippo's get excelled in western riding, just as he did.)

Zippo Ltd, a 1987 gelding out of Ima Blister Bug, had a decade-long winning streak in trail, pleasure, showmanship, and western riding. He is a multiple year-end high-point horse who, as of September 1999, had earned 60 AQHA awards and more than 3,000 points in youth, amateur, and open competition. Zippo Ltd earned nearly $36,000 in AQHA Incentive Fund money between 1990 and 1998.

Keep in mind that whatever is printed here will be obsolete by the time you read it. By the beginning of 1999, Zippo Pine Bar's get had earned three-quarters of a million dollars in AQHA Incentive Fund money alone. Add to that the pleasure futurity and derby purses won through NSBA, Quarter Horse, Appaloosa, Paint, Palomino, and open competition, and you find that Zippo's get have won an estimated $5 million.

Zippos Betty Bea, for example, won almost $35,000 in prize money, while Zipped Tight, Cant Stop Zipping, Mr Magnolia Zip, and Zippo Can Do have earned more than $20,000 each, according to Equistat. Zippos Rockin Robin and Zippos Bandana each earned nearly $20,000 in AQHA incentive bonuses. But this short list doesn't even begin to scratch the surface of what Zippo Pine Bar has sired. One day, it will require a book.

"Most sires are either broodmare sires or they produce sons who carry on the bloodline," noted Ann Perry. "What's amazing to me is that Zippo

Almost without exception, his sons and daughters seem to have his same innate desire to please.

OK Im Zipped earned the 1998 youth world championship in western riding and reserve championship in western horsemanship with rider Quincy Cahill, pictured, the daughter of Texas trainer Nancy Cahill. The 1990 gelded son of Zippo and Oklahoma Reject, by Dingo Dial, was a top 10 placer in western riding at both the open (1994 and 1997) and youth (1996 and 1997) world shows. **Photo by Jennifer Barron, Courtesy** *The Quarter Horse Journal*

has a phenomenal record with both his sons and his daughters."

With Zippo Pine Bar gone, his legacy is being carried forward by a legion of great mares and stallions. At any given time, usually a half dozen of his sons can be found on AQHA's Leading Performance Sires list. Zips Chocolate Chip, for instance, has become a leading sire of pleasure and performance horses, often switching places with or running a close second to his famous daddy. On the feminine side, as of late summer 1999, more than 400 of Zippo Pine Bar's daughters have produced offspring with more than

15,000 AQHA points and 300 ROMs.

Without question, Zippo Pine Bar revolutionized the pleasure industry. But with his pedigree and performance ability, it could have been any event.

"He kept alive those working qualities that we really need in the horse industry," concluded Ann Perry. "He produced horses for everybody."

17 DOC O'LENA

By Betsy Lynch

He was the quintessential cow horse: kind, intelligent, fleet, and powerful.

Born of cow horse royalty, Doc O'Lena sired a dynasty of horses who have dominated cow horse competition. His offspring have won NCHA, NRHA, and NRCHA titles; AQHA, APHA, and ApHC world championships; and more than $14 million in earnings.

Photo by Tony Leonard, Courtesy *The Quarter Horse Journal*

DOC O'LENA was indeed a gift to the horse world. That he existed at all is testimony to the dedication of his breeders, Dr. Stephen and Jasmine Jensen; the perseverance of veterinarian Dr. Frank Whalen; and the heart of his mother, Poco Lena. That Doc O'Lena fulfilled his destiny is a tribute to horseman Shorty Freeman. That he was able to perpetuate a cutting horse dynasty is one of those

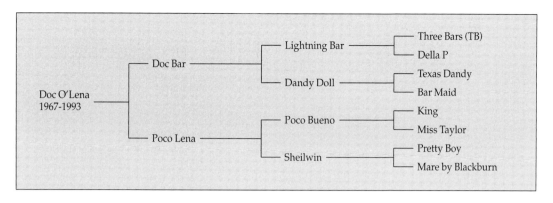

inexplicable wonders of genetics.

Doc O'Lena's story is nothing short of remarkable. It begins near the end of his dam's life, and brings home the notion that greatness is more a matter of choice than chance.

Cow Horse Royalty

Doc O'Lena's dam, Poco Lena, was the daughter of AQHA Champion Poco Bueno and Sheilwin, by Pretty Boy. Poco Lena was not only an AQHA Champion, but she was also the first horse to be inducted into the National Cutting Horse Association Hall of Fame. She was the NCHA world champion cutting mare in 1959, '60, and '61. Between 1954-1961, she was the NCHA reserve world champion cutting horse five times. By the time her cutting career ended, tragically and abruptly, Poco Lena had earned nearly $100,000 in NCHA competition—during an era when purses were little to nothing. So great were Poco Lena's accomplishments, she was also inducted into the American Quarter Horse Hall of Fame.

But fame did not ensure Poco Lena an easy existence. In 1962 her owner B.A. Skipper Jr. was killed in a plane crash on his way home from a cutting. A hired driver, who was to bring the horses home, left them in a trailer without food or water. In the mayhem following the disappearance of Skipper's airplane, it was days before the horses were missed and located. The episode nearly killed Poco Lena, and crippled her so severely she would never compete again.

Despite her condition, Poco Lena was sold in Skipper's estate dispersal early in 1963. She was on her way to Louisiana when the buyer reneged on the deal. The mare was left stranded at a cattle station at the Texas-Louisiana state line

Halter and Performance Record: 1970 NCHA Futurity Champion; 1971 NCHA Derby, 3rd Place; NCHA Earnings, $21,991.

Progeny Record: (As of September 1999)

Foal Crops: 24	Halter Points Earned: 77.5
Foals Registered: 1,329	Halter Registers of Merit: 2
AQHA Champions: 1	Performance Point-Earners: 405
World Champions: 7	Performance Points Earned: 5,803.5
Halter Point-Earners: 14	Performance Registers of Merit: 112
National Cutting Horse Association Earnings (as of February 1999): $14,142,205.96	

while the sales managers tried to figure out what to do.

Yet it was this sad state of affairs that ultimately led to Poco Lena's next date with destiny.

California horse breeders Dr. Stephen and Jasmine Jensen heard the plight of the great mare, and decided they would like to purchase her. Their hope was to rehabilitate Poco Lena and breed her to their champion halter stallion, Doc Bar. However, when Poco Lena finally hobbled off the trailer in California, her condition was so pitiable that the Jensens' first inclination was to have her humanely destroyed. Veterinarian Dr. Frank Wayland persuaded the new owners to give Poco

Doc O'Lena's sire, Doc Bar. A son of Lightning Bar and the Texas Dandy mare Dandy Doll, Doc Bar was bred to run but washed out early at the track. Instead, the stallion stood grand champion at halter 10 times and sired both halter and performance winners, passing on cow sense, charisma, and athleticism to his offspring. Doc Bar's story is told in the first Legends *book.*

Photo by *Western Livestock Journal*

Halter horse sire Doc Bar was an interesting match for Poco Lena, the queen of cutting.

Lena one last chance. He felt they might be able to breed her to Doc Bar yet.

Resectioning her hoofs did alleviate some of Poco Lena's pain, but it was far from a cure. Equally discouraging was the mare's reproductive health. For years she had been given medication to keep her out of heat. Making the situation more dire was Poco Lena's age. She was already 14 years old and had never had a foal.

"She was a nonfunctioning broodmare," recalled Stephenie Ward, the Jensens' daughter. "When they first got her, her ovaries were the size of peas.

But Dr. Wayland and Dr. Gary Deter worked tirelessly—not only on her feet but also on her reproductive tract. Every month it was a new project."

It took two years, but finally, in 1966, Poco Lena conceived. She was in foal to Doc Bar for the first time.

Without question, Doc Bar was an interesting match for Poco Lena. Although he was bred to run, he had no speed. Instead, he made his mark in the halter horse world. Yet the Jensens liked the working lines, and in particular the Poco Bueno-Poco Tivio mares. Just such a cross had produced the great cutting and working cow horse mare Fizzabar. But even with Fizzabar's phenomenal success, Doc Bar's get weren't being shown on cattle in any numbers. In fact, by the time the cutting horse world discovered Doc Bar's prepotency for producing cagey, athletic cow horses, his most famous son had already hit the ground.

On June 21, 1967, Doc O'Lena was foaled on the front lawn of the Jensens' Double J Ranch in Paicines, California. The Jensens, who made their residence in Orinda to the north, were at the ranch the weekend Poco Lena's small bay colt arrived. Stephenie Ward recalled her

The immortal Poco Lena was an AQHA Champion by AQHA Champion Poco Bueno and out of a Pretty Boy mare. She was also a three-time NCHA world champion, a five-time NCHA reserve world champion, and an inductee into both the NCHA and AQHA halls of fame. She produced only two foals after being severely foundered. Both sons, Doc O'Lena and Dry Doc, were by Doc Bar. Poco Lena's story is told in Legends, Vol. 3.

Photo Courtesy *The Quarter Horse Journal*

Doc O'Lena as a yearling, at the California ranch of Dr. Stephen and Jasmine Jensen, who owned both Poco Lena and Doc Bar at the time.

Jensen Photo

*Doc O'Lena and
Shorty Freeman in
action in Arizona,
1975. Shorty retired
the stallion after
a few years of cam-
paigning, for fear
of injuring the horse
so he couldn't breed.*

**Photo by Frank Conrad,
Courtesy NCHA**

*Shorty Freeman and Doc O'Lena. "It was almost like they developed a kin-
dred spirit," explained Shorty's biographer, Gala Nettles. "But that doesn't
even begin to touch it. Although he had ridden some great horses, this horse
made him. He always had the belief that Doc O'Lena would bring him financial security. And sure enough, he did. But it was more than that. He loved
that horse, and I think their attachment grew over time."*

Photo by Dalco, Reprinted from *Just Shorty* **by Gala Nettles**

mother commenting that the colt was so
tiny he could walk under his momma's
belly without even touching her.

Because Poco Lena was so badly
foundered, the Jensens kept her in
the yard, on the soft grass and safely
fenced away from the other horses.
Doc O'Lena quickly learned to nurse
when Poco Lena was lying down because
his dam spent so much time that way
to relieve her aching feet. But just because
Poco Lena had to be isolated didn't
mean her colt did.

"We have a pipe fence around the house
and there was another old mare and her
colt on the other side," said Stephenie.
"So my parents took the bottom two pipes
out of one section so Doc O'Lena could
go in and play with the other colt, and
then come back over to Poco Lena to
nurse. It was just a small opening, but he
knew exactly where the gate was. He
was a smart little guy."

Doc O'Lena's keen intelligence and
nice disposition were evident early,
Stephenie remembered.

"He was a sweet colt, not nippy, and
he didn't have much silliness about him.

194

Started under saddle by the Jensens' son-in-law, Charlie Ward, Doc O'Lena was trained and campaigned by Shorty Free-man. The stallion and Shorty swept the 1970 NCHA Futurity, winning both go-rounds, the semifinals, and the finals. Shorty co-owned the stallion at the time with Adrian Berryhill (center), receiving the trophy from Jim Calhoun.

Photo Courtesy *The Quarter Horse Journal*

He was the kind of colt who wouldn't shy or jump away from things. If he saw something strange, he would just stop and look at it."

Training

Charlie Ward, Stephenie's husband, started Doc O'Lena under saddle in the spring of his 2-year-old year. Charlie was immediately impressed by how trainable the colt was. Charlie had been a roper all of his life, but had developed a fascination for cutting horses. He had taken a Doc Bar colt to Texas for futurity practice the previous year, and attended a couple of Buster Welch's cutting schools. That was where Charlie first met Shorty Freeman. Charlie also showed his first NCHA Futurity horse the year before he started Doc O'Lena. He was beginning to get a feel for the sport. When he began riding Poco

Lena's colt, he felt certain the stout bay colt had the right stuff.

"I think there was a little resistance every now and then when Charlie first started him, but Doc O'Lena wasn't mean or stupid about it," recalled Stephe-nie. "He had his own way. He was one of those thinking kind of horses. He'd kind of test the saddle, and then test the person. Then he'd say, 'Oh, all right, I'll go along with you.' "

After about 30 days of training, Charlie began to work Doc O'Lena on cattle.

"Doc O'Lena was a smart, cowy horse, and Charlie knew it right away," explained Stephenie. "Charlie always said

Charlie Ward always said Doc O'Lena had a connection with the cow that you could feel from day one.

Si Olena is a 1986 sorrel stallion by Doc O'Lena and out of Reisa Rey, by Rey Jay. Shown here winning the reserve championship at the 1990 NCHA Super Stakes with Kathy Daughn, Si Olena won the AQHA world championship in senior cutting in 1998, with Teddy Johnson as his rider. **WH File Photo**

Doc O'Lena had a connection with the cow that you could feel from day one."

Charlie reported to his in-laws that Doc O'Lena seemed to be everything his pedigree promised. The Jensens began to selectively put the word out that Poco Lena's colt was for sale.

"They were asking $10,000 for him,"

Stephenie remembered. "It was phenomenal at the time, but now it sounds like nothing. My parents knew how valuable he was going to be, since he was out of such a fantastic mare. They always said that everything on the place was for sale—but probably not Doc Bar," she laughed. "But the reason they bought Poco Lena was to breed her and get a colt who could continue to make a reputation for Doc Bar."

Shorty Freeman was training cutting horses for Adrian Berryhill in Scottsdale, Ariz., and his reputation was looming large in the industry. Shorty had been

Trained and shown by Shorty's son, Bill Freeman, Smart Little Lena became a superstar when he won the Triple Crown of cutting: the NCHA Futurity, Super Stakes, and Derby. The chestnut stallion out of Smart Peppy, by Peppy San, is Doc O'Lena's top money-earning offspring, with a bankroll close to $750,000. Smart Little Lena has two NCHA Futurity champions to his credit, Smart Date and Smart Little Senor, and one NRCHA Futurity winner, Smart Little Calboy. **Photo Courtesy** *The Quarter Horse Journal*

successfully campaigning horses such as Hoppen and King Skeet for National Cutting Horse Association world championship titles. Charlie had seen Shorty handle horses at Buster's and had watched him show. Charlie knew the man had an uncanny touch. He was one of the first people the Jensens contacted about their special colt.

"Doc O'Lena was already working cows by the time Shorty came," Stephenie explained. "But most of the riding we do here is not in an arena. We're on this big ranch; it's about a half-mile to the cutting pen. So there's a lot of riding out. You have to cross the river, and jackrabbits run out from underneath you. Doc O'Lena had been through all of that. We'd already hauled him to friends who had a cutting pen over in Escalon, and a

lot of people saw him work a cow before Shorty took him."

Shorty Freeman came to California in July to show horses, and on the return journey stopped by the Double J to try Doc O'Lena.

"It was funny. We saddled the horse there at the barn," Stephenie recalled, "and, as I said, it's a half-mile ride down to the cutting pen. We had to go by this pen of cattle, where we had just put some black and white Holsteins. When Doc O'Lena walked up and spotted those Hol-

CD Olena is one of Doc O'Lena's three NCHA Futurity champions (the others are Lenaette in 1975 and Smart Little Lena in 1982). CD Olena, out of a Peppy San Badger mare, won the 1994 Futurity with rider Winston Hansma, shown. The sorrel stallion's earnings total more than $100,000.

WH File Photo

steins, he just stopped and looked. Then one of them moved and he jumped. He'd never seen black and white cattle before."

In the telling and retelling, Shorty's first ride aboard the young stallion evolved into a yarn about how Doc O'Lena ran off the first time he saw a cow.

"He didn't run off with Shorty in the cutting pen," Ward clarified. "He just rode by those black and whites and went, 'OH!' "

Runaway or not, Shorty told the Jensens he definitely wanted the horse. He would work out the financial arrangements with his boss Adrian Berryhill. The Jensens waited, but the check didn't arrive. Doc O'Lena remained at the Double J Ranch and Charlie kept riding him.

In September, Shorty convinced the Jensens to put the colt in training with him, which would give Mr. Berryhill a chance to see the horse work. To facilitate the sale, the Jensens sent Doc O'Lena to Arizona.

Several months went by and still the transaction didn't materialize. Finally, Dr. Jensen lost patience and sidestepped Shorty. He called Adrian Berryhill and asked him directly if he wanted to buy Doc O'Lena.

Perhaps the timing was right. Freeman had just won the 1969 NCHA Futurity reserve championship on Berryhill's

Doc Bar mare, Doc's Kitty. Shorty was equally confident that the 2-year-old bay colt he was riding for the Jensens was destined for greatness. In fact, Shorty longed to have a partnership interest in the stallion. But although Shorty was long on talent, he was short on cash. He simply didn't have the money to buy half-interest in Doc O'Lena.

When Dr. Jensen called Berryhill, Berryhill not only agreed to buy Doc O'Lena, he decided that Shorty deserved to own a part of him. When the registration papers were transferred to Berryhill, Shorty's name went on them as well.

"Berryhill, exhibiting faith in his trainer, agreed to pay the entire price, now $15,000, for the partnership purchase of the young stallion," wrote Gala Nettles in her book, *Just Shorty*. "Where and when, though, was he (Shorty) going to obtain $7,500 to pay Mr. Berryhill his half of the $15,000?"

The answer would come a year later.

The Futurity

Shorty Freeman spent the next 12 months preparing Doc O'Lena for the NCHA Futurity. Because he was on the road so much hauling for another NCHA world title, Shorty always said Doc O'Lena trained himself.

"Good horses are that way," observed Stephenie Ward. "Everything seems natural and easy. But the truth is, Shorty was the trainer, and Doc O'Lena was a perfect fit for Shorty's training style.

"Shorty let a horse learn; he didn't force one to learn," she continued. "He let his horses do a lot. He let them make mistakes. And as intelligent a horse as Doc O'Lena was, if he made a mistake and Shorty corrected him afterwards, he learned by it. If he jumped too far beyond the cow, Shorty would hurry him back, show him that he missed the cow, instead of grabbing him before it happened. Some trainers can get by with horses who aren't quite as smart because they teach them a pattern, and as long as they stay within that pattern, they're safe. But Doc O'Lena was smart enough to learn from his mistakes. That whole idea of letting the horse learn instead of forcing him to learn is something that we

all admired about Shorty."

When the time came, Shorty loaded up his horses and headed to Sweetwater, Tex., for the prefuturity practice sessions. It was an opportunity for him to see just how ready his entries were.

"There were about 60 or 70 horses there for the practice, and we drew places to see where we'd work. Well, when it came time to work Doc O'Lena, I rode him slowly into that herd of cattle feeling real confident in him, but he sure fooled me. He never even saw a cow. He didn't know there was one in Texas! All he could see was the bleachers and the lights and everything going on. He was *so* country. I was sick. But he got it all out of him that first day, and from then on, he was just fine." (Excerpted from *Just Shorty* by Gala Nettles.)

"Just fine" was a typical Shorty Freeman understatement.

At the 1970 NCHA Futurity held in Fort Worth, Doc O'Lena and Shorty made history and set a record that has stood for more than 30 years. They won all four go-rounds, scoring a 220.5 in the first go, a 218 in the second go, a 219.5 in the semifinals, and a 223 in the finals— three points ahead of the reserve champion, Miss Holly Deer.

From that moment forward, Shorty Freeman and Doc O'Lena's names became inseparable. The win was especially significant to Shorty because his share of the $17,357 winner's purse paid off his debt to Adrian Berryhill. His half-ownership in Doc O'Lena was free and clear.

So impressive was Doc O'Lena's Futurity sweep that people often forget the stallion competed the next year in the 1971 NCHA Maturity (what is now the Derby). Shorty and Doc O'Lena finished third and added another $2,500 to their lifetime earnings. In 1972 Doc O'Lena won an additional $438 in weekend competition, including a championship at the Illinois State Fair, but by this time, Shorty had

At the 1970 NCHA Futurity, Doc O'Lena and Shorty Freeman set a record that has stood for 30 years: They won all four go-rounds.

become reluctant to show him.

"After the Derby, Shorty didn't ride him much," confirmed Shorty's son-in-law, Terry Riddle. "He took him to Columbus to the Congress and was going to show him there, but Doc O'Lena slipped on the concrete in one of the walkways, so Shorty didn't get to show him. As far as I know, he never showed him anywhere after that. What Shorty said to me is that he couldn't take a chance of crippling the horse so he couldn't breed, or take a chance of a truck running over him on the highway."

Breeding

After the Futurity, Shorty and his wife, Gay, stood Doc O'Lena at stud in Arizona for $750. They advertised the stallion's services in the *Cuttin' Hoss Chatter,* and were immediately overwhelmed by mares.

"People were sending three and four mares, which was unheard of back then for breeding cutting horses," recalled Gay. Doc O'Lena was booked full, and every square inch of the ranch overflowed with broodmares and horses in training. The next year, Berryhill and Freeman decided to double Doc O'Lena's fee, thinking it would discourage breeders. But still the mares came.

The workload became so overwhelming, in fact, that when race horse owner Jake Bunn offered Shorty a job in Illinois managing his Thoroughbred farm, the Freemans packed their bags and moved to the Midwest. As part of the agreement, Bunn bought out Adrian Berryhill's half-interest in Doc O'Lena for $20,000.

Shorty quickly discovered that Bunn had no real interest in the cutting horse stallion, so Shorty sent Doc O'Lena to stand at the B.F. Phillips Ranch in Frisco, Texas. When breeding season ended,

Terry Riddle brought the stallion back to Shorty in Illinois. Bunn, however, refused to let Doc O'Lena reside at his Thoroughbred facility. Doc O'Lena was then moved down the road to George Bunn's farm. Shorty commuted several times a week to ride the stallion and train his cutting futurity entry.

It didn't take the Freemans long to realize that the move had been a mistake. After the 1973 Futurity, they made arrangements with the Berryhills to return to Arizona. The only complication was the matter of Doc O'Lena. Shorty wanted to buy Bunn's partnership interest, but he needed $20,000 to do it. He talked to banker and fellow cutter Dick Gaines, but Gaines could not finance an out-of-state loan. Instead, Gaines loaned Shorty the money for the stallion out of his own pocket, telling Shorty, "I hope you can't pay for him."

"That statement scared me to death," Shorty told Gala Nettles in one of their extensive interviews.

But Shorty did pay Gaines back, and for a time, he was the sole owner of Doc O'Lena—which suited Shorty just fine. That changed again when his friend and employer Adrian Berryhill died. Bend Inn, the ranch where the Freemans had trained and lived for so many years, was being divided. Mrs. Berryhill asked Shorty and Gay if they wanted to buy part of the estate. To make the down payment, Shorty again sold half interest in Doc O'Lena, this time to longtime friend and client Walter Hellyer. Shorty and Hellyer remained partners on Doc O'Lena until the stallion was syndicated in 1978.

The responsibility of owning and standing Doc O'Lena was an awesome one, to be sure. Yet it is one that Shorty thrived on.

"It was almost like they developed a kindred spirit," explained Gala Nettles. "But that doesn't even begin to touch it. Although he had ridden some great horses, this horse *made* him. He always had the belief that Doc O'Lena would bring him financial security. And sure enough, he did. But it was more than that. He loved that horse, and I think their attachment grew over time."

The Freemans had built the stallion his own adobe barn in the middle of

Doc O'Lena's ability to stamp his foals— regardless of the cross—enhanched his reputation as a sire.

Todaysmyluckyday proved that Doc O'Lena offspring could rein as well as cut. This 1992 bay stallion out of a Doc's Sug mare won the 1995 NRHA Futurity with Todd Bergen, shown. The stallion later won two AQHA world championships: junior reining in 1996 and junior working cow horse in 1997.

Photo Courtesy *The Quarter Horse Journal*

Bend Inn. Every night after Shorty was through working horses, he'd go down to check on Doc O'Lena or take him out for a ride in the round pen.

Offspring

By the mid-1970s, Doc O'Lena's first offspring were coming of age, and the talent they possessed further fueled the demand for breedings.

Terry and Sharon Riddle, for example, owned a Doc O'Lena daughter named Lenaette, out of Bar Socks Babe. They bought the filly as a yearling after Shorty sold her dam to a customer in Canada. Terry Riddle began training her for the NCHA Futurity. He felt the little mare had so much talent that in May of her 3-year-old year, he sent Lenaette to his father-in-law to finish. At the 1975 NCHA Futurity Lenaette lived up to her heritage. She won the second go-round, the semifinals, and the finals, keeping at bay some really bad cows that would

have eaten a lesser horse alive.

"I'd have to say that I was a lot more nervous just watching than I ever have been showing," chuckled Terry Riddle. When his talented little mare claimed the $30,000 winner's purse with a score of 224, Riddle's turmoil was over.

Lenaette's victory was simply the next stage in the Doc O'Lena phenomenon. The next year, Shorty won the NCHA Derby with Lena's Bonita, and in 1979 was the reserve Derby champion on Moria Lena. From that point on, Doc O'Lena's sons and daughters began to dominate

Throughout the 1990s, the dynamic Tap O Lena racked up awards and winnings in excess of $450,000 for breeder-owner-rider Phil Rapp. By Doc O'Lena and out of the Doc's Oak daughter Tapeppyoka Peppy (herself an accomplished cutting horse), Tap O Lena is shown winning the 1994 Augusta Futurity non-pro division with Rapp aboard.

Photo Courtesy Morris Communications

the sport, and Doc O'Lena himself began giving his own sire, Doc Bar, a run for his money on the leading sires lists.

As Doc O'Lena's fame and fortune grew, it became harder and harder for the Freemans to keep up with the demand for breedings. It was also frustrating that many of the mares were not of the caliber they felt he deserved. Yet Shorty never had the heart to turn anyone away. Even when Doc O'Lena's stud fee reached $2,500 in 1977, there was no shortage of mare owners willing to ante up. That's when B.F. Phillips stepped in to offer Shorty a solution to his growing dilemma: syndication.

B.F. planted the seed in Gay and Shorty's mind during a horse sale at the Phillips Ranch. He also discussed the idea with Jim Reno, a good friend of the Freemans. Even though it made perfect sense, Shorty balked at the idea. It took Reno months to convince Shorty that it would solve a lot of his problems.

"It wasn't a good time for him," explained Gala Nettles. "Jim (Reno) would list the advantages and disadvantages, and the conflicts would often make

Shorty go off into a rage. It was like he was being asked to give up his child. He knew it was the best thing for the horse, but letting him go was very hard."

But let him go he did. In 1978 Doc O'Lena was syndicated for $2.1 million. Fifty shares were sold for $30,000 each, with Shorty and Walter Hellyer retaining another 10 shares apiece. B.F. Phillips orchestrated the sale. Each shareholder was entitled to one breeding a year for the life of the stallion. The Doc O'Lena Syndicate sold out in 30 days. Later, shareholders would find they could sell a single year's service to Doc O'Lena for $20,000 or more—if they were willing to part with the opportunity of having another Doc O'Lena son or daughter. Most weren't willing to make that sacrifice.

When you examine the records, it's easy to understand why.

During his lifetime, Doc O'Lena sired 1,311 Quarter Horses, six Appaloosas, and 12 Paints. His offspring have won more than $14 million in cutting competition, including three NCHA Futurity championships—Lenaette in 1975, Smart Little Lena in 1982, and CD Olena in 1994—and a record 36 finalists. Doc O'Lena has sired champions in almost every major cutting event held, both open and non-pro. His get have also won major titles in reining, working cow horse, and roping competition.

According to a 1999 Equistat report, at least 25 Doc O'Lena sons and daughters have earned more than $100,000 in competition, including: Miss Elan, Dox Lena Rey, Dox Time And Again, Doctor Wood, Perry San, Sugar Olena, Travalena, Todaysmyluckyday, Smart Peppy Doc, Dox Abilena, Dolly Olena, Doctor What, Marcellena, Lenas Telesis, Data Lena, Lenas Lucinda, CD Olena, Fannys Oskar, Sanolesa, Sonitalena, Scarlett O Lena, Lenas Dynamite, Tap O Lena, and Smart Little Lena.

Smart Little Lena

Smart Little Lena, who tops the list of money-earners, has been a phenomenon in his own right. The chestnut stallion out of Smart Peppy, by Peppy San, became a superstar when he won the Triple Crown of cutting: the NCHA Futurity, the NCHA Super Stakes, and the NCHA Derby (co-champion). Smart Little Lena was also a Masters cutting champion. Bill Freeman (Shorty's son) trained and showed the stallion. Several months before the Futurity, Bill asked his dad to ride Smart Little Lena for a short time.

"I was going to some shows out west, and I didn't want the horse to be left unattended for that period of time, so I sent him over to my dad," explained Bill Freeman. "He rode Little Lena for that two weeks, and he really did help him."

Although it would seem the natural thing to do, Shorty never compared Doc O'Lena and Smart Little Lena.

"He never would compare horses—not just those two, but any horses," said Bill. "He was a true believer in the moment, not one to reminisce in the past or speculate about the future."

It would have been hard for anyone to predict just how successful Smart Little Lena would be. By the time his show career ended, he had won nearly $750,000. Like his sire, Smart Little Lena was syndicated and has gone on to sire cutting, reining, and working cow horse champions who have won millions, with champions in virtually every major event, including two NCHA Futurity champions, Smart Date in 1987 and Smart Little Senor in 1988.

Another Smart Little Lena son, Smart Little Calboy, won the 1988 National Reined Cow Horse Association World Championship Snaffle Bit Futurity. Doc O'Lena himself sired an NRCHA Snaffle Bit Futurity reserve world champion when Me O Lena claimed the title in 1981.

Legacy

Both Bill Freeman and Terry Riddle have successfully trained and shown a number of Doc O'Lena's sons and daughters. They're very familiar with the qualities that set them apart from other family lines.

"They're a little bit hotter than most horses, so you have to be more careful

Doc O'Lena's top money-earner with $750,000 in earnings, Smart Little Lena won cutting's Triple Crown: the NCHA Futurity, Super Stakes, and Derby.

One of Doc O'Lena's two Appaloosa world champions, Ima Doc O'Lena won the Pacific Coast Cutting Horse Association Derby and two ApHC cutting world titles. The first Appaloosa son of Doc O'Lena, the stallion has sired cutting, reining, and working cow horse champions, including Ima Jo's Doll, the only Appaloosa to win the NRCHA Snaffle Bit Futurity. Ima Doc O'Lena, shown here with Hanes Chatham at the 1983 NCHA Super Stakes, has been inducted into the Appaloosa Hall of Fame.

Photo by Fred Miller, Courtesy Jimmie Miller Smith

with them," observed Bill Freeman, "They're a little more hyper, which fits my program because I like a real active horse. They've got a lot of cow and the willingness to please. They're the kind of horses who don't require a lot of chastising, but by the same token they can't stand any, either."

Riddle concurred. "I'd have to say that they're fragile-minded horses. They have a lot of natural cow sense, but you can't be rough with them. You have to handle them easy and let them develop themselves—show them what to do, but don't ever try to force anything on them. They mature quick enough, as a general rule, but they get mentally better with age."

During his lifetime, Doc O'Lena bred all types of mares. His ability to stamp his foals—regardless of the cross—enhanced his reputation as a sire.

"Doc O'Lena was a dominating sire," confirmed Riddle. "I think most mares put 75 to 80 percent of what a colt is into that colt. Doc O'Lena put 75 to 80 percent of Doc O'Lena into his babies.

"He was one of the few studs I've seen in my lifetime who could dominate a mare," Riddle continued. "You could see the Doc O'Lena characteristics in the colts out of just about any kind of a mare. Granted, some were better than others. For example, nobody knows yet today why Bar Socks Babe crossed so well on him, but she did. So did those two mares of B.F. Phillips', old Moira Girl and Gin Echols."

Bar Socks Babe, foaled in 1966, was by Bar El Do, by Sugar Bars, and out of Dusty Socks, by Gold King Bailey. She produced 12 foals by Doc O'Lena: Lenaette, Bardoc O'Lena, Bar O' Lena, Maybellena, Havealena, Lizzielena, Tamborlena, Makinyourmark, Travalena, Keys To The Moon, Quanah O Lena, and Lady Rolena. Almost all of her daughters were NCHA Futurity finalists. In addition to open Futurity Champion Lenaette, Bar Socks Babe also produced an NCHA Futurity Non-Pro Champion when Bar O'Lena won the title in 1977. Bar Socks Babe's sons were also outstanding performers, earning well over $300,000 in cutting competition.

Moira Girl, by Mora Leo, by Leo, and out of Sonoita Queen, by J B King, produced such great offspring as Shorty Lena, Moria Lena, Stay With Me, and Okay Bye. Gin Echols, by Ed Echols and out of Gin Squirt (TB), produced 1979 NCHA Derby reserve champion Gins Lena, Spot O'Gin, Shot O' Gin, and one of Shorty Freeman's personal favorites, Tanquery Gin.

Although most of Doc O'Lena's offspring headed to the cutting pen, 30 of his sons and daughters have won more than $300,000 in National Reining Horse Association events. Todaysmyluckyday was the 1995 NRHA Futurity Champion and earned over $100,000. The bay stallion out of Doc Alice is also a two-time AQHA World Champion, winning titles in both reining and working cow horse.

As of September 1999, Doc O'Lena's get had won 14 AQHA world championships, 11 reserve world championships, and three year-end high-point titles. His world champions include: Diamond Lena Bars, Doc O Leo, Doc's Rosie, Doc Athena, Tamulena, Dunna Doc, Si Olena, Marcellena, Todaysmyluckyday, Anna Paulena, Made To Boogie, Rosezana Lena, and Chex In My Pocket. He also produced Spark O Lena, the 1996 AQHA Reserve World Show Superhorse, and one AQHA Champion, Mr Sun O Lena.

Doc O'Lena also sired two Appaloosa world champions, Ima Doc O'Lena and Miss Doc O'Lena. Ima Doc O'Lena, a two-time ApHC world champion cutting horse and a Pacific Coast Cutting Derby champion, is also a member of the Appaloosa Hall of Fame. In addition to his show ring accomplishments, Ima Doc O'Lena sired Ima Jo's Doll, the only Appaloosa ever to win the prestigious National Reined Cow Horse Association Snaffle Bit Futurity. He also sired multiple national, world, and futurity champions.

Doc O'Lena's Paint offspring include three world champions: Delta O Lena, Electrolena, and Gay O Lena. Doc Doll, one of Doc O'Lena's best-known Paint sons, earned more than $37,000 in NCHA events.

There are so many outstanding sons and daughters of Doc O'Lena that it would be impossible to name them all. More than half of all his get have earned money in competition, be it cutting, roping, reining, or working cow horse. When he died in 1993 at the age of 26, his legacy was already secure in the genes of his offspring. In 1997 Doc O'Lena was inducted into the American Quarter Horse Hall of Fame.

Although Doc O'Lena was not known for his beauty, he was the quintessential cow horse: kind, intelligent, fleet, and powerful. Cutting horse legend Buster Welch once described the way Doc O'Lena worked a cow as "poetry in motion."

One last thing that can be said for certain: Doc O'Lena surely did his momma proud.

AUTHOR PROFILES

Mike Boardman

MIKE BOARDMAN has deep roots in the detailed world of pedigree research. A transplanted Australian now living in Corning, Calif., he studies breeding nicks as his hobby, and makes his living breeding horses and running auctions. Mike has combined the hobby and the breeding into a successful business, and is called on by knowledgeable horsemen across the country for pedigree consultation.

Mike and his wife, Elizabeth, owned Dual Doc. For the last years of the stallion's life, they stood him at their Southern Cross Ranch, when they lived in northern Washington State.

Writing when time permits and the subject interests him, Boardman has been published in Canada, Australia and the United States. He's currently working on a book about "The Master," Greg Ward.

Diane Ciarloni

DIANE CIARLONI authored the original *Western Horseman* book *Legends* under the byline of Diane Simmons.

Diane grew up in an agricultural area outside Memphis and began her career in journalism with the Scripps-Howard newspaper chain, while still working on her degree at Memphis State University.

She began her career as a free-lance writer in 1975, concentrating on horse-related subjects. By 1980, Diane's work had been carried in 12 publications, including *Western Horseman, American Horseman, Horse of Course, Horse & Rider, California Horse Review, Paint Horse Journal, Rodeo News, Horse Illustrated*, and *Speedhorse*.

She was one of the first equine journalists to begin working directly with veterinarians, providing medical and health articles in layman's terms for a number of magazines. She's also written feature material for *Art West* on equine and/or western artists.

Although Diane's writing accomplishments have involved almost every segment of the horse industry, she's concentrated on racing since 1978.

Now living in north Texas, she currently serves as editor for *Speedhorse/The Racing Report*. Her race-related editorials have won her several awards, including the American Quarter Horse Association Sprint Award twice, and her work was also reviewed in The Best American Sports Writing of 1991.

She's a multiple contributor to *Chicken Soup for the Horse Lover's Soul*, released in 2003.

Alan Gold

ALAN GOLD got his introduction to the horse world when he took a job with *The Australian Stock Horse Magazine* in the mid-1970s. He also got hooked on horse racing while living in Australia. "People pull over to the side of the road to listen to the Melbourne Cup on their car radios," he says. "I learned a lot about enthusiasm for horses while I was in Australia. I even met people who could repeat the call of a race the way a student might recite Shakespeare."

When he returned to the States in 1982, Alan took a job with *The Quarter Racing Record*, and eventually became that magazine's editor. His stories have appeared in dozens of magazines on three continents. His novel, *The White Buffalo*, tells about a cutting horse trainer whose buffalo gives birth to a rare white calf. Alan is also the co-author of *Pride in the Dust*.

Alan founded Fifth Leg Publishing, which offers a selection of quality books for horse lovers at www.fifthleg.com. "An Aussie race caller inspired the name," he explains. "When the favorite made up a hopeless deficit in the homestretch, the announcer shouted, 'He grew a fifth leg!' Sometimes, that's all it takes."

Alan is currently the director of publishing for the National Cutting Horse Association.

Jim Goodhue

JIM GOODHUE is highly qualified to write on any subject dealing with the history of the American Quarter Horse.

Jim went to work for American Quarter Horse Association in 1958, immediately after receiving an advanced degree from Oklahoma State University. Originally hired to work for *The Quarter Horse Journal*, Jim went on to spend 11 years as head of the association's performance division and 22 years as AQHA registrar. For years, Jim wrote monthly columns for the *Quarter Running Horse Chart Book* and *Journal*. He also contributed feature material to the Journal on a regular basis.

A great deal of Jim's historical knowledge of the Quarter Horse breed was gained on a firsthand basis. He remembers, for instance, his first exposure to Grey Badger II, one of the horses profiled in *Legends 2.*

"It was in the late 1940s, and Walter Merrick was match-racing Grey Badger II in Oklahoma," he recalls. "Walter was down on the track, getting the horse ready to go, and Tien, his wife, was up in the stands, taking bets. Tien had bills wrapped around every finger and she was sure doing her best to see that anybody who wanted to lay some money down on the race had the opportunity to do so."

Jim retired from AQHA in 1991.

Sally Harrison

SALLY HARRISON has been writing about and photographing horses since 1981. Her articles and photographs have appeared in numerous publications and she's written three books: *Cutting: A Guide for the Non-Pro Competitor; Matlock Rose, The Horseman;* and *The Cowboy Life of James L. Kenney.* She also co-authored *Pride in the Dust.* Her writing is familiar to tens of thousands of racing fans who've enjoyed her articles in *Lone Star Today,* the daily racing program for Lone Star Park at Grand Prairie, Texas.

Since Sally began writing about horses in the early 1980s, when she owned and bred Arabian horses, she's had hundreds of stories published in numerous magazines. Her readers have found that Sally's curiosity, rigorous research, and insight bring her subjects to life. She won the American Quarter Horse Association's Steel Dust award for best feature article of 2002.

"I started writing about horses and people because I wanted to find out their stories myself," says Sally, a former high school English teacher. "My goal has always been to write from a reader's perspective, and never intrude on the material myself."

A nationally recognized equine photographer, Sally has turned her lens on countless great Quarter Horses and Thoroughbreds over the last 20 years.

Says cutting legend Buster Welch, "Sally Harrison is the only person I know who can head a cow and take a picture at the same time."

Sally also operates a busy equine advertising and marketing agency in Arlington, Tex., where she lives with her husband, writer Alan Gold.

Frank Holmes

FRANK HOLMES has been penning horse-related feature articles and historical books for more than 37 years.

He sold his first feature article involving Quarter Horses to *Hoof and Horns* magazine in 1965. Frank is also considered one of the foremost historians of the Appaloosa and Paint breeds, as well as Quarter Horses. His many features on the sires and dams of all three breeds stand as benchmark contributions to the collective lore of the western horse.

After 18 years of working for the federal government, Frank pursued a full-time career as a free-lance writer in 1991. Then, between 1994 and 1996, he was a staff writer for *Western Horseman.* During that time he contributed to the *"Legends"* series and wrote the *WH* book *The Hank Wiescamp Story.*

In 1996, he became the features editor of the *Paint Horse Journal* in Fort Worth.

There, through his articles and photographs, he combined his love for history, horses and the horsemen and horsewomen behind them.

"There is a common thread that's shared by the major stock horse breeds," he notes. "Often, while pursuing research on one breed, I find myself gaining insight into the history of another.

"It's interesting to take note of the common heritage shared by the different breeds and to observe how they branched off to form the separate and distinct breed registries that exist today."

Frank returned to Colorado in 2000 to rededicate himself to his first love — researching and writing horse history. He has since written two books: *Wire to Wire, The Walter Merrick Story* and *More Than Color, Paint Horse Legends.*

Betsy Lynch

BETSY LYNCH heads up her own marketing and communications firm, Third Generation Communications, which specializes in horse-related products and services. She's the editor of *Performance Horse Magazine*, a national publication that targets the specialized interests of cutting, reining and working cowhorse enthusiasts.

With a degree in agricultural journalism from Colorado State University and a lifelong involvement with horses, Betsy has devoted her career to writing, photography, editing, marketing, advertising, public relations and special events management. She's the co-author of the book, *Bits & Bridles: Power Tools for Thinking Riders*, and founded a publication for the reining industry called *Showtime Reports*. She's worked on staff for a number of publications and her articles and photography have appeared in numerous magazines in the United States and abroad.

While growing up, Betsy had the opportunity to watch riders such as Dale Wilkinson, Bill Horn and Clark Bradley set the arena ablaze. She remembers the thrill of meeting Wilkinson and Mr Gun Smoke during a 4-H tour of Wilkinson's farm. Those early experiences made a lasting impression in many ways. When the opportunity arose, Betsy took a hiatus from journalism to work on a cutting horse ranch in Texas.

Betsy resides in Fort Collins, Colo., with her husband, two sons, two dogs, four cats, six horses and a flock of chickens. When's she's not writing, she's riding.

A.J. Mangum

A.J. MANGUM spent his childhood on a central Oregon horse and cattle ranch, where handling horses was a part of everyday life. After putting in seven years on the Pacific Northwest horse show circuit, he studied at Northwestern University and Oregon State University before beginning his writing career as a reporter for a newspaper in Alamosa, Colorado.

In 1993, A.J. joined the staff of the *Appaloosa Journal*, serving first as assistant editor, then as editor of the award-winning breed publication. Under his leadership, the magazine garnered the top American Horse Publications honor, the general excellence award.

After a year as a field editor with *The Quarter Horse Journal*, A.J. joined *Western Horseman* in 1998. Today, he's the magazine's editor.

Writing about horses and horsemen has taken A.J. all over North America and to the Netherlands, Belgium and France to cover major events, profile influential breeders, and gather instructional material. A lifelong rider and horse owner, A.J., like many of this book's authors, has found a way to combine his equine hobby and his career. He's also written a *Western Horseman* booklet titled *Ranch Roping* with trainer-clinician Buck Brannaman.

A.J. married Roy Jo Sartin in 2003 and the couple live near Colorado Springs.

Susan Scarberry

SUSAN SCARBERRY researches pedigrees and performance records when she's not keeping records for the Arkansas ranch where her husband, Benny, trains calf and team roping horses. Susan enjoys showing cutting horses, and also runs the family's insurance agency.

"I really enjoy watching or reading and hearing about good performance horses – today's performers and yesterday's equine heroes," she says. "Their dispositions and abilities, their offspring and their pedigrees are always interesting to me."

Susan's ties to her chapter subject, Harlan, hit close to home: The Scarberrys raise performance horses, specializing in Harlan bloodlines, and show some of their prospects at American Quarter Horse Association shows. In 2002 their good show mare, Harlans Bobbi Jo, earned AQHA Superior awards in heeling and calf roping, was third at the 2002 AQHA Championship show in junior heading and placed in year-end standings in all three events.

Susan and Benny have two teenage sons, Matt and Casey, who help train colts and with farming duties.

Larry Thornton

LARRY THORNTON started with a serious interest in equine pedigrees in the mid-1960s and wrote his first article for *Speedhorse* in 1984. He then became a regular contributor to that magazine, writing a monthly column and features. His interest in performance horses led to a series of stories for the National Cutting Horse Association's *Cutting Horse Chatter* on famous cutting horse bloodlines.

Since 1989, Larry has written a column for *Southern Horseman* magazine called "The Working Lines," which is also published in several other horse magazines. Larry's book by the same name is a compilation of some of his articles on great horses and breeders.

"I credit any success I have as a writer to the people I have interviewed," states Larry about his writing career. "B.F. Phillips Jr. was the first great horseman and breeder to give me an interview, and it was his input that made my first story a success. I've been able to visit with many of the great horsemen in our industry, giving me an opportunity to learn about famous breeding programs and great horses.

"It seems that with every article, I find something new and interesting," says Larry. "Learning something new and then reporting on what I find is a very rewarding way to be a part of the horse industry."

Larry, a graduate of the University of Nebraska, is an agricultural instructor at the Area Vo-Tech Center in Russellville, Ark. He lives in London, Ark., with his wife, Judy. They have a small breeding program that specializes in cutting and reining horses.

PHOTO INDEX

A

Alouette, 165
Annie Echols, 27
Arizona Junie, 165
Arizonan, 23

B

Bioninic, 170
Blondy's Dude, 42, 44, 45
Bob Cuatro, 16
Bradley's Hank, 109
Bras d'Or, 18

C

Cash Rate, 134
CD Olena, 198
Chapparita Menada, 14
Cherry Echols, 30

D

Dash For Cash, 126, 127, 129, 130, 131, 132
Dashingly, 135
Dashs Dream, 135
Deb's Smokey Joe, 111
Denim N Diamonds, 87
Diamonds Sparkle, 56, 58, 59, 60
Dimonds Ms Sparkle, 55
Dixie Beach, 105
Doc Bar, 192
Doc O'Lena, 190, 193, 194, 195
Doc's Oak, 173
Doc's Remedy, 173
Dollie Pine, 176

Dude Lit, 46
Dude's Ada Sue, 52
Dudes Baby Doll, 47
Dudes Banjo, 53
Dude's Dream, 48
Dude's Gaucho, 51
Dudes Mr Kim, 49
Dude's Showdown, 54
Dusty Boss, 166

E

Easy Reb, 83
Ed Echols, 20
Ed Heller, 25

F

Fair Lady Tonto, 100
Fancy Zippin, 184
Fantacia, 76, 77
Fantasy, 75
Fillinic, 162, 164
Fillynic, 171
Find A Buyer (TB), 128
First Down Dash, 133
FL Lady Bug, 118
Frog W, 98

G

Garrett's Miss Pawhuska, 140
Geeper Creeper, 85
G F's Punchinello, 167
Gin Echols, 26

Ginger Echols, 27
Gotum Gone, 137

H

Hank H, 97, 104
Hank's Dial Doll, 101
Harlan, 102, 103, 105
Harlan Crocker, 113
Harlan filly, 106
Harlan Okmulgee, 110
Harlan Sport, 112
Harlan's Tyree, 108
Harlaquita, 106
Harlene, 107
Home Remedy, 172
Hula Baby, 22
Hula Girl P, 22, 23

I

Ima Doc O'Lena, 204
Impressive, 150, 152, 153, 155, 161
Impressive Chase, 158
Impressive Dottie, 156
Impressive Prince, 159
Impressive Reward, 160
Impressor, 154

J

Jerry's Bug, 121
Joe Barrett, 12
Joe Blair, 141
Johnny Boone, 82
Justanold Love, 133

L

Lady Bug's Moon, 114, 116, 117
Leo San, 9, 10
Leo's Showman, 120
Little Joe, 8

M

Masked Lass, 89
Melody Zipper, 185
Mighty Michelle, 86
Mike Echols, 28
Miss Bank, 69, 72, 73, 74
Miss Mighty Bug, 122
Miss N Cash, 136
Miss Princess, 66, 68, 69, 70, 71
Mr Diamond Dude, 46
Mr Hay Bag, 123
Mr Master Bug, 125

O

Okie Star Dude, 50
OK Im Zipped, 189

P

Pale Face Dude, 49
Parker's Trouble, 23
Peppy San, 11
Peppy San Badger, 12
Poco Lena, 193
Pokey Pat, 145

R

Rebel Cause, 78, 80, 88
Rebel Rocket, 84
Reprise Bar, 39, 54
Rocket Wrangler, 128, 130
Rose Bug, 124

S

San Siemon, 9
San Sue Darks, 9
Shawne Bug, 120
Shining Spark, 63
Si Olena, 196
Small Town Dude, 47
Smart Little Lena, 197
Sonny Kimble, 13
Spark O Lena, 64
Sparkles Rosezana, 60, 61
Sparkles Suzana, 38, 62
Sport, 15
Sporty Pedro, 17
Springinic, 168
Spring Remedy, 172
Sugarnic, 169
Sugar Remedy, 172
Sugar Vandy, 167

T

Tap O Lena, 202
The Barn Burner, 157
Tiny Circus, 59
Todaysmyluckyday, 201
Tonto Bars Gill, 95
Tonto Bars Hank, 90, 92, 93, 94, 96, 99

Top Deck, 81
Top Moon, 119
Travel Echols, 29
Turf's Best, 83

V

Van Decka, 147
Vandy, 138, 139
Vandy's Flash, 144, 149
Vanetta Dee, 142
Vanguard, 146
Vannevar, 143
Vansarita Too, 148

W

War Chant, 24
Woven Web (see Miss Princess)

Z

Zandy, 14
Zans Diamond Sun, 41
Zan Gold Chevas, 40
Zan Gold Jack, 37
Zan Parr Bar, 32, 34, 35
Zan Parr Jack, 36, 37
Zantanon, 6, 8
Zantanon Jr., 13
Zipabull, 187
Zippo Can Do, 186
Zippo Pine Bar, 174, 177, 178, 179, 181, 182
Zips Chocolate Chip, 183
Zorena, 19

NOTES

Books Published by
WESTERN HORSEMAN®

ARABIAN LEGENDS by Marian K. Carpenter
280 pages and 319 photographs. Abu Farwa, *Aladdinn, *Ansata Ibn Halima, *Bask, Bay-Abi, Bay El Bey, Bint Sahara, Fadjur, Ferzon, Indraff, Khemosabi, *Morafic, *Muscat, *Naborr, *Padron, *Raffles, *Raseyn, *Sakr, Samtyr, *Sanacht, *Serafix, Skorage, *Witez II, Xenophonn.

BACON & BEANS by Stella Hughes
144 pages and 200-plus recipes. Try the best in western chow.

CALF ROPING by Roy Cooper
144 pages and 280 photographs. Complete coverage of roping and tying.

COWBOYS & BUCKAROOS by Tim O'Byrne
176 pages and over 250 color photograps. The author, who's spent 20 years on ranches and feedyards, explains in great detail the trade secrets and working lifestyle of this North American icon. Readers can follow the cowboy crew through the four seasons of a cattle-industry year, learn their lingo and the Cowboy Code they live by, understand how they start colts, handle cattle, make long circles in rough terrain and much, much more. Many interesting sidebars, including excerpts from the author's personal journal offering firsthand accounts of the cowboy way.

CUTTING by Leon Harrel
144 pages and 200 photographs. Complete guide to this popular sport.

FIRST HORSE by Fran Devereux Smith
176 pages, 160 black-and-white photos, numerous illustrations. Step-by-step information for the first-time horse owner and/or novice rider.

HELPFUL HINTS FOR HORSEMEN
128 pages and 325 photographs and illustrations. *WH* readers and editors provide tips on every facet of life with horses and offer solutions to common problems horse owners share. Chapters include: Equine Health Care; Saddles; Bits and Bridles; Gear; Knots; Trailers/Hauling Horses; Trail Riding/Backcountry Camping; Barn Equipment; Watering Systems; Pasture, Corral and Arena Equipment; Fencing and Gates; Odds and Ends.

IMPRINT TRAINING by Robert M. Miller, D.V.M.
144 pages and 250 photographs. Learn to "program" newborn foals.

LEGENDS 1 by Diane Ciarloni
168 pages and 214 photographs. Barbra B, Bert, Chicaro Bill, Cowboy P-12, Depth Charge (TB), Doc Bar, Go Man Go, Hard Twist, Hollywood Gold, Joe Hancock, Joe Reed P-3, Joe Reed II, King P-234, King Fritz, Leo, Peppy, Plaudit, Poco Bueno, Poco Tivio, Queenie, Quick M Silver, Shue Fly, Star Duster, Three Bars (TB), Top Deck (TB) and Wimpy P-1.

LEGENDS 2 by Jim Goodhue, Frank Holmes, Phil Livingston, Diane Ciarloni
192 pages and 224 photographs. Clabber, Driftwood, Easy Jet, Grey Badger II, Jessie James, Jet Deck, Joe Bailey P-4 (Gonzales), Joe Bailey (Weatherford), King's Pistol, Lena's Bar, Lightning Bar, Lucky Blanton, Midnight, Midnight Jr, Moon Deck, My Texas Dandy, Oklahoma Star, Oklahoma Star Jr., Peter McCue, Rocket Bar (TB), Skipper W, Sugar Bars and Traveler.

LEGENDS 3 by Jim Goodhue, Frank Holmes, Diane Ciarloni, Kim Guenther, Larry Thornton, Betsy Lynch
208 pages and 196 photographs. Flying Bob, Hollywood Jac 86, Jackstraw (TB), Maddon's Bright Eyes, Mr Gun Smoke, Old Sorrel, Piggin String (TB), Poco Lena, Poco Pine, Poco Dell, Question Mark, Quo Vadis, Royal King, Showdown, Steel Dust and Two Eyed Jack.

LEGENDS 4
216 pages and 216 photographs. Several authors chronicle the great Quarter Horses Zantanon, Ed Echols, Zan Parr Bar, Blondy's Dude, Diamonds Sparkle, Woven Web/Miss Princess, Miss Bank, Rebel Cause, Tonto Bars Hank, Harlan, Lady Bug's Moon, Dash For Cash, Vandy, Impressive, Fillinic, Zippo Pine Bar and Doc O' Lena.

LEGENDS 5 by Frank Holmes, Ty Wyant, Alan Gold, Sally Harrison
248 pages, including about 300 photographs. The stories of Little Joe, Joe Moore, Monita, Bill Cody, Joe Cody, Topsail Cody, Pretty Buck, Pat Star Jr., Skipa Star, Hank H, Chubby, Bartender, Leo San, Custus Rastus (TB), Jaguar, Jackie Bee, Chicado V and Mr Bar None.

LEGENDS 6 by Frank Holmes, Patricia Campbell, Sally Harrison, GloryAnn Kurtz, Cheryl Magoteaux, Heidi Nyland, Bev Pechan, Juli S. Thorson
236 pages, including about 270 photographs. The stories of Paul A, Croton Oil, Okie Leo Flit Bar, Billietta, Coy's Bonanza, Major Bonanza, Doc Quixote, Doc's Prescription, Jewels Leo Bar, Colonel Freckles, Freckles Playboy, Peppy San, Mr San Peppy, Great Pine, The Invester, Speedy Glow, Conclusive, Dynamic Deluxe and Caseys Charm

NATURAL HORSE-MAN-SHIP by Pat Parelli
224 pages and 275 photographs. Parelli's six keys to a natural horse-human relationship.

PROBLEM-SOLVING, Volume 1 by Marty Marten
248 pages and over 250 photos and illustrations. Develop a willing partnership between horse and human — trailer-loading, hard-to-catch, barn-sour, spooking, water-crossing, herd-bound and pull-back problems.

PROBLEM-SOLVING, Volume 2 by Marty Marten
A continuation of Volume 1. Ten chapters with illustrations and photos.

RAISE YOUR HAND IF YOU LOVE HORSES by Pat Parelli w. Kathy Swan
224 pages and over 200 black and white and color photos. The autobiography of the world's foremost proponent of natural horsemanship. Chapters contain hundreds of Pat Parelli stories, from the clinician's earliest remembrances to the fabulous experiences and opportunities he has enjoyed in the last decade. As a bonus, there are anecdotes in which Pat's friends tell stories about him.

RANCH HORSEMANSHIP by Curt Pate w. Fran Devereux Smith
220 pages and over 250 full color photos and illustrations. Learn how almost any rider at almost any level of expertise can adapt ranch-horse-training techniques to help his mount become a safer more enjoyable ride. Curt's ideas help prepare rider and horse for whatever they might encounter in the round pen, arena, pasture and beyond.

REINING, Completely Revised by Al Dunning
216 pages and over 300 photographs. Complete how-to training for this exciting event.

RIDE SMART, by Craig Cameron w. Kathy Swan
224 pages and over 250 black and white and color photos. Under one title, Craig Cameron combines a look at horses as a species and how to develop a positive, partnering relationship with them, along with good, solid horsemanship skills that suit both novice and experienced riders. Topics include ground-handling techniques, hobble-breaking methods, colt-starting, high performance maneuvers and trailer-loading. Interesting sidebars, such as trouble-shooting tips and personal anecdotes about Cameron's life, complement the main text.

RODEO LEGENDS by Gavin Ehringer
Photos and life stories fill 216 pages. Included are: Joe Alexander, Jake Barnes & Clay O'Brien Cooper, Joe Beaver, Leo Camarillo, Roy Cooper, Tom Ferguson, Bruce Ford, Marvin Garrett, Don Gay, Tuff Hedeman, Charmayne James, Bill Linderman, Larry Mahan, Ty Murray, Dean Oliver, Jim Shoulders, Casey Tibbs, Harry Tompkins and Fred Whitfield.

ROOFS AND RAILS by Gavin Ehringer
144 pages, 128 black-and-white photographs plus drawings, charts and floor plans. How to plan and build your ideal horse facility.

STARTING COLTS by Mike Kevil
168 pages and 400 photographs. Step-by-step process in starting colts.

THE HANK WIESCAMP STORY by Frank Holmes
208 pages and over 260 photographs. The biography of the legendary breeder of Quarter Horses, Appaloosas and Paints.

TEAM PENNING by Phil Livingston
144 pages and 200 photographs. How to compete in this popular family sport.

TEAM ROPING WITH JAKE AND CLAY by Fran Devereux Smith
224 pages and over 200 photographs and illustrations. Learn about fast times from champions Jake Barnes and Clay O'Brien Cooper. Solid information about handling a rope, roping dummies and heading and heeling for practice and in competition. Also sound advice about rope horses, roping steers, gear and horsemanship.

WELL-SHOD by Don Baskins
160 pages, 300 black-and-white photos and illustrations. A horse-shoeing guide for owners and farriers. Easy-to-read, step-by-step how to trim and shoe a horse for a variety of uses. Special attention is paid to corrective shoeing for horses with various foot and leg problems.

WESTERN TRAINING by Jack Brainard
With Peter Phinny. 136 pages. Stresses the foundation for western training.

WIN WITH BOB AVILA by Juli S. Thorson
Hardbound, 128 full-color pages. Learn the traits that separate horse-world achievers from also-rans. World champion horseman Bob Avila shares his philosophies on succeeding as a competitor, breeder and trainer.

Western Horseman, established in 1936, is the world's leading horse publication. For subscription information: 800-877-5278.
To order other *Western Horseman* books: 800-874-6774 • *Western Horseman*, Box 7980, Colorado Springs, CO 80933-7980.
Web site: **www.westernhorseman.com.**